# WHEREVER

## NO LIGHT . . .

Whatever it was that had surrounded me so completely, it had no size or shape. One minute, it seemed huge, the next minute, it was floating in the dark and I had become one with it.

That floating feeling gave way to the sudden feeling of movement. Ahead and slightly above me, I could vaguely sense a light at the far end of a long tunnel. The blackness was churning, moving through itself. Instead of pitch blackness, I could see alternating shades of black and gray along the sides of this tunnel. Everything was moving in the same direction—toward the light.

The light was above me but I became fascinated by a strange feeling in my hands. They were expanding, nothing hurt, but my hands seemed to be expanding beyond their normal size. At the same time, I was being caressed by a gentle breeze and could hear a low-pitched, droning noise. It was calling me, guiding me somewhere toward the light, but this time I didn't follow it. . . .

This is not a metaphor for what happened. Close your eyes, open your heart. This all exists . . . over there . . . through the portal we label death.

—Barbara Harris

# FULL CIRCLE

## THE NEAR-DEATH
## EXPERIENCE
## AND BEYOND

### Barbara Harris and
### Lionel C. Bascom

Commentary by
Bruce Greyson, M.D.

**POCKET BOOKS**

New York   London   Toronto   Sydney   Tokyo   Singapore

Quotes from *Heading Toward Omega* reprinted with permission from Kenneth Ring, Ph.D.

While this book is an accurate accounting of the author's life and experiences, patients' names have been changed in order to protect their privacy.

An *Original* Publication of POCKET BOOKS ·

POCKET BOOKS, a division of Simon & Schuster Inc.
1230 Avenue of the Americas, New York, NY 10020

## THIS BOOK IS DEDICATED

To the wonderful warm memories of Mary (May) Doherty.

To Mary Ellen Doherty Layden for her huge open heart.

And, proudly, to my three children, Beth, Steven, and Gary, for their courage to stand by me and for their wisdom when I have needed it.

*Time is Unconscious Eternity*

—Sam Keen, *The Passionate Life*

# Contents

# CONTENTS

# Acknowledgments

While there are three names on the cover of this book, the list of people who are also responsible is actually "fifteen years long."

Both IANDS chapters in Florida deserve my thanks for their support when I needed it. My special thanks to Carol Lewis for all her encouragement and to Jack Cuthrall for becoming the regional coordinator after I left. I also want to thank Nancy and Alan Shenk, M.D., Luba and David Aaronson, and Shelley and Bob Katrosar for helping and encouraging me. Larry and Bev Brawer and their children are always there, constant friends. Sherwin Harris and I share three beautiful children and good memories through the twenty-six years we shared, too.

I am deeply indebted to those thirty-two brave people and the helpers at the IANDS Clinical Approaches Conference and to all those hundreds of people since then who have written to me about their experiences.

My special thanks to my friends in Connecticut: Steven Price, Diane Mann, Laurie Peters, Sharon Batey, David Doherty, Roy McAlpine, Ric Bach, Sandy McGibbon, Marsha Aaronson, and the Friends of IANDS chapter here. Nancy Bush, Leslee and Ed Morabito, and Lynn and Jim Crum opened their hearts and their homes to me. Nancy and Leslee have helped guide me.

I would like to thank three other people for sharing their experiences—Audrey Harris, Tom Sawyer, and Ron Chester.

Kim Clark Sharp helped me to laugh when I really needed to and couldn't. Sharon Grant has been a constant friend. She has read this manuscript over and over from the perspective of a near-death experiencer and from the perspective of a reader who has never heard of an NDE. Her talents at bringing out subtlety are throughout this book.

Kay Allison of the Quest Institute is a soul sister and one of the best networkers on the East Coast for healing the planet.

Adele Leone, my literary agent, has believed in this story from the beginning. Kathy Bradley Sullivan, the editor of this book, was incredibly skillful in finding the areas, and there were many of them, that needed to be clarified. I am grateful for her expertise.

I saved two important men in my life for last because this is hard to put into words. Ken Ring has been my brother and my mirror. He took my memories of who I was in my near-death experience and showed me my "Self" clearly— so I could be that person again. Bruce Greyson has been a constant friend, a trusted colleague, and my mentor these past seven years. When I have needed a brother, he has always selflessly been there. And he has shared his incredible knowledge as a scientist for this book. These two special men have never tired of listening to my stories and helping me gain clarity. Bruce Greyson and Kenneth Ring deserve my eternal thanks.

And, last, I must thank the Universe; not just for my near-death experience but for all the lessons, all the guidance, all the synchronicities that have brought me to the point of writing this book so that I may share with you its beauty.

—Barbara Harris

# Preface

"I was gone, asleep, nonexistent, or I just wasn't remembering anything. I awoke and found myself out in the hospital corridor. The hallway was empty.

"I was supposed to be in bed, and if I was caught out there, I'd get into trouble, so I headed back to my doorway. I was startled by my view of the P.A. speaker next to my room just above my door—I was at eye level with it. I knew that speaker had been way above my head when I was admitted to the hospital, and now I was looking straight at it.

"I moved through the doorway and into my room, and there I was, lying in bed. I had a clear, vivid view of my body in that awesome bed. I felt good, clear, calm, and free of pain. Then I was in blackness. There was a gentle caressing breeze wrapped around my invisible body. A low *droning noise was beckoning me. This is not metaphor for what happened to me that night.*

*"Close your eyes, open your heart. This all exists . . . over there . . . through the portal we label death."*

—Barbara Harris

# Introduction

## by Bruce Greyson, M.D.

Six years ago I was asked by a public broadcasting TV station in Detroit to provide scientific perspective for a late-night talk show on which a woman was to tell about her near-death experience. I had been approached because I was research director of the International Association for Near-Death Studies.

I accepted the invitation largely because the woman who was to appear on the show, Barbara Harris, had been patiently completing questionnaires for me from her home in Florida for a couple of years. I was grateful to her for her participation as a volunteer subject in my research, and I was curious to meet this person whom I knew mainly as Subject #1066.

I actually knew a fair amount from Barbara's questionnaire responses about her near-death experience, or NDE, about her chronic back problems, her corrective surgery and nearly fatal complications, and from that spotty information I had imagined meeting a rather dispirited invalid, confined to a wheelchair and weakened by years of painkillers and infirmity.

I should have guessed from the fact that the show was scheduled for April Fool's Day that I was in for a surprise. Instead of my fantasized invalid, I was confronted by a vibrant and dynamic person full of childlike joy and wonderment, who over the intervening years has continually challenged my own intellectual biases and breathed into my research the reality that comes only from experiencing.

Now, after six years and many, many miles together, Barbara has asked me to provide scientific perspective to this book. Though I know her so much better now—as a constant friend, an inspiring colleague, and, yes, still as a tireless research subject—I find the scientific perspective so much harder to provide now than before I knew so much. In the intervening years I have been a witness to and participant in this story, a story that involves phenomena that can't even be put into words, let alone examined under a microscope.

Let me hasten to say, however, that this is not a far-out story. Barbara's near-death experience is not extraordinary, as near-death experiences go. I have heard and read hundreds of accounts that are more fantastic, more otherworldly, and more awe-inspiring than hers. I say that to try to put her account in perspective, for it will certainly seem to many readers fantastic, otherworldly, and awe-inspiring.

It is a paradox that while NDEs are extraordinary, they are also so ordinary: a 1981 Gallup Poll estimated that about eight million adult Americans have had one. It is also paradoxical that while NDEs are so awesome, so grandiose, they are also so intimate. The value of Barbara's story for us is not that it is unusual, but that it is so typical of what millions of others have gone through, are going through, and will go through.

Many near-death experiencers (NDErs) insist that the NDE itself can never fully be conveyed to someone who has not experienced it, since it is not of this reality. As a non-NDEr I can respect that opinion. However, the aftereffects of the NDE definitely *are* of this reality; in fact, that's part of the problem. This book accordingly does not dwell on the otherworldly features of Barbara Harris's NDE, fascinating though they are. Instead, it focuses on the worldly aftereffects, those aspects that not only can be conveyed to others, but must be if we are to learn anything at all from these extraordinary experiences.

Much has been made of the fact that certain near-death experiences are "negative" or unpleasant, in contrast to the prototypical "positive" or pleasant NDEs like Barbara's. It has been objected that few near-death researchers are willing to deal with the "negative" NDE. Negative NDEs certainly happen, but I'm not convinced that they need to be "dealt with" as unique experiences distinct from "positive" NDEs.

Many of the aftereffects that Barbara Harris describes in this book are negative and unpleasant, and many of them will be familiar to NDErs, regardless of what kind of NDE they experienced. While I recognize that there may be some value for a researcher to categorize NDEs as positive or negative, my interest as a clinician in helping NDErs leads me to focus on the aftereffects and ways of coping with them, rather than on the type of NDE itself.

Before I attempt a scientific explanation of what Barbara and millions of people like her experienced, let me address briefly the thornier question of whether science *should* try to explain NDEs. Let me start by playing devil's advocate, and list the reasons why science perhaps shouldn't try to mess with the NDE.

First is the concern about how we'll use what we learn about NDEs scientifically. Science is without values. Scientific information and conclusions have given us tremendous power over our planet, but no guidance as to how to use it. Our industrialized society, blessed with four centuries of phenomenal discoveries and material progress, is plagued by the runaway consequences of that progress: polluted air and water, overpopulation, man-made diseases, the threat of nuclear war, depletion of our limited energy reserves and of the earth's ozone layer and in fact its very crust.

When you consider the tremendous power the NDE has to transform the individual NDEr, do we really want to give scientists access to that kind of power? The NDEr comes away from the experience with a deep spirituality and a sense of values and priorities. Will the scientist?

Author and physician Walker Percy had a character in his novel *Love in the Ruins* recite "The prayer of the scientist if he prayed, which is not likely: Lord, grant that my discovery may increase knowledge and help other men. Failing that, Lord, grant that it will not lead to man's destruction. Failing that, Lord, grant that my article in *Brain* be published before the destruction takes place."

Second, will a scientific explanation of the NDE violate its very nature? Empirical science proceeds for the most part by breaking things down into their component parts. Many NDErs insist that a basic message of the NDE is that things can't be broken apart without losing their essence, that in fact what we usually see as individual objects, including ourselves, are in fact parts of a whole, and that we can appreciate our own selves only by realizing the whole and ceasing to think of ourselves as separate individuals. Can you explain a forest by studying individual leaves and twigs? Can a verbal recitation of the sequence of musical notes convey the essence of a symphony?

Finally, how will scientific study of NDEs affect individual people? Will it encourage NDErs to think of themselves as different from others and isolate themselves? Will it make them feel violated or degraded by having an ultimately unexplainable part of themselves subjected to a superficial attempt at explanation? Will explaining the positive aspects of NDEs and their aftereffects make non-NDErs intolerant of NDErs' human frailties?

These are difficult questions, and since many of them deal with abstractions that are not observable, I don't have answers for them all. But I do have a counterargument for why science should—indeed, why science must—try to explain NDEs. Again, it's based not on observations, but on an assumption. That assumption is that NDEs occur for a reason, and from watching the changes in NDErs, I believe that we have NDEs in order to learn from them how to help others.

Scientific explanations of NDEs can help individual NDErs come to terms with what happened to them and figure out how to make the most of that experience. Scientific explanations of NDEs can help dying people prepare for what lies ahead, can help grieving families live again after the death of a loved one, and can help suicidal individuals find meaning in their lives.

Only if NDEs can be explained in scientific terms will they be accepted and respected by those health-care providers who need to understand them in order to help their patients, by the policy makers who decide how we order our priorities, and by society at large, which is so enamored of the scientific method.

The scientific method, with its limitations, is the best method we have for establishing something as being consistent and reliable enough to be meaningful to others. A near-death experiencer may not feel the need for science to explain the NDE, but a scientific explanation of the NDE is the only way of extending the benefits of NDEs from the individual NDEr to non-NDErs and to society at large.

And finally, science must try to explain the NDE, because therein lies the key to its own growth. Advances in the scientific method come about because the existing method for answering questions has met its match, and new techniques have to be developed to account for our increasing knowledge of the universe. History tells us that only in trying to explain phenomena currently beyond its reach does science evolve new methods.

I believe the NDE is one of those puzzles that just might force scientists to develop a new scientific method, one that will incorporate all sources of knowledge, not only logical deductions of the intellect, and empirical observations of the physical, but also direct experience of the mystical.

# I

## THE END

My soul sits, looking out of time,
Telling my mind to not worry, time heals.
—Barbara Harris

# 1

## Memories

A truly upwardly mobile Michigan auto executive proudly drives a top-of-the-line Buick, owns a sprawling four-bedroom house in a suburb like Bloomfield Hills, and marries a dutiful wife. His neighborhood has everything: beautifully landscaped property, maids, gardeners, pool attendants, and exactly 2.3 children per house.

This was the life that Sherwin Harris and his wife, Barbara, had.

Their dream of belonging there, however, had several flaws.

The first distinction that made the Harrises different was the fact that Sherwin wasn't just another junior auto-industry executive hoping for annual pay raises, promotions or a golden parachute when he retired. In his early thirties Sherwin was already a managing partner in the thriving family-owned business his father had founded in the 1920s.

The second distinction was the fact that they were Jewish. Barbara, however, wasn't a loner, and belonged to several neighborhood clubs and community organizations, including the garden club, and she was genuinely liked.

Although Barbara went to temple on Saturday and her children were being raised in the Jewish tradition, she was not a religious person. Secretly she was a self-avowed atheist. God had stopped existing for her back when she was Barbara Silverman and lived with her parents, Florence and Julius.

As far as Barbara was concerned, her ancestors might have walked the Red Sea with Moses, but God had not delivered his people to the promised land. God couldn't even protect one little girl from the psychological stress caused by her mother's repeated hospitalizations.

Her father, Julius Silverman, worked long, hard hours as a truck driver servicing cigarette vending machines in the inner city of Detroit. Her mother, Florence, stayed home and took care of the family. Marshall, Barbara's brother, was six years older than she, so that while they had little in common, they found much to fight about. The arguments were unpredictable and, more often than not, got physical. Barbara was often separated from her mother for weeks at a time when Florence was hospitalized. Her mother's mood swings and her relationship with her brother created an incredibly stressful situation for the small child. Already insecure, she also kept a big dark secret: she wet the bed until the age of seven or eight. Her secret clouded her self-esteem and kept her from being happy.

The one happiness she did have came from her grandmother, whom she affectionately called Bubbie. Her visits with Bubbie and her aunts and cousins were the best part of her childhood.

A year after Barbara married Sherwin, all of her dreams came true. Barely twenty years old, she gave birth to a beautiful baby girl, whom they named Beth. Beth was born one month after they moved into a small but pretty house in Oak Park, just off Oak Park Boulevard in Detroit. As Barbara went through labor at Mount Sinai Hospital, Sherwin's books and notes were spread all over her bed as he studied for finals. Luckily, the timing was good; he would graduate a few days after Beth was born and go to work in the family business, a job that would afford them a comfortable life-style.

Two years after Beth came Steven and a move to a better neighborhood in Southfield, Michigan. Gary was born four years later. By that time Sherwin was running the family business. They moved up again, this time to a sprawling tri-level home in fashionable Bloomfield Hills. By the age of twenty-six, Barbara had three beautiful children of her own to love and care for.

In 1973, however, this all began to unravel after a freak fall in a swimming pool. A curvature in Barbara's lower spine was diagnosed as congenital sclerosis, a curvature that ran in her family. Her mother had been operated on several times for it. Now Barbara suffered from the same condition, and her swimming-pool injury exacerbated it. Shortly before Christmas 1974, she was plagued by constant back pain. She had already been hospitalized repeatedly for this condition and it was just getting worse. Nothing seemed to help, except drugs. Unfortunately, the pills she took just deadened the pain; they did nothing to improve her health.

Secretly Barbara was terrified that her pain would become as bad as her mother's had been. As she opened her eyes in the morning and tried to move off the bed, it would seize her: first the physical sensation and then the deadening fear.

Barbara was given Valium, first five milligrams, then ten, four times a day. Empirin with codeine controlled the pain if she took it along with the Valium. As long as she swallowed the little blue tablet and the round white pill four times a day, the pain would stay in the background. If she stopped the medication, it would grab her—just below the waist—and sometimes squeeze her breath away.

She lost weight rapidly; the codeine nauseated her as the Valium suppressed her appetite. Anyone who knew Barbara before, knew her personality was rapidly changing, withdrawing. Only Barbara couldn't tell because she wasn't aware of anything anymore. The medication dulled her senses as much as the pain did. She felt trapped, overwhelmed by a terrible feeling of doom.

*I was nervous. I had never done anything like this before. This was the first time I was responsible for a charitable art auction. Robin, my close friend, was the president of the board. She coached me all the way through. I knew I couldn't have done it without her.*

*I was irritable and depressed. I had withdrawn weeks earlier, after my third hospitalization. Besides traction, the chief of neurosurgery had performed a rhizotomy, a nerve block on my lower back, to try to stop the pain from getting worse. My doctor was highly respected, a legend at Beaumont Hospital. My mother was also seeing him, and she was admitted at the same time I was for the same procedure. We laughed about the coincidence, but it seemed weird to me. She asked that we share a semiprivate room in the admitting office as I sat next to her. The woman behind the desk had said no almost immediately. I was relieved. I knew I needed to take care of myself. No one knew what would happen, and I just didn't have the strength to take care of my mother now.*

The neurosurgeon had inserted four large-gauge needles into the facet joints of my spine. They couldn't give me a pain reliever because I had to tell them exactly where the needles would create pain as it radiated down my legs. When the line of radiation was the same as the pain I usually felt, they would know they were in the right place and then insert a fluid to soothe the painful nerves. As the needles were pushed into my spine, the pain was intense. The procedure took much longer than it should have, but they had to arrange the needles at equal depths. I had to lie facedown on a hard cold X-ray table for over an hour, and was feeling nauseated from the probing needles. I got sick to my stomach and everyone had to wait for me to stop vomiting. Actually, everyone left the room except the doctor. He gently put the weight of his body over my shoulders and upper back. While I was in the middle of being sick, I vaguely heard him telling me that he had to pin me down because if I moved, they would have to start positioning the needles all over again. When I finally stopped vomiting, the three technicians and another doctor returned. One of the techs leaned over and put her face close to mine. Touching my face gently, she asked if I was okay. Then she told me how she could feel what I was going through and she praised me for my courage. Her comment focused me. I didn't know about courage or composure. I just kept thinking about how I wanted to stop hurting, and I was so sure, or almost sure, that this procedure would help.

Then they injected a fluid into my spine, and the pain went away. It disappeared for a few weeks. In total amazement and disbelief, I stopped taking all my pills. By that time I was off codeine and on Percodan. In the hospital I had been getting shots of Demerol.

Thrilled to finally be off the drugs, I was devastated when

*the pain slowly crept back. With it came the inevitable dosages of Valium and pain pills. With it also came the crushing burden that soon I would have to prepare for my fourth hospitalization in less than two years. The neurosurgeon told me that this time he would use electricity to deaden sensory nerves that had merely been soothed by the last treatment. The first treatment had done nothing to help my mother, and she wouldn't be trying it again. But I was younger, stronger. Besides, I needed it. I wasn't a mother to my kids anymore. I wasn't a wife. I wasn't anything.*

*Sherwin told me I looked good as we drove to the country club where the art auction I had organized was being held. He was happy that I was involved in the community again. He loved me skinny. I now weighed 103 pounds. I had dropped twenty pounds. It was easy to be thin when my back hurt. I had no appetite.*

*Sherwin wound up doing a lot of my tasks, like grocery shopping. When the pain was really bad, Sherwin would do the dishes after dinner. My friend Robin took over my car-pool duties.*

*As we drove through Bloomfield Hills, heading for the fund-raiser, it began to snow. It was a beautiful, peaceful evening and I wished we were now driving home instead of just going out. I wanted the event to be a success so I could feel good, because I had forgotten what feeling good felt like. My back ached—a dull throbbing pressure that invaded the small of my back like a huge toothache taking over my lower body. It traveled down my right leg, attacking my ankle and weakening my foot.*

*Robin and I shouldn't have put all those heavy plants from the greenhouse into her car and unloaded them. As we arrived at the club, I popped a Valium into my mouth. I took a deep breath and walked in.*

# 2

# The Circle Bed

In the spring of 1975, Barbara couldn't be weaned from the drugs until her back problems were cleared up. Her doctors hospitalized her again for the fourth time in less than a year. Barbara was fitted with a thirty-pound body cast. It was an attempt to stabilize her back, in the hope that the pain would disappear. It did, but only temporarily. Now she was to be hospitalized for the fifth time for a spinal fusion.

At the end of May, Barbara was admitted to Beaumont Hospital. In her private room she found what doctors later told her was a Stryker Frame Circle Bed. A short time later, she underwent a surgical procedure that took five and a half hours, after which she was placed in the bed that looked like a Ferris wheel, with two chrome hoops that encased a stretcherlike bed in the middle. Barbara was suspended in the stretcher on her back. Three times a day two nurses would place pillows over her, then a duplicate stretcher.

They would secure the "human sandwich" with straps; then the bed would be rotated by an electric motor until she was lying facedown. She'd stay in this position for twenty minutes. The procedure allowed her skin to breathe and kept fluid from building up in her lungs.

"This bed's not so bad," she thought. "I can't even feel the mattress. They said it was like a hammock. It's better." She was still groggy after the surgery, and drifted in and out of sleep. Visitors sometimes came and went without her knowing.

"Hi, Doctor. Great Demerol," she said the morning after her surgery. "No pain."

"We're giving you morphine," he told her, looking at her chart. "Your back was broken through," he said. "Like a kid's loose tooth!"

She was too weak to respond. She just looked around the room, noticing all the bags of clear intravenous liquids hanging on either side of the bed. She was being fed and medicated by these fluids now. She fell asleep and slept through the night.

About eight o'clock the next morning, a male technician came into her room, pulling a portable breathing device behind him. Her breathing had been labored during the night and doctors decided to put her on a ventilator three times a day for twenty minutes because she couldn't take deep breaths on her own anymore.

"I'm not here for my lungs," she told the young man. "I'm breathing all right," she insisted.

"It'll make things easier for you," the young man said as he plugged the machine into the wall outlet.

"Be a good patient," she told herself, "or he'll get annoyed." He put the mouthpiece in place.

When he was sure the machine was working properly,

he told her he was taking a break but would check on her in a few minutes.

He watched the machine for a few seconds longer, then left the room. There was a mouthpiece between her gums and lips. The machine filled her lungs and stopped itself, with a steady, natural rhythm.

Minutes later, something went wrong mechanically. The machine wouldn't stop and continued filling her lungs with air, too much air. Barbara couldn't scream with the mouthpiece in place. She began to panic and passed out. She didn't regain consciousness until late that night.

When she awoke, the room was dim-lit and she knew something was seriously wrong with her. Looking down at her stomach, she noticed that the bedcovers were raised. Her stomach was swollen, and at first she imagined that she was pregnant.

She had developed an air pocket known in medical terms as an "ileus." Air had inflated her stomach and blown up her intestines like balloons made from human tissue.

"My incision is pulling. Make my stomach go down," she yelled. She lay there for several minutes, just screaming hysterically.

When help arrived, Barbara's condition was critical. Doctors and nurses flooded into her room. They worked frantically to stabilize her. Her vital signs—heartbeat and blood pressure—had weakened considerably and her blood volume had dropped to a dangerously low level. Shock waves of pain racked her body.

"Give me a shot of something, anything," she screamed. "That machine blew me up." Why were they sticking those tubes in her nose? They were making her worse. "Let me die," she screamed. "Let me die." Her heart rate was erratic. Her blood pressure fell rapidly and she slipped into unconsciousness.

Medically speaking, Barbara appeared to be sleeping. Some part of her, however, was awakened, although anyone looking at her frail body wouldn't have noticed anything unusual. The floor she was on was quiet, the way hospitals are between midnight and dawn. Her body lay motionless, closely monitored by all sorts of high-tech machinery calibrated to register her life responses and any change in her condition. Anyone monitoring these devices that night would not have noticed anything out of the ordinary. But something unusual was about to happen, something that would change her life forever.

A part of her drifted upward and left her broken body lying in the Circle Bed. Call it her soul, her spirit, or whatever your belief system is most comfortable with. Barbara was having what is commonly referred to as an out-of-body experience. Her body lay still in that bed while some other conscious part of her found itself out in the hallway of the orthopedic floor in Beaumont Hospital. It was Barbara, or at least some perceiving part of her that was now conscious and awake, and for a minute she didn't realize that she had left her body.

"Must be late," she thought. "If I get caught out here, I'll get in trouble." Effortlessly she headed toward her room. She was a little surprised at first because she was floating, not walking. She hadn't felt this good in months. It was a liberating feeling; she felt more energy than she could ever remember having. She turned around and found herself face-to-face with the speakers of the hospital public-address system—up near the ceiling.

Those speakers had been three or four feet above her head when she checked into the hospital. Moving back into her room, she saw her own body still lying in the Circle Bed. The fact that she had somehow been separated from it puzzled her, but the first thing that struck her was how bad she looked lying down there in the bed.

"I look funny with that tape on my nose and all those tubes sticking out of me," she thought, feeling very calm. Amazingly, her thoughts were clear and focused. As alien as these scenes were to her, there was no confusion or panic about the situation. She seemed able to view everything around her in an objective, nonjudgmental way, as if she were a third entity commenting on all that was happening. She was acutely aware of how different things appeared to be, but there was also a strong sense of familiarity about it all. Time and space became immeasurable and she had a laissez-faire attitude about everything, an intense indifference that no drug could duplicate.

After a time, that feeling merged with the comforting feeling that she was no longer alone. She wasn't. Something or someone had enveloped her, cuddled her, comforted her in the same way her grandmother, Bubbie, had done so many times when she was a little girl. Bubbie had died ten years ago, yet Barbara felt herself being pulled closer and closer to her, and the feeling was the same as those times when she had buried her face in Bubbie's huge bosom for comfort.

This was no dream or trick of the imagination; Barbara knew her long-dead grandmother had found her and was holding her, and she could feel the love engulf her.

"Is it really dark, or are my eyes just not working?" she asked herself as she became more and more a part of the lush softness that embraced her. It never occurred to her that her eyes were closed as her physical body lay somewhere below in that Circle Bed. She merged now with whatever it was that had surrounded her.

Wherever she was, there was no light. Whatever had

surrounded her so completely had no size or shape. One minute it seemed huge; the next minute it was microscopic. It was floating in the dark and she had become one with it.

This floating feeling gave way to the sudden sensation of movement. She felt herself gently moving forward. Ahead and slightly above her, she felt drawn toward something now at the far end of a long tunnel. The blackness had now become tunnellike, and it was churning, moving through itself. Instead of pitch blackness, she could see alternating shades of black and gray along the sides of this tunnel. It was churning and separating into light that was moving, and she was moving too—toward a pinpoint of light at the end of the tunnel.

She could feel her physical body in much the same way an amputee whose leg is amputated can sometimes still feel the presence of severed limbs.

Though the light was above her, she became fascinated by a strange sensation in her hands. They were expanding, painlessly, beyond their normal size. At the same time this was happening, she was being caressed by a gentle breeze and could hear a low-pitched droning noise. The sound was calling her, guiding her somewhere toward the light, but this time she didn't follow it.

# 3

## A Second NDE

Barbara awoke the next morning—back in her body. It would take nearly seven years for her to find adequate words to describe what would later be termed by researchers a classic near-death experience. She didn't know it then, but she had been whisked through the portal we call death and had lived to talk about it. All she really knew that next morning was that she had somehow left the Circle Bed the night before and no one would believe her.

It was about seven o'clock in the morning, and day-shift nurses were busy waking patients who needed bathing, morning medication, and breakfast. It was business as usual on the floor, and a young nurse breezed into Barbara's room and quietly opened the drapes on her window to let the sun in.

"Close them, please," Barbara asked. "The light hurts my eyes." It was a strange request. Barbara's room had a beautiful view and she had always liked looking out the window. It was a way to pass the time.

"It's a beautiful day," the nurse told Barbara.

"The light hurts my eyes. Please close the drapes and keep them closed."

Thereafter Barbara's room stayed dark, both night and day. Her hearing, too, had become more acutely sensitive, so she requested that the nurses keep the door to her room closed, blocking out the hall noises and the sound of the P.A. system. Every sound seemed magnified now.

Several times a day she would be rotated. For part of the day she'd lie facedown in this strange bed. For the rest of the day she would lie on her back.

About five days after her first out-of body experience, another crisis triggered a second near-death experience.

During one of her routine rotations in the Circle Bed, the nurse placed pillows under her to make her more comfortable. Then she left the room, closing the door behind her as Barbara had asked all the nurses to do. A few minutes later, Barbara had to urinate. She couldn't use the bedpan without help, and she couldn't find the call cord. When the nurse had turned her, she'd forgotten to pin the cord back to the bed.

Quietly she waited until she had to urinate so badly that she ached.

"Oh, please hurry," she said to herself, almost whimpering aloud. Suddenly she could feel herself losing control.

"Oh, God," she cried, "I can't wet the bed! Don't let me wet this bed," she screamed hysterically.

As a child, wetting the bed meant punishment and public censure. When, as an adult, the childhood feelings resurfaced, she became hysterical. As she felt the moisture spread through the bed, Barbara could physically feel herself being separated from her body. Either her body was now moving away from her or she was moving away from it. She couldn't tell. In any case, she found herself about fifty feet above the Circle Bed, which was physically impossible because the ceiling wasn't that high. Below, she could see herself weeping frantically in a way she had not done since childhood. She heard her own screams, but the whole scene now seemed to be encased inside a transparent bubble.

At the same time, she was also back in the tunnel, enveloped by blackness. In one direction she saw a bubble that contained her thirty-two-year-old body lying in the Circle Bed.

In another direction, she saw a cloudlike formation with thousands of other transparent bubbles. She moved closer to the cloud and realized that each of these bubbles contained an event that had occurred in her life. One of them caught her attention immediately.

It was Barbara as a baby. She wasn't more than a year old, and to her amazement, she was lying facedown in her crib, crying just as hysterically as the thirty-two-year-old version of herself. The striking similarity of these two scenes mesmerized her.

In the Circle Bed scene, her nurses appeared and immediately tried to console Barbara. They took the urine-soaked pillows away and tried to make her comfortable. But there was no comforting this woman, just as there seemed to be no relief for the child.

As Barbara looked down on all this, it seemed as if the two scenes were happening simultaneously.

After looking back and forth several times between the scenes, Barbara moved even closer to the cloudlike formation and began moving through the bubbles, scene after scene. She wasn't just a passive observer, and again, she wasn't alone. Something unexplainable was moving with her. It was a force or some sort of intelligent energy that was taking her on a guided tour of her life as if it were segments of a long motion picture.

In one she saw herself as a teenager going out with Sherwin. In another she saw her mother fly into a rage, standing in the doorway of their northwest Detroit home. She remembered that day again, and could feel her mother's fear. As she watched this and other scenes, something miraculous happened.

Barbara had always viewed herself a victim. She believed she had been the victim of a stern mother and passive father, and had often felt unloved by both parents, just as she had sometimes felt unloved by Sherwin. Her perception of these things was different now. That wasn't what she was seeing in these bubbles, even though the facts in the scenes were in no way altered from what she remembered. Her mother had screamed at her, and that's what Barbara was seeing now. When her father seemed to ignore her, she saw that too. But the difference now was how she felt about what she was seeing. Barbara no longer saw herself as the only victim in these scenes. As she watched, she felt an overwhelming compassion for her ailing mother, whose pain thus became Barbara's pain. And there were times when Barbara wasn't sure if she was merely watching the bubble-encased scenes or was somehow actually being allowed to relive each of these moments.

Suddenly she seemed to understand the reasons for things clearly for the first time. She found herself saying "No wonder, no wonder," over and over again. In bubble after bubble, scene after scene, she could feel her mother's pain and anguish and understand her father's helplessness.

She had a clear perception that she had always understood

all this but had never been able to connect with it until now. She felt omniscient and knew the presence she felt was God. There was no image of a gray-haired old man with a beard, or even of a separate being. God was both with her and a part of her. She was both with God and a part of God.

In another bubble Barbara saw herself at the age of six, sitting in Miss Hamden's second-grade class at MacDowell Elementary School. Miss Hamden was standing on a small chair, putting things on a bulletin board. Suddenly, and without warning, she fell, just as Barbara remembered her doing. Barbara had disliked Miss Hamden intensely, and hated being in her class. When Miss Hamden fell that day, Barbara had had to stifle her laughter, and that is what she saw herself doing now.

In the bubble, Miss Hamden was on the floor writhing in pain. She screamed for someone to get help. Barbara looked around and saw that no one was moving. She raced out of the room, heading toward the principal's office, while her classmates stood in the room looking on, horrified.

As she peered into the bubble from the blackness that enveloped her, Barbara could smell the pungent odor of that classroom. Miss Hamden never used deodorant, and her body odor filled the room with a musky smell. Floating high above this scene now, that same awful smell returned to her as strong as if she were again sitting in Miss Hamden's classroom.

As she watched herself run out into the hall, she immediately picked up the strong smell of the heavily waxed floors at the school. As she watched herself race down the metal-tipped stairs, she could clearly hear the pinging noise they always made when anyone went down them. Her senses were sharper than mere imagination, more distinct than memory. She was reliving these experiences.

When she got to the principal's office, another smell came rushing in and she recognized it right away—rubber boots, the old-fashioned ones with the noisy buckles. She remembered why. Lost boots were kept in the principal's office, under the wooden bench.

When Barbara told Assistant Principal Levitsky about Miss Hamden, he dashed out of the office, leaving Barbara behind. Now she remembered the crisis that had occurred that day. When he left, she found herself shivering with fear over the fact that she was now stranded without a hall pass. She remembered thinking, "If I try to go back upstairs without a pass, I am going to get in trouble. I laughed when Miss Hamden fell." And the little girl internalized a feeling of being bad.

"No wonder," she thought as she moved among the bubbles. She could see clearly now that she had always believed that she was an unworthy child who felt undeserving and bad. As these scenes of her life were paraded before her now, she could see herself acting out this role. In this review, it became clear to her that this feeling of low self-worth had affected every relationship in her life. This realization had a profound and immediate healing effect on her. It was like years of psychotherapy in an instant.

Perhaps the most profound thing that occurred as she bounced from bubble to bubble, scene to scene, was the powerful gift she was receiving—the gift of her own forgiveness. Embracing herself, forgiving herself, seemed to free her from a lifetime of self-inflicted wounds.

Somehow, when the review was over, Barbara knew that she had committed only one sin. She had failed to love herself.

There is no way to measure how long she lingered in this altered state of consciousness. Like before, she eventually found herself out in the hall again. This time, however, her out-of-body experience allowed her to overhear some conversations that concerned her medical treatment and the nurse who had been taking care of her.

When her nurse discovered Barbara screaming hysterically because she had wet her bed, she became so upset that she was sent home early. Barbara overheard two other nurses talking about this in a laundry room behind the nurse's station during her out-of-body experience. She also saw them put her urine-soaked pillows in a clothes dryer without washing them first.

"Does she know once she gets out of the Circle Bed that she's going to be in that body cast for at least six months?" one nurse asked as Barbara listened intently.

"I doubt it," the other nurse said. "Her doctors are telling her six weeks. She's going to be in that thing for a long time, once she gets out of here."

Barbara floated over the nurse's station and returned to her room. When she awoke, her out-of-body experience was over and she had returned to the Circle Bed.

A short time later, when one of the nurses she had overheard talking came into the room, she told her about this second unauthorized flight she had just taken.

"I left the bed," Barbara said.

"You didn't leave this bed," the nurse said, trying to soothe her.

"I don't mean my body left the bed, *I* left the bed," Barbara said, knowing how ridiculous this sounded. But it had happened.

The nurse just assumed her patient was either hallucinating or had experienced a feverish dream and the images from it were still dancing around her head.

The other nurse Barbara had seen in the laundry room

earlier came into the room too. The two talked quietly together in a corner of the room for a second; then one of them left. She returned shortly with a sedative.

"I can't explain this. I know it sounds crazy, but I left the bed," Barbara told them, speaking slowly. She was exhausted and her speech was a little jumbled. She kept pausing, trying to choose her words carefully so that what she wanted to say wouldn't sound as crazy as it seemed, even to her.

She couldn't explain what had just happened; she just knew that it had happened. Unfortunately, the more she tried to explain it, the more jumbled her words became. Finally, when she realized the nurses didn't understand, she gave up trying.

Then something occurred to her. She knew something that could prove she wasn't crazy. They knew she couldn't have dragged that broken body of hers out of the Circle Bed. An out-of-body experience, although she didn't call it that then, was the only logical way to explain the things she had overheard in another part of the hospital. It would also serve as a reality check: if she was just going crazy or having hallucinations, they'd tell her none of the things she'd seen and overheard had ever happened.

"Please call my day nurse and tell her I'm all right," Barbara said. "I know she went home upset, and I'd like her to know that I am all right."

Both nurses were stunned. Barbara couldn't have known about the nurse who'd become a little hysterical in the nurse's station after the crisis with Barbara. Judging from the expressions on their faces, Barbara knew she had her facts straight.

They sedated her heavily, hoping she'd sleep. Besides morphine they gave her Valium and Vistaril.

"You know," Barbara said, "you should tell me the truth. I know I'm going to be in this body cast for six months. Tell the doctors I want to know the truth."

"You need to sleep, Barbara. You need to rest now, honey," one of the nurses said. "That little cocktail I just gave you will help."

Barbara began to feel a familiar warmth as the morphine coursed through her body and she began to drift off. But she remembered one more thing she had to say.

"You really should have washed those pillows before you put them in the dryer." Then she closed her eyes and slept.

# 4

## A Chrysalis

"For about a week I faded in and out of consciousness," Barbara remembered. She was heavily sedated and often had difficulty acknowledging people who visited her in the hospital.

Barbara was given Demerol and sometimes morphine to stave off pain. Drifting in and out of consciousness, she would have drug-induced hallucinations and frightening nightmares.

"There was a picture in my room of sand dunes and the seashore," she said. "When I was hallucinating, I kept seeing John Kennedy in that picture drowning. I knew I was hallucinating, and that he had already died many years ago."

There was also a recurring nightmare prompted by a television movie in which vicious Doberman pinscher dogs repeatedly tried to attack some people in a supermarket.

"I was strapped in that bed with both stretchers used to hold me in an upright position to orient me to standing before they put the body cast on. The TV was right in front of me on the wall, and I was forced to look straight into it—then I kept dreaming of those dogs." The image of former President Kennedy drowning and those attacking dogs stayed with her for some time, but eventually faded.

"John Kennedy's body and face in the water would fade. What I remembered about it was disjointed," she said. The memory of her tunnel experiences, and the out-of-body experience that preceded it, however, returned clearly to her again and again.

Her nightmares and hallucinations faded in time, but sharp chronological sequences of her near-death experience seemed to grow more vivid each time she tried to recreate it in her mind.

Barbara remained hospitalized for several weeks.

"I told all my doctors that I had left the bed. That's all I was telling them," she recalled years later.

"Just forget about it, dear," they told her—or said she was hallucinating.

"The only doctor who seemed to listen to me was my internist. When I told him what happened to me, he wrote down his home telephone number on the tissue box next to my bed and told me to call him if it happened again."

Encased in a body cast and armed with an array of pain-killing drugs, relaxants, and sleeping pills, Barbara was finally released from the hospital in late June. The cast came down from her armpits, ending around the groin area, and extended down her right leg to her knee. The cast weighed about thirty pounds and Barbara weighed only eighty-five.

"I had to lie down in the back seat of the car all the way home. Actually, Sherwin and a nurse had loaded me into the back like a piece of furniture. As we approached the house, I was able to pull myself up enough to see the front, and as we came up the drive, the back of our home. Our house sat far back from the road on an acre of beautiful land. I suddenly realized that flowers had been planted all around the house. Impatiens, pansies, and geraniums were arranged in the usual way I had planted them every year. Sherwin told me the women from the garden club had planted them all in one day; several of my friends did it as a get-well gift. I was so filled with joy. What a wonderful, thoughtful gift. The colors seemed more brilliant than I remembered them. Every time I looked out a window that summer, the colors of those flowers filled me with the caring of those friends who had planted them.

"I was too weak to manage the cast and the stairs. Sherwin had to drag me up. The house looked beautiful inside. The colors pulled me in, welcomed me back. I needed to cry. I needed to rest. But I never needed to check for dust, to make sure my house was 'in order.' That part of me was gone."

The next six months were spent in bed at home. From her armpits to her knees, Barbara was encased in plaster. She watched people living and moving and talking when she could, but most of the time she was alone in her bed.

Barbara convalesced slowly, still aided by painkilling drugs and sleeping pills.

"I was on Valium and I had two kinds of sleeping pills," she recalls. "I was taking so many drugs I was in a constant dreamlike state. My heart was overflowing with this incredible love for everyone and everything around me. But I couldn't connect with anyone."

Her children, twelve-year-old Beth, Steven, who was nine, and five-year-old Gary, had been without their mother on and off for two years because of her illness. Now that she was home, she was still separated from them because she spent most of her time lying in bed. The body cast made free movement around the house impossible. For six months she lay there with thoughts of her grandmother, the tunnel, the love, her childhood, John Kennedy drowning, and threatening Dobermans. Barbara held all these images in, unable to define any of it.

"The only memories I have of my children then are of them waving to me from my bedroom door. The place I held in our family—mother, wife, and friend—was gone. Sherwin and the kids had done the best job they could do, and I had the feeling they didn't know how to move over and make room for me again." Despite these sad thoughts, Barbara says she began to feel unexplainable happiness.

"I had such wonderful feelings of joy bubbling up in me like a geyser. When I expressed thoughts that seemed wonderful to me, my eyes would fill with tears. I had to learn not to let the children see me cry," she said, "because tears to them meant pain, and they'd plead with me to take another pill. No one understood that my tears were happy tears," she said. "I wanted them to know that I was back, but no one seemed to hear," she said.

Feeling disconnected and lonely, Barbara sought the help of a psychiatrist.

"There was a lot of static about my wanting to see a psychiatrist. My family was really against psychiatry. It was something to be ashamed of, but I got my brother to take me to see a psychiatrist at Beaumont Hospital. I was still in the body cast, and again I had to be loaded into a station wagon like a piece of furniture," she said. "During the first four or five sessions, I told the doctor I was having problems communicating with my family. I wanted to tell him that I felt differently about things too, but I had trouble explaining myself. There were no words to explain what I felt then.

"In my life review, I immediately clicked into things clearly for the first time. I had felt like a victim of the people around me for most of my life. In the life review, I could see that we were all victims. All those wounds and scars were suddenly healed after the life review. It was like having years of therapy in an instant. I now had this strong urge to hug and love everyone." This is what she wanted to say to the psychiatrist, but couldn't find the words.

"Every other doctor I had talked to just wrote prescriptions for more drugs when I brought it up, so I was afraid to talk about it until the sixth session. Finally I told him about leaving the bed that night, and I started describing my life review. He just listened."

Finally he told her: "Barbara, your doctors were afraid you weren't going to come out of this." Above all, he said, she needed to remain quiet and rest until her body healed. Then, she could come back, when she was stronger, and go back into her childhood through analysis.

"He wrote a prescription for antidepressants, little red pills, and sent me home," Barbara said.

About a week after she got home, Sherwin and a neighbor arrived with a present.

"Sherwin and Don Madigan brought me a walker. It had a big bow on it, and Don told me I'd need it at the end of the week because he was having a picnic and baseball game at his house with my son Gary and his son Rusty, who was four."

That weekend, Barbara was hauled down the street to the Madigans' house and propped up against a car so she could watch the game.

"Some of the kids were still in Pampers," she said. "I couldn't stand and watch much of it because I was still weak, but Don did everything he could to make me feel I was still part of things. For a few wonderful moments that day I was able to laugh and put my ordeal behind me."

Although in a cumbersome body cast, Barbara found some freedom with her walker. One night, about a week later, she looked at her nightstand, which was covered with bottles of pills. The bathroom counter was covered with medications too.

"I went to the mirror and realized that I looked so unhealthy. I took out some rouge and started putting it on my cheeks to put some color on my face. Suddenly I looked at the pills and the rouge on my face," she said. "I started opening bottles of pills and pouring them down the toilet."

Soon after, Barbara began experiencing meditation or silent prayer, although at the time she had no name for it.

*If anyone had told me then that I was meditating, I would have denied it. Meditation wasn't something I knew about or cared to try. We weren't "into that kind of thing" and I wasn't trying to be interested in anything weird.*

*I was able to go back in the tunnel, where I was enveloped by the blackness again. In one direction was the bubble that contained my thirty-two-year-old body. In another direction I saw a cloudlike formation with thousands of other transparent bubbles.*

*I believed I had been the victim of a stern mother and a quiet father. I had often felt unloved by my parents. I felt overwhelming compassion for my mother, whose pain became mine as I watched these scenes. There were times when I wasn't sure if I was watching events or reliving them.*

*Somehow, I seemed to understand the reason for things clearly. I knew the presence I felt was God's.*

This was her memory of her experience in the hospital. It was as clear and vivid as if it had occurred yesterday. It had been more than six months, and she had little difficulty remembering details of that night. The hallucinations and nightmares had long ago disappeared, but the images of this profound experience stayed with her.

Remembering it left her with an understanding she couldn't explain until years later.

*I was acting. My whole life I was acting because I always had the feeling that if people found out who I really was they wouldn't like me, that I was really very bad. I had walked around for thirty-two years hiding the fact that I was bad. As a child, when I got spanked I felt I was bad. And when something good happened, I felt I really didn't deserve it.*

*Up to this point, my whole life had been an act, an act to be good so people would believe that I was a good person, and if I could win everybody over, then I would finally like myself.*

*When I came back, I really understood that I was a good person, and if people would get to know the real me, they would like me. I met my real self during the experience in the hospital. It was the most important incident of my life. I had really been born again, not in a religious sense but in a spiritual sense.*

Even years later, Barbara could vividly remember who she had been before her NDE and compare that Barbara with the woman she was becoming.

*I could put myself into that mental state and see a totally different human being than I am now. If I still had to be that other Barbara, I wouldn't want to be walking around. I would probably find something else that hurt just as badly as my back, and I would probably have a tremendous need for all the pain medication to fill that emptiness that was so much a part of me.*

Without knowing exactly how, Barbara knew she was changing, and changing rapidly.

*That emptiness had been filled up by something in my being that I can only call love. I don't mean the kind of love I had thought of until then. Before, love was what made Sherwin and me want to get married and own each other; it kept us loyal. Everything we owned, we loved: our kids, our home, our airplane. We loved what we possessed. I loved being accepted in the community, working for good causes, being a Girl Scout leader. All of that is important, but this was new, this was overflowing, this brought tears spilling out every time I thought of it.*

The final few days in the body cast were pure agony. Barbara's skin had rubbed so raw that the cast's plaster had become stained with blood. She spent hours using a hand-held dryer set on cool to circulate fresh air inside the cast.

Some areas, especially directly around the leg, couldn't be reached. The itching was unbearable. All of her muscles had atrophied. Only meditation—memories of her childhood as relived through the NDE—and a sense of connection with something greater than herself kept her sane. After five and a half months, the body cast was removed.

*The body cast came off in November. I was so thin. My ten-year-old son's blue jeans fit me. I started eating hot-fudge sundaes and pastry, plus the usual meals, and began to put on weight. My orthopedic surgeon told me I had to build my muscles again by swimming and walking. I couldn't do anything else. I signed up at the YMCA for different swimming classes that wouldn't push me too hard, classes suitable for pregnant women, heart-attack cases . . . and me. I was at the pool three times a week. Gary and I would go in the evening for family swims. I remember one evening that winter when it was below zero. We bundled up and went swimming. My six-year-old was my companion, in wool hats, scarves, leggings, and boots. We giggled as we ran through the snowflakes into the car, but our teeth chattered for the fifteen-minute ride home.*

*I could walk when it was clear. I was warned repeatedly not to go out when it was slippery. One fall, and I could crack the still-fragile fusion in my spine.*

Encouraged by Sherwin to reward herself, Barbara went back to school. She enrolled in a personal-growth workshop at Oakland University in nearby Rochester. She emerged from the two-week seminar determined to find new ways to communicate.

"Sherwin and I had been childhood sweethearts," she said. "As adults, he was in the role of parent and I was still a child," she recalled years later. "Now I wanted equality. I wanted to be on the same level, and suddenly the workshop had given me a language with which to express this to him.

"I was still searching for a language to explain what had happened to me in the Circle Bed. I needed words to explain how I was changing too. Sherwin wanted me to go to school. "See if you can find it there,' he said.

# 5

## First Inklings

While all of this was going on in Barbara's life, Dr. Bruce Greyson, a professor of psychiatry at the University of Virginia, was involved in parapsychological research with Dr. Ian Stevenson and was about to turn his attentions to work in near-death studies. Dr. Raymond Moody had just become a resident, working under Dr. Greyson; his book *Life After Life* was soon to be published. The book was to become a landmark work in the field of near-death studies, and Bruce Greyson's interest in the subject had been ignited by Moody's research. Meanwhile, Dr. Kenneth Ring was busy with his own research at the University of Connecticut.

Together these researchers were learning that the near-death experience itself has a profound mystical aftereffect on survivors. There was a great deal more to explore, and their research was accelerating at a rapid pace. Barbara knew none of this at the time. Even if she had heard the phrase "near-death experience" back in 1975, she would not have been able to connect it to what had happened to her that year. She was the wife of a wealthy midwestern businessman—that was her reality.

The Harrises' private plane was still hangared at a nearby airport. Sherwin was working toward upgrading himself as an instrument pilot. In 1976, he decided to fly the family to Washington in their Cessna for the Bicentennial Weekend, a celebration of the nation's two hundredth anniversary. It was a weekend of exhibits at the Smithsonian Institution, parties, and parades.

"I would have been very excited about a trip like that before," Barbara said, "but I just didn't feel part of things anymore. Things I used to enjoy no longer held my interest. I didn't talk about it. I appeared to be having a good time, but I was really out of it and just didn't know how to reconnect."

The old Barbara might have cried in frustration, as if she'd been jilted and abandoned by those she was closest to. Instead, she simply attributed the estrangement to her long illness and absence from the family's lives.

Her reasoning, however, was incorrect. The old wife and mother was a memory. Without knowing how or why, Barbara Harris had taken her first steps on a long road toward change. A radical transition in life-style had already been set in motion without her knowing it, by forces she would not have been able to accept at the time.

The changes in her began gradually, but she started noticing isolated, often odd occurrences around her. She was also overcome by strange feelings that had never happened to her before. It slowly dawned on her that a change was occurring in her, but she could not identify it.

"Suddenly television became noise to me, I couldn't take the violence," she said. "I stopped reading the newspapers and spent a lot of time, three or four times a week, just sitting quietly listening to classical music. I had never listened to classical music in my life, but I suddenly joined a record club and was buying Beethoven and Bach records. Beethoven's Ninth Symphony became my favorite piece of music.

"Then something else started happening. I'd be lying in the living room reading and suddenly get this surge of anxiety," she said. "I'd go from being totally relaxed into overdrive and I'd get unexplainable bursts of energy. It was an uncomfortable feeling. I wanted to just shoot myself off the sofa, and the only way I could overcome this feeling was to sit on the floor with my legs crossed in an odd position and wrap my arms around my body." The position she found most comfortable resembled the seated lotus position meditators use.

"This happened without warning, and the only way I could relieve that feeling was to sit like that until it subsided."

About the same time, she began getting severe headaches.

"I can remember getting four or five headaches, and I'll never forget them because they got so bad I'd sometimes start vomiting and see flashing white light," she said. "I had heard that people who got migraine headaches sometimes saw lights, and I just assumed that was what was happening to me."

At one point the pain was so intense that Barbara drove to the office of the internist who had given her his home phone number that night in Beaumont Hospital when she told him she had left the bed.

"He gave me a shot of Demerol and another shot of

Companzine. Sherwin had to come down and drive me home,'' she said. The medication had little effect for most of the evening, but just before midnight, the headache began subsiding.

"He said he was prepared to admit me to the hospital again if my headache didn't stop," she said. "Then he said something strange. 'The barometric pressure began falling at eleven-thirty, Barbara. Sensitive people sometimes get bad headaches when the barometer readings are high.'

"I felt so alienated from my family and friends at that time. I knew they were the way they had always been, but I felt so confused. I wasn't interested in the old stuff. I was scared of headaches and finally went to have an EEG, a test to record brain waves for any abnormalities. I was angry with myself for needing more medical tests, and while I was in the waiting room of the lab I developed another headache that was so bad I left, went home, and sobbed until it stopped. I couldn't understand what was happening to me."

Barbara inadvertently found an unexpected and unorthodox way to relieve the pain in her head. She decided to take up volunteer work. She went back to Beaumont Hospital and was assigned to work in the emergency room. Her doctors approved, as long as the work was light.

"I had an especially bad headache the morning I started, and thought it was because of the excitement of being there for the first time as a volunteer. I didn't know what to expect, and naturally just thought the headache was brought on by anxiety," she said. "An old woman who came in complained of being cold, so they told me to get her a blanket from the warmer. I got her one, put it over her, and tried to soothe her by smoothing the blanket with my hands. For a couple of minutes I stroked this beautiful old gray-haired woman, trying to make her more comfortable, and my headache just disappeared. I could almost feel the pressure in my head drain out through my hands.''

With different patients under different circumstances, Barbara had this experience repeatedly. ''I'd feel pressure building up inside my head, but it always went away when I put my hands on the patients,'' she said. ''I couldn't explain it then, but helping them somehow always helped me too. Even when the headaches stopped, I'd come home after being on my feet for eight hours and I was supercharged. I knew it was because I was touching these people. I didn't know why, but it gave me an enormous amount of pleasure and energy.''

Volunteer work became Barbara's new addiction. Sherwin appeared to be happy that his wife wasn't just sitting home alone any longer, but he wasn't happy about what she was doing instead. ''I think Sherwin was turned off by my volunteer work. Hospitals, especially emergency rooms, upset him. I looked like a wealthy, bored housewife from Bloomfield Hills, and the staff and other bored Bloomfield Hills housewives joked about it.''

Sherwin tolerated rather than enjoyed her emergency-room tales over dinner or while chatting before they fell asleep at night.

''We never talked about it, but he knew that something was going on because when he had a headache, he would ask me to put my hands on him. Somehow, I knew I was supposed to put my right hand at the base of his neck and my left hand on his forehead. Without knowing how or why it worked, I would put my hands on him and his headaches disappeared too,'' she said.

Other odd things happened to Barbara, for which she had

no logical explanation. At thirty-five she began to notice pockets of heat in various parts of her body. "My big toe would get hot, or a spot on my right hip would heat up, while the skin around it remained cool," she said. "Sherwin and I never talked about it in detail, but I would ask him to feel my hands or hip, and he felt the heat too."

She also began seeing things that no one else could see. "I'd suddenly see flashes of light. When that happened at night while I was trying to get to sleep, I always just assumed it was lightning outside." One night, when the flashing lights began, she asked Sherwin if he had seen them. "We both watched for bolts of lightning outside. I saw the flashes. Sherwin didn't."

At about the same time, she also began awakening spontaneously at about two o'clock in the morning—as if by someone or something. "This didn't happen only occasionally; it happened every night during this period. It was like being called awake by a silent voice or nudged by an invisible finger. It wasn't like insomnia. It didn't disturb me, it felt natural, and I'd just lie there for two hours, until four o'clock every morning. The only way I can explain it, even now, is to say it felt like I was being plugged into something and getting invisible lessons every night," she said. "Whatever it was, it energized me."

Barbara was getting only four or five hours' sleep, but she had more energy than she used to have after eight hours of undisturbed sleep. She was taking college courses at Oakland University, was cooking for the first time in years, was doing things with her kids again, and was doing volunteer work with the Cub Scouts, the school, and the hospital.

*The moment I got out of my car and strolled through the campus of Oakland University, I took a deep breath. Maybe*

*I had never breathed before. For sure it felt like I had never really lived before. This was it. I was a newborn human being in a whole new environment. I wanted to be a sponge and absorb all the knowledge I could. I wanted the library to be my second home. I never wanted to do another fundraiser again. That was too many levels away from helping someone. I wanted to help myself first—become something, someone who could help other people directly. I was so thankful Sherwin wanted me to go back to school. Not even back; to start school. I had missed all this, and now I was going to do it. I promised myself I wouldn't abandon Cub Scouts and my other activities—they were still important.*

*After I got the catalog of classes, I sat on a bench in the middle of the campus and read. This was better than the Neiman-Marcus Christmas catalog could ever be!*

While much of her life seemed to be changing, something that had always been a part of her marriage remained the same. Sherwin had been her steady "boyfriend" now for more than twenty years, and every Saturday night they had a date. One Saturday they planned to go to Barbara's garden-club cocktail party. Barbara had some difficulty fitting into the swing of things, but she still felt close to some of these women. Their children went to the same schools and played outdoors together. They had had a lot in common.

It was at the party that something else unexpected happened, an experience that would be a precursor to future profound precognitive experiences. This one involved Don Madigan, the neighbor who had coaxed Barbara out and onto the walker he and Sherwin bought when she was first discharged from the hospital. Barbara had always been close to Cindy, Don's wife, but hadn't been particularly close to him. Like the other men in the neighborhood, Don was a successful businessman and spent much of his time traveling.

It was a warm night, so Barbara and Sherwin walked to the party just down the street. The house was typical of the neighborhood: the living room had an expansive picture window that overlooked gardens and nearby woods. The house could easily accommodate the thirty-five couples who had been invited to the party.

"I looked across the room at a group of men, and Don was sitting in the middle of them," she said. "For reasons I couldn't explain, I studied him intently, and an ominous feeling overcame me. There was something urgent about it. I walked over to the group and started talking to him. It was almost as if no one else was there.

"I was about to sit in an empty space next to him when a woman took it, so I just sat in his lap," she said. "This was an odd thing for me, because we were friends, but I had never shown him this kind of affection before."

"Don," Barbara said, "I feel that I just have to tell you that I love you," surprising both herself and the husband of a close friend and neighbor. But Barbara wasn't professing romantic love. It was a strong platonic admission, more like caring, more like universal love, not a sexual or romantic love.

As shocking as what she heard herself saying was, Barbara continued, unable to stop.

"You helped me more than you'll ever know when you insisted I come to your picnic when I first got out of the hospital," she said. "I want you to know I think you're a wonderful man."

"Nobody ever said anything like that to me, Barbara," he said sheepishly. "I don't feel very good about myself at all. In fact, I never really quite made it to the places I wanted to go, and for some reason, I know I've gone as far as I'm going to go."

"More than any other man in this room, you should be proud of yourself, Don Madigan. You're self-made, got no help from anyone. You run with all the biggies in your field, you've got three great kids, a wonderful wife. You've made it, and you managed to stay human doing it," she said, lost in their conversation. When she looked up, Cindy gave her a limp smile then signaled Barbara to get off her husband's lap. Barbara, flush with embarrassment, immediately got up. The feeling that had driven her to be so intimate, so friendly with another woman's husband, had passed. What lingered, however, was a feeling of doom and foreboding that she couldn't explain.

A week later, Don was dead. The victim of a massive heart attack, he had collapsed in front of Barbara's house while jogging, and died at the age of thirty-five.

# 6

## Go Where You Shine

In her work at the hospital, Barbara gravitated to needy strangers, as part of some unspecified but urgent mission. This need to help others soon became the dynamic core of her personality. She had first noticed it when she was compelled to approach Don.

"I didn't know Don Madigan was going to die, but now that I look back on it, I knew *something* wasn't right for him and I had to tell him I loved him," she said.

But now this need was spreading to people she knew only casually or not at all. It caused unnecessary friction in a family about to be plagued with a series of conflicts—all in one way or another related to Barbara's changing attitudes.

When she tried to tell Sherwin how she had helped a critically ill patient relax or comforted a dying man, he received these stories coolly. Barbara had become comfortable working with the dying. What was fulfilling to her sounded morbid to Sherwin.

"I wasn't trying to be that way," she said, "but I'd know when people were dying. I could tell them that dying wasn't painful. I could tell them that there was nothing to fear. For some reason, I knew how to comfort them, but Sherwin said I talked about death and sickness all the time," she said. "He couldn't understand why I felt so much for people I hardly knew, and I knew it upset him."

Nevertheless, Barbara loved her volunteer work and didn't seem to have a conscious choice over whether or not she was doing the right thing. She was acting on newly discovered urges and instincts that compelled her to befriend just about everyone she came in contact with, for reasons she couldn't explain. "I felt connected to everyone, whereas before I was feeling distanced," she said. For instance, in 1976 a chance meeting with a couple from New Zealand living in Michigan temporarily turned into a close friendship. Karen Collins had simply answered a classified ad Barbara had run, hoping to sell their old dining-room table and chairs. The friendship began over a cup of coffee and it lasted for almost two years, until Karen, Chris, and little Gina moved back to their Pacific island home.

"They didn't know the old Barbara, so I could just be me with them. I found the friendship liberating, because in New Zealand there isn't as much emphasis on material things," she said. "I found them refreshing. They saw everything differently than Americans. They joked about status-seeking and materialism."

*For the two years that they were in Michigan, we cele-brated all the holidays together, their country's, this coun-try's, and the Jewish holidays. I remember one Passover seder, they bought us Blue Nun wine and we laughed so hard as we explained this Jewish holiday and its rigid dietary laws to them. They bought a house near us. We celebrated holidays together and would even return, the day after big events, to eat all the leftovers and help clean up. We spent days hanging wallpaper in their house. Both Karen's and Chris's parents came to visit and we had dinner parties for them and showed them around Michigan. We took trips in the plane to many parts of the United States that we had been to before. But we saw things again, as if for the first time, through their eyes. For the first time since my NDE, I could pour my heart out to a girlfriend who really understood. She wasn't locked into any of the old beliefs. We giggled all the time. We socialized with other people from all over the world that were part of the Burroughs International Group, the company that had brought Chris, Karen, and three-year-old Gina Collins into our lives. We spent a fun summer by our pool with them and a group of French, Italian, Australian, and British people.*

*In November we flew with the Collinses to Florida to visit Sherwin's parents. Sherwin's dad had cancer and shortly after that Thanksgiving together, he died.*

*Karen and Chris were so taken with Florida, they couldn't believe that we wanted to live in Michigan. They constantly told us stories about how wonderful it is to live by the sea. They painted wonderful scenes for us of the wonder of living naturally in a warm climate all year long.*

*We took a trip to Disney World with them, and again they talked about how much happier we would be in Florida. Sherwin had wanted to move years ago. I was the one who needed convincing.*

*Then, in the spring of 1978, the Collinses moved back to New Zealand. As they were preparing to leave, Sherwin put the business up for sale and I handled the sale of the house. Both sold within two weeks.*

*These wonderful fun-loving people came into our lives at a unique time, and when they left two years later, nothing was the same for us. As we moved to Florida, I prayed that this would be a new beginning for Sherwin and me, that we would find common goals in settling our family in a whole new environment. We both agreed that this would be a fresh start.*

*One night in that short span of time after the Collinses left and before we did, I was sitting up in bed starting a new book. As I turned to the first page, my eyes froze. The two main characters were called Karen and Christopher Collins! I started laughing, and then tears streamed down my face.*

When the Harris family moved to Florida, they bought a home in Pembroke Pines, just a few miles north of Miami. Like their house in Michigan, this was a rambling four-bedroom home, this time on a lake with palm trees. Shortly after they moved in, they built a swimming pool with adjacent whirlpool on a screened-in terrace. Barbara quickly fell in love with her new surroundings.

Sherwin passed the Florida real-estate exam and worked in an office six blocks from the house. Barbara took classes in real-estate law, hoping they could develop a new common interest, but by the time she finished, he had bought a furniture-manufacturing business. She forgot real estate and followed her first love, seeking out the sick and dying. She enrolled at the Respiratory Therapy Institute near downtown Miami. Respiratory therapy was a new and exciting branch of nursing with a focus on critical-care units and emergency-room training.

During her two and a half years of training, Barbara continued to have encounters with strangers. As part of the training, students were assigned to clinical practicums in Miami-area hospitals. Barbara did a series of rotations at Mount Sinai Medical Center in South Miami Beach and at Mercy Hospital in Coconut Grove. As in Michigan, she continued to have odd encounters with the people she met. One of them was a black woman who worked in the nursery at Mount Sinai.

*One morning, while I was assigned to the neonatal unit, I put on a sterile gown and worked with this tiny baby who couldn't have weighed more than three pounds. My gaze was fixed on this infant for a long time, so I wasn't aware of my surroundings. When I finally did look up, a huge black woman in white was watching me. We made eye contact and smiled at one another.*

*When I looked up again, she was outlined in light. A golden aura surrounded her body, and the longer I looked, the brighter the light became.*

*Nothing was said for some time, but when I finished caring for the infant, I walked over to the woman and we began talking.*

"Working with these little babies doesn't scare me, but I can't seem to go into a burn unit," Barbara confessed.

"Child, each one of us has an area where we shine," the woman told her. "I shine with these babies. I know which ones are going to make it, and I know which ones won't be going home. Go where you shine." She put her hands on Barbara's shoulders. "Don't force yourself to go anywhere you don't feel right!"

Officially, because she was a student at the Respiratory Therapy Institute, Barbara was no longer a volunteer. As part of her course of study, she worked with the terminally ill at Mount Sinai. This lasted for two and a half years. In a one-on-one situation, she found she could quickly tune in to those patients who had come near death. On a floor filled with critically ill patients, Barbara, like the black woman in the neonatal unit, somehow knew which patients would recover and which would not. This was where Barbara could "shine."

Barbara knew from her own experience that most doctors and some of the nurses ignored a patient's reports of seeing "light at the end of a tunnel." They believed the patient had been hallucinating. Barbara knew differently. While the doctors tended to the physical needs of these patients, Barbara listened to their stories and shared their awe over the experience. A few garbled sentences about leaving the bed, about sighting dead relatives, or about feeling able to live or die by simply choosing, and Barbara knew that they had had experiences similar to her own a few years before.

Her memory of that time was as vivid as it had ever been, and although she still did not have any formal language for these experiences, she could relate easily with these patients and comfort them.

Whenever patients recovered enough to talk about their experiences, Barbara always found she had one thing in common with them. Their fear of death, like her own, had disappeared. If they spoke of seeing "the light," a serene, peaceful smile accompanied the conversation. If they recalled having a life review, the conversation was punctuated with new understanding about loved ones.

It was under similar circumstances that she met Bernie Hirsch. Hirsch was a poorly dressed man she stumbled into one morning in front of the school on Biscayne Boulevard, a section of Miami populated by homeless alcoholics and an occasional prostitute.

"I parked on the side street next to the school and locked the car. As I approached the front entrance, I saw a man sitting on the steps slumped over. He was perspiring heavily, more heavily than he should have been at that time of the morning, even in Florida. He wore shoes without socks and was dressed in mismatched clothes.''

"Are you all right?" Barbara asked, feeling the same need to talk to this stranger she had felt for Don Madigan that night back in Michigan.

He answered her, but his speech was garbled and disjointed.

Tom Green, Barbara's six-foot-five-inch black instructor, walked up the stairs. Tom was wary of the drunks and street hustlers who populated the neighborhood. " Class will be starting," he said as he passed the two on the steps. "Come inside, Barbara," he said, walking through the glass doors without her.

"My glance darted back and forth, looking at Tommy standing inside and this man slumped at my feet," Barbara said. "He must have been between fifty and sixty years old. He looked like a lot of the bums who panhandled in the area, but I knew this man was in trouble. Without thinking, I bent down and touched him. I took his pulse. It raced so fast it was impossible to count.''

"Barbara, get in here," Tom yelled, sticking his head out the door.

"I raced up the stairs inside and tried to get Tommy to listen to me. He's in trouble," she pleaded. "He needs help.''

"He's a drunk," Tom said.

"No, I tried to take his pulse and its racing. He's disoriented. He needs our help.''

Outside, Tom took the man's pulse. Without speaking, he walked up the steps and headed toward his classroom.

Barbara went in too, but couldn't just forget about the

man outside, so she went back out. The man tried to speak, saying something about his wife. His words were still garbled.

"I am going to call an ambulance," she told him.

"That'll scare my wife," she understood him to say through his slurred speech. "Take me to the Miami Heart Institute."

The Heart Institute was no ordinary health-care facility. It was an exclusive hospital. What did this man know about such a place? she wondered.

Tom emerged through the glass doors again. "That's it," he shouted. "Get in here now, Barbara, and leave that drunk alone!"

"I can't," she pleaded. "I'm taking him to the hospital."

"No you're not," Tom shouted, acting like a big brother and the friend that he had been. "He could die in your car and some relative will sue you and Sherwin. They didn't care about this bum when he was alive, but if something happens to him now, they'll sue you anyway. Get in here. I'll call 911 and let them worry about him."

Tom called and she stayed outside with the stranger. Whatever was wrong was getting worse.

"We're getting you some help," Barbara told him.

"No," he shouted, and scrambled to his feet. He started running, and Barbara chased after him. He ran out into the heavy traffic on Biscayne Boulevard. She caught him just as he crossed the yellow line. Back near the curb, he started running parallel to the parked cars. Tom emerged from nowhere and wrapped his big frame around this ailing older man.

The emergency medical team arrived minutes later and took their captive away.

Tom was obviously annoyed with Barbara but said nothing. He took his position at the blackboard and began teaching. Barbara sat through the class without hearing a single word he said that morning. When the class ended, she bolted out and headed for the Heart Institute, half an hour away on Miami Beach.

*The hospital looked more like a luxury hotel than a place where they practiced medicine. At the front desk I explained what had happened three hours earlier. No, I didn't know his name. I wasn't even sure the EMTs would bring a disheveled man like that to a hospital like this. It took some time, but we finally located him. When I entered the room, a petite well-dressed woman was standing by the bed.*

*The patient, Bernie Hirsch, was in a private room. He had been hooked up to various monitoring devices, he had been washed, and his hair was combed. The woman was his wife, Laura.*

*"I found him this morning," I told her.*

*"He's lucky," she said. "He was in arrhythmia and could have had a heart attack. He'll be here for a week or two. This has happened once before."*

*I stayed only a short time, then drove out of Miami Beach over the Broward County line out of Miami, heading home.*

*I checked in to see Bernie about a week later and he was discharged shortly after that brief visit. For some reason, I felt strangely connected to the Hirsches. About a month after Bernie got out of the hospital, I called their house and asked if I could visit them.*

*What I found when I got there surprised me.*

*They lived in the penthouse of a fashionable condominium that overlooked Biscayne Bay. A valet parked my car. There were a doorman and security guards. Whoever Bernie Hirsch was, he wasn't the drunk we had mistaken him for* weeks earlier. Although he had looked the part that morning in front of the school, Bernie Hirsch wasn't your run-of-the-mill street person. The school was just a few blocks away from this luxury condo, but Biscayne Boulevard was worlds away from this swank residence, located on what was commonly referred to as the Gold Coast.

The apartment opened up to a roof garden with a panoramic view of Biscayne Bay, Miami Beach, and the ocean. The interior was austere but well-appointed, with original works of art and hundreds of books. I stayed only a few minutes because I could tell they were both uncomfortable in my presence. Who was I, after all? What did I want from them? I tried to quell their fears, telling them that Sherwin and I owned a furniture-manufacturing business in Hallandale. It didn't work, so I left.

For reasons I can't explain, I still wanted to know these people, so I visited them once more months later. They were moving to California, I was told. Bernie looked ill and needed a change. They had already sold the penthouse and were buying a small studio on a lower floor, where they would stay when they returned to visit friends and relatives. Again I left with an uncomfortable feeling.

Bernie Hirsch called me a year later. He was back in Florida and asked if we could meet for lunch. When I saw him, my heart sank. His health was obviously failing. We lunched at a small restaurant he and his wife had often gone to when they lived here. After all this time, I finally found out who he was—a retired attorney. Bernie was well-known in the Miami area for his community work:

"I started a halfway house for prisoners released from the Miami County Jail," he told me. "When they're released, they spend a few months with retired lawyers in the Miami area."

"Why were you so poorly dressed the morning I found you?" I asked.

"The neighborhood isn't safe, so I dressed that way to blend in," he said. And then he told me about his personal life, about Laura and his children. He told me he was afraid his time was limited, and he felt so weighted down and confused. I told him about my back problems and how I had resolved my feelings of being different; how lonely it had been for me. As the day wore on, his coloring seemed to get better.

The following June, Bernie Hirsch died. His wife called to tell me, and she invited me to Bernie's memorial service in South Miami. I drove to the church alone. It was an unusual service, with no casket, and people stood and gave testimonials about the Bernie Hirsch they had known. One of his best friends, another attorney, said, "Bernie was such a good guy, the best, but that always worried him. He told me once that he was afraid of being too good—that after he died, we'd call him Saint Bernard." Everyone laughed. A singer sang his favorite song, "Summertime," from the opera Porgy and Bess.

I spoke briefly, saying that I had known Bernie only a short time but he had told me how much he loved his family and how concerned he was over leaving his wife and children behind. When I finished, Laura looked directly at me; our eyes met and I smiled.

We walked out silently as the singer sang another song Bernie had chosen to leave us with: "Cabaret."

# 7

## A View from the Circle Bed

Barbara knew that medical science refused to acknowledge such near-death experiences as seeing tunnels or being visited by long-dead relatives as real. While she still didn't recognize the fact that she had had an NDE, she knew these unexplainable levels were real.

Now, five years after her experience in the Circle Bed, as she was immersed in course work at the respiratory-therapy school in Florida, she wondered if perhaps the decision to go back to school had been prompted by an unconscious need to find out for herself what actually had happened to her medically in the hospital. Her doctor had denied any wrongdoing on the part of any attending hospital personnel, and had told her the ileus could not have been caused by the respirator. She had never been given a logical reason for it, so she was determined to find out herself.

Her suspicions were confirmed one morning as she drove

to school with Jana, an instructor at the school. Jana, who lived in a modest condominium fifteen blocks from Barbara's house, had always been a little puzzled by Barbara. Why would someone who lived on Pembroke Lake choose respiratory therapy as a profession? Most of the other students enrolled in this technical training course were people right out of high school.

Jana was visibly shocked when she heard that Barbara had been in a Stryker Frame Circle Bed and survived. "Most people who wind up in those beds don't make it," Jana said, "or they are crippled for life."

Barbara, telling her the story, finally said, "I blew up like a balloon while I was strapped in that thing. I developed an ileus."

"How did that happen?" Jana asked.

"The technician left me alone in the room while I was getting intermittent-positive-pressure-breathing treatments to keep my lungs clear," Barbara said as they drove along the I–95 to Miami. "I passed out when the breathing machine wouldn't stop. When I woke up, I thought I was having another baby, but I realized quickly that something was terribly wrong."

"An ileus is one of the negative effects of IPPB treatments," Jana said. "When we get to that unit, you'll learn all the side effects. I want you to tell this story when we cover IPPB treatments in class."

"Okay," Barbara said nervously.

"In fact, I think you should write about it. Give all our students an idea what it's like from the patient's point of view. Tell them how terrified you were in that bed. I want them to know so they won't leave their patients unattended."

Jana made it a daily habit to ask Barbara if she had written the paper. One Friday night at eleven-thirty, Barbara sat down to write it.

*Five years ago I was hospitalized several times for what was thought to be congenital scoliosis exacerbated by a fall. A few months later, a nerve block was done, followed by traction and muscle relaxants. Four hospitalizations and two years later, I was living on drugs in constant pain. It became apparent that permanent immobilization of my spine via a lumbar fusion was the best chance I had to get back to a normal life. Everyone involved—doctors, my husband, and I—knew that this was a necessary procedure. It may, in fact, have been delayed too long. . . .*

Wednesday, two P.M.: *What room number is this? Who cares? A private is a private. I was lucky to get back on orthopedics this soon. Same chair, same TV. Who cares about the bathroom? They say I'll never use it after tonight. Why did they put that dumb-looking bed in this room? It's crowded enough already. I'll be in that thing tomorrow. Why look at it today?*

*Oh, well, the view's pretty. The other times, the view wasn't like this one. I've never been on this side of the hospital. All those times they tried to help me. They are so nice. Most of them, that is. If I'm really good and don't cause any problems, then even the mean ones will be okay.*

*It's time for my Valium. I wonder if I'm supposed to get fives or tens? They really relax me when I get them with the Demerol shots.*

Wednesday, eight P.M.: *It feels so good now that they took the cast off. Wow! No cast for a month! That dumb Circle Bed will be a picnic after the cast. Maybe they'll let me take a bath before the surgery.*

*That was sweet of the chaplain to come in and talk to me, even though I'm not Christian. I hope he understood. If they don't help me tomorrow, I really do want to die, and I mean it. He looked at me funny. Well, maybe his God thinks you can be happy in pain. But if God is there and really loves me like he says, he'll let the surgeons fix my back—or he better let me die. I'm not going home to live like I have.*

*The Demerol's great. No pain anymore.*

Thursday, seven P.M.: *Wow! Surgery is far-out! I love what they're wearing. This shot is a riot. They look like spacemen. They really are breathing in those suits.*

Visiting hours: *Mmmm. This bed's not so bad. I can't even feel the mattress. They said it was like a hammock. Well, it's much better than that.*

*Oh, look, there's Bob. Isn't that nice? He's on his way home from work and he came to see me. Hi, Bob!*

Late Thursday: *Hi, Doctor. Great Demerol. No pain! Morphine! Is that right? Hmm. Is that stronger than Demerol? Like a kid's loose tooth? My back? Oh! It's broken through. Like a kid's loose tooth, huh?*

*See you tomorrow. Say hi to your wife for me.*

*Look at those bags. Three of them! My arm doesn't even feel all the needles.*

Friday or Saturday, eight A.M.: *Hi! You're so young and cute to be working here. (Is he old enough? What's that machine? Is he kidding? Why cough? I'm not sick. I'm not here with a cold. Breathe for me? Can't he see I'm breathing on my own? Oh, well, be good, Barbara, or he'll tell some-*

*one else.) Sure, put it in my mouth. Wow! Again? Oh, well, I'll humor him. He's so young.*

*Oh, sure, you can leave. I'll do it myself. There's nothing to it. Don't worry. Have a break. I'm very cooperative. I've been here five times now. They all know me. You can ask them. I'm very cooperative. You go do what you have to and I'll let this thing breathe for me.*

*Okay, I'll take a little sip and . . . hmmm. So . . . stop. Too much . . . stop! Oh, God!*

Late P.M.: *What time is it? It's dark in the halls. So many people in here! I'm having a baby! Look at my stomach! Oh, oh. My incision is pulling! My skin is going to burst. Make my stomach go down. My incision is going to explode! Please, all of you. Can you hear me? Help, please!*

*What's that? Am I pregnant? What's an ileus? That machine blew me up. I remember now.*

*A shot, please, anything! Why put a tube in my nose? You're sticking tubes and pipes and bottles all over me. But I've been good. Oh, please. They're making me worse! Let me die!*

Next day: *Hi! What? Oh, I don't care. There's room up there for another plastic bag. Just stick it up there. I wonder whose blood that was? Hi, Jeanine, you drove all the way here to see me. Traffic must have been bad. She looks sick. She's rubbing my arm. Oh, that feels good. Thanks. I wish someone would touch me again. No one touches you when you're in here. I'm not contagious.*

Days later: *Boy, this is becoming a drag. TV's boring and doesn't even make sense. Oh, well, almost time for a shot.*

*Hey, don't open those drapes. It's too bright! It'll hurt my eyes. I don't care what's out there. Nobody's going to open those drapes.*

*Time to rotate me? Okay. Make sure the bedpan's out of the mattress. Straps. Plug it in. Boy, I'm getting good at this. I bet I could do it myself, but they'd get mad. Here goes . . . and over we go!.*

*Feels good. Maybe my back'll stop sweating for a while. Thanks, Nurse. You're both sweet. Remember to close the door. I can't stand the noise of the hospital's page system. Okay, thanks. I'll see you in twenty minutes. Yes, I'm fine.*

Later: *Longer than usual, I think. I wish they'd hurry. I have to go to the bathroom. Not to the bathroom, in the pan. Don't know why I have to pay for a bathroom I can't use.*

*Where are they? Oh, please come open the door. Where's the button? No button. They forgot to pin it on! Please come back. Please, Nurse. Please, someone! Oh, God, I don't want to be bad. I'm thirty-two years old. I can't wet this bed. Help! Total hysteria, followed by shots.*

*Nurse, where's my nurse? Was she sick? She usually doesn't leave early. Is she okay? Is she mad at me?*

Next week: *Why am I crying? Stop crying. They'll be upset with you. Hi, Nurse. Please go away. I'm crying and I shouldn't be. I've been so good. I never cried the whole time, and now I'm ruining it . . . Don't tell me it's okay. It's not okay. I should see a psychiatrist because I think I'm too depressed. I shouldn't be. The guy in the next room is dying of cancer. Now, he can be depressed, but me, I'm lucky. Tomorrow I get the body cast, and I won't be able to move for a long time, but that's okay, because I'll be out of this dumb bed. So I have no right to cry. I want to be good.''*

Postscript: *When I was in the Circle Bed, everyone thought I was unaware and no one communicated with me. I thought I was communicating, but most of the time the words stayed in my head.*

*When I did get them out, no one understood me. So I decided to put my story into words in the hopes that it can create more empathy and compassion among practitioners in this field I have learned to love. As I walk into a patient's room, I am instantly aware of his or her fear and feelings of helplessness and even isolation from the rest of the human race.*

When Barbara finished the article about one A.M., she went into the den, where Sherwin was watching a movie. She read it aloud to him and he was stunned. He said he had never realized she was alert enough to understand so much of what had been going on around her when she was so critically ill.

*Sherwin's reaction to what I had written sent a bolt through me. So, what I did remember was true. I had the scenes in the Circle Bed straight. Those moments weren't hallucinated. I suddenly had an affirmation that my outer vision in the Circle Bed was accurate. Jana had confirmed that IPPB treatments done wrong could create an ileus. I had passed out when the ventilator wouldn't reverse, and so I couldn't remember when the technician came back. I could only remember waking up sometime later in horrible pain and screaming. Oh, how I wanted to die at that moment. The feelings inside me then were so strong I will never be able to forget them. I had no idea that I was starting to die, but I certainly wanted to. I was an atheist, I believed in nothing, nothing beyond this, but nothing would have been better than two years of Valium and painkillers and Circle Beds and body casts.*

*I kept my inner vision tucked safely in my heart. I never dreamed of putting it on paper. How could I tell anyone? I hadn't believed in anything; would anyone believe me? I didn't put my inner experience in the memories I had just written. I didn't try to tell anyone, not after trying to tell the psychiatrist while I was in the body cast in Michigan. I felt it was impossible to explain the kind of love I had felt. There was no man with a long white beard. There was this sense of love that we have no words for here, that I have no other experiences to fall back on to explain, except maybe it was my grandmother's love multiplied by a million or more. That energy, that feeling that held me up while I relived my life, loved me for all I had done. I was the one who had always judged me poorly. In that life review, I could feel my pain, and everyone else's pain too. That part was horrible, but behind our ignorance that created the pain, there was love, there was promise. And it was the same love that was with me, helping me to see me, and to see it in everything.*

*I never thought of trying to explain that inner journey in the paper I read to Sherwin. My heart never let me take it up to my head, for my heart knew devotion, whereas my head threatened to violate it. It was safely held in my heart and occasionally would trickle out when it could do some good. You couldn't talk about it; you could share it with people who needed it.*

Barbara read her paper in class. At Jana's urging, she mailed a copy of it to the American Association of Respiratory Therapists in Dallas, which published a monthly magazine. Within a month the editor wrote back asking if he could publish it in the November 1980 issue. It was to be published for the national convention of several thousand respiratory therapists later that year in Dallas.

Barbara was planning to go to Dallas in December 1980 for that convention when another life-changing experience occurred.

# 8

# Resurrection

Barbara's enthusiasm over the fact that her stream of consciousness article would appear in a national respiratory therapy magazine didn't interrupt her daily routine. A few weeks before the Dallas trip, Sherwin's cousin Carol Jefferson came to town on business. Carol still lived in Michigan, but she and her husband had bought a condo in Boca Raton. Barbara planned to take her shopping at Sherwin's furniture store.

The first night of her visit, Carol asked Barbara to see a movie called *Resurrection*, a new release starring Academy Award-winning actress Ellen Burstyn. Writing about her memories of the Circle Bed had already pushed all of Barbara's emotional buttons. Little did she know that the spontaneous decision to see *Resurrection*, a film neither of them knew anything about, would trigger recurring visions of the images she'd seen during the NDE.

The film begins with Burstyn planning to buy a birthday gift for her husband. She surprises him with a new red sports car one night after work. They drive off and head down a highway. Suddenly, without warning, he swerves the car to avoid hitting a boy on a skateboard. The car smashes through a guardrail and plunges down a steep embankment. The screen fades to black. The scenes that followed were flashed on the screen in rapid-fire succession:

A hazy view of a hospital operating room, with doctors and nurses in green gowns working on someone.

A flashback, reviewing the automobile crash.

An insider's view of a swirling tunnel of light. The tunnel is smoky and you can see shadowy images of people, all pointing toward a bright light at the far end of the tunnel. . . .

Burstyn's character was having a near-death experience, and Barbara sat watching it transfixed. At the same time, she began to relive her own NDE.

Without warning, the film is thrown into reverse, and the scenes are played backward.

Burstyn awakes in a hospital room and hears someone say, "Welcome back." Her husband has died in the crash, she is told. Her back has been badly damaged and she is confined to a wheelchair. The nerves in her spinal cord have been severed and she's told she'll never walk again.

"All of a sudden I had the same feeling I had during my experience, and I was back there again," Barbara recalled years later. "I was back there again and I was peaceful. I couldn't communicate what I was feeling to Carol. I was just back there again."

There was a scene in the film after Burstyn returns home to her harsh father's house when a child gets a sudden nosebleed during a town picnic.

"She's a bleeder," someone shouted. The town doctor, who had been playing horseshoes, rushes over and is unable to stop the bleeding. Just as the girl's mother is about to rush her to a hospital miles away, Burstyn asks if she can put her hands on the girl. She does, and the bleeding stops.

"She was looking at her hands just as I had been looking at my hands, and in the movie Ellen Burstyn's grandmother takes her hands and holds them," Barbara said. "They're hot," her grandmother said, talking about Burstyn's hands. Then the old woman told her about a woman who, fifty years earlier, had almost died, and when she recovered, she had become a healer.

"I was sitting there saying to myself: I knew all of this before, somehow, I knew all of this but never really put it together. That's what happened when I touched my patients." When Sherwin picked them up, Barbara climbed into the car and immediately blurted out details of the movie and how closely it matched her own experience.

"I had so much enthusiasm about it. It all made perfect sense, even the part about her hands heating up," Barbara said.

The following day, Carol and Barbara drove to Sherwin's factory showroom and shopped for several hours. Five minutes after they left, like Ellen Burstyn, they were involved in a car accident. Their car was hit at an intersection by another car that ran a stop sign. Barbara's right knee smashed through the plastic glove compartment and her left side was slammed into the steering column. Carol's face was covered in blood. Barbara was hurt too, and judging from her pain, she thought one of her lungs had probably collapsed. They were treated at Hollywood Memorial Hospital, where Barbara allowed technicians to X-ray her chest and neck, but she refused to let them X-ray her back. She denied she had reinjured it. That would be her worst nightmare revisited. The idea of facing surgery again was too much for her, so she denied any pain in her back.

"I stayed home for two weeks, hoping the pain would just disappear," Barbara said. It didn't. She was anxious to go to the convention in Dallas. Barbara and Sherwin had also been planning a trip back to Michigan to see Bill and Jeanine Hande, old friends who lived in Flint. She considered putting that trip off and also scrapping the trip to Dallas. After two weeks of thinking about both trips, however, she decided she was going to stay on her course despite her renewed problems.

"I know I'm off-track somehow," she said, praying aloud one day in her yard. "I know I'm hurt again. I promise I won't be bitter, but you've got to guide me," she prayed. She pleaded, then packed her bags and left for Dallas.

At the convention, she found the respiratory-therapy magazine everywhere she looked on the convention floor. One of the lecturers, Dr. Loren Bensley, a professor of health sciences, was speaking about caring for the emotional needs of the critically ill patient when she arrived.

"He thoroughly understood the subject," Barbara recalled. "Medical professionals," he said, "are so busy with the technical aspects of illness, they forget that patients float in and out of consciousness." He said patients needed to be touched and to be oriented, which was the reason Barbara had written her article in the first place.

After his talk, Dr. Bensley asked for questions and comments. Barbara stood and complimented him, saying she had written the article in the magazine and just wanted to confirm what he was saying. "It should be you up here speaking, not me," Bensley told her. She flushed with embarrassment and sat down.

"I wanted to talk to him afterward, but when I got to him, he said he had to leave to catch a plane almost immediately," Barbara said. "He gave me his card and told me to write to him." After he left, I glanced at it and couldn't believe what I read. He was at Central Michigan University, about an hour's drive away from Bill and Jeanine Hande's home in Flint.

When she wrote to Bensley, he invited her to visit him. She went a few weeks later, during her already scheduled trip to see Bill and Jeanine.

*I wasn't there five minutes when Loren led me to his class of health-care students, handed me a copy of my article, and told me to read it to them.*

*Everyone responded excitedly after I finished. We had a wonderful discussion on how to communicate with critically ill patients. The comments flew around the room, and suddenly class was over and a whole group stood around me in the hall and we continued. A nurse who had gone back to school had dinner with me in a nearby restaurant and we just kept going. When I drove back to my friends in Flint, Bensley's words kept going through my head:*

*"Your story shook them and opened them up. Keep writing, and by all means keep talking to classes, start applying to speak at conferences. We need more people with experiences like yours speaking in health-care education."*

She returned to Florida a few days later, determined to speak to hospital staffs and wherever else she could.

Barbara's chest and back problems persisted. So when she got back home, she consented to have her back X-rayed. The first chest films had shown no bone fractures, but four fractured ribs showed up this time. The spinal fusion had been damaged. Her doctors told her as gently as possible that she couldn't do any more direct patient care. Barbara was labeled as totally disabled now.

"I had three more months before I graduated from my respiratory training, and I was determined to finish," she said. She walked outside and stood by the lake she lived on, looked up into the sky, and again cried: "Okay, I was off-track—and you're putting me back on again. I promise not to be bitter if you promise to guide me."

Every day thereafter—after school and hospital clinicals—she drove to her doctor's office, where she underwent treatments; pads placed on her lower back sent electrical impulses traveling back and forth to either side of the new spinal injury. It was an attempt to relieve the pain. This was followed by twenty minutes of hydrocollator heat treatments that soothed the muscles around the spinal column. These treatments had a cumulative effect. One day, as she lay there, she could hear the hum of the ventilation system in the room. It hummed quietly, but she could hear it plainly.

"I was totally relaxed from the treatments and my hearing just absorbed the humming sound," she said. "The tone put me into a relaxed state of consciousness and it triggered an out-of-body experience. All of a sudden I could see my body down on the table and the sound of the humming noise was exactly like the sound I heard when I was in the tunnel. I also heard faint music," she said.

When she was not having these treatments, Barbara was aware of pain. She had heard about biofeedback as an alternative to drugs and was willing to do anything to avoid taking painkilling drugs again.

She found a book called *Beyond Biofeedback* by Elmer

and Alyce Green, researchers at the Menninger Foundation in Topeka, Kansas. They said in the book that the body will do what you tell it, if you learn how to tell it. They explained what visualization is and how to use it to communicate with your body. And then the Greens explained how this research fit in to pain control through biofeedback, a monitoring technique in which patients tune in to their own body rhythms—heart rate, brain waves, blood pressure, galvanic skin response and body temperature. After reading their book, Barbara decided to try it. She was able to borrow her first biofeedback machine, a little device equipped with goggles that had synchronized flashing lights and earphones. The lights and music were timed to flash in sync with a theta or alpha tone. Then she wrote away to a catalog company for a hand-held biofeedback machine known as a GSR unit. The object was to get the machine to emit a low tone, which meant you were relaxing. A high-pitched tone indicated that the patient was tense. Later, she found an inexpensive feedback device that fitted on a fingertip and gave a temperature readout. Using it, she trained herself to go into a deep state of relaxation by sitting with it three times a day. It relaxed the tense muscles around her spine so she didn't have to use muscle-relaxant medication. Eventually she could relax without the biofeedback apparatus. Barbara did this three times every day and was able to release her pain. At will, she could put herself into a deep trance.

This type of "free-form meditation" was giving her the actual experience of the healing energies and altered states of consciousness and it was also bringing her back to scenes she had been in during her near-death experience.

It was the beginning of a holistic approach aimed at healing herself. She also walked at least four miles a day, and often up to twelve miles when the weather was good. The pain in her chest from the four rib fractures disappeared, and the pain in her back began to subside.

In the fall of 1981 Barbara came across some old issues of *Omni* magazine. In one she found an article about a professor in Connecticut, and it immediately caught her attention.

"Knowing about people who have had near-death visions or other experiences is no guarantee you will have one yourself," the *Omni* story said. "In fact, according to a University of Connecticut psychologist who has completed an extensive study on the subject, just the opposite seems to be true.

"Dr. Kenneth Ring and his associates made this discovery after interviewing 102 persons who had come close to death through illness, accident, or, in some cases, attempted suicide," the brief article said.

"He did find that almost half, forty-eight percent, had what he calls a core experience, a sense of deep peace, reevaluation of their lives, a vision of unearthly lights, or even a confrontation with spirits," *Omni* said. "Among the men, he found that accident victims were most likely to have had these experiences. Women had their core experiences through illness. Attempted suicides had few of the experiences, and, curiously enough, the same was true of those who held religious beliefs in an afterlife or who had previously known of the near-death phenomenon," it said. "Most of those who had the experience had no such religious beliefs and had never heard of Elisabeth Kubler-Ross, the foremost researcher of near-death visions. That ruled out what Ring designates the 'wishful thinking' theory, that those aware of near-death are more likely to have them.

Ring's own theory is that somehow people who are near death achieve an altered state of consciousness.''

That article marked the beginning of Barbara's own resurrection. She hastily wrote to Ring, beginning a long and fruitful correspondence with one of the world's leading investigators of near-death experiences.

She told him in her first letter that his term ''core experience'' was what she had had, never considering it a near-death experience because she didn't actually die. Dr. Ring sent her his first book, *Life at Death*, and she read that people heading toward death can have an NDE.

Suddenly, Barbara was getting so much information— and finally it became clear to her that she really had had an NDE.

# 9

## Healing in Our Time

*At the same time Ken Ring and I started exchanging letters, it was finally sinking in that my back injury was making it impossible for me to do any more direct patient care in a hospital setting. I had a few dying patients that I was visiting in their homes several times a week, but I enjoyed the camaraderie of working in a hospital and now that was gone. One evening Sherwin brought up the fact that I seemed blue and suggested that I go to a workshop. Traveling to a workshop sounded so refreshing, and then it hit me. A week ago I had received a flier for a conference called "Healing in Our Time" to be held in Washington, D.C., and it was sitting right there next to the bed. I grabbed it and showed it to him and he looked it over and said, "Go!" I hugged him and kissed him and hugged him again. I was so excited, and I wasn't even sure why.*

*When this particular flier had come, I saw Elisabeth*

*Kubler-Ross, M.D. listed as the keynote speaker and it made me think how many times I had wished to hear her in person. I loved reading her books. She understood so much about helping people die. But I had to be nuts to fly to Washington, D.C., alone and not know a soul in the city or anything about the group I was going to be with. They called themselves "Sufis," whatever that was. Oh, well, I'd find out more when I got there. I really wanted to hear Elizabeth. I was going to do it.*

*The day before I left, I received a letter from Ken Ring confirming his trip to Florida in early December. So when I came home, I could look forward to meeting Ken.*

*I flew into Washington in the morning and immediately went to the Shoreham Hotel. It is a wonderful hotel and I was glad the meeting was there, so I wouldn't have to venture out alone. My room was decorated the way I would decorate a room for my daughter Beth. It was wallpapered with yellow and bittersweet wildflowers and the bedspreads on two big beds had the same flowers. The carpet was yellow and there were light yellow and white curtains covering four big windows with a beautiful view of Washington and the Washington Monument.*

*I went to the coffee shop for lunch and could hardly contain my excitement. I started talking to a lady at the next table and she turned out to be the head of the Sufi order in California. I told her, "I'm so excited to be here and I don't even know why. I really wanted to hear Elisabeth Kubler-Ross but I must be here for more reasons than that. I have never traveled alone to one of these and I don't even know who or what the Sufis are."*

*She laughed and told me all about the Sufis. They are healers who have developed their unusual powers of self-regulation and an unusual awareness of other people at a normally unconscious level. She told me that the order is relatively unknown in the West, but the tradition comes from the Middle East and is an esoteric branch of Tibetan Buddhism and esoteric Indian yoga. Anyone at this conference could be a Sufi just by developing his awareness. She also said. "Lots of people are led to these types of gatherings and don't know why at first, but they learn a lot and understand more about why they came when they leave. Give yourself a chance, and you'll find out as it unfolds. Now, take a few deep breaths and try to relax. Let me give you my room number, and if you have any more questions or just feel that you want to, come and visit me." And she got up and left.*

*Registration started at five o'clock. I was in line at four. The first speaker, Pir Vilayat Inayat Khan, wasn't scheduled to start until eight. I was in my seat for the evening program shortly after five. I had the first seat on the middle aisle in the first row behind the VIP section. The auditorium started filling up a little while later.*

*Inayat Khan started speaking at exactly eight o'clock. He talked for almost two hours. Although much of what he said referred to physics, it was quantum physics and I had read enough to grasp bits and pieces here and there. He was inspiring this huge audience—several thousand people striving to get in touch with their own uniqueness, creativity, and self-confidence.*

*Then Elisabeth came. She stood for a while and then sat on the wood table that held a pitcher of water and two glasses, one of which contained a bunch of zinnias. I was surprised by her size. She is a tiny woman, but that in no way hinders her incredible power.*

*At the same time that I was spellbound by her stories, I was also very much aware that I was witnessing one of the most powerful women of our time. If I had had to leave the next morning and not hear another thing, Elisabeth's talk would have been enough. She told one story after another about her dying patients:*

*"I was about to leave my home just north of San Diego to go to the airport to catch a plane for a talk. Time was of the essence, and my phone rang. A young woman from a town just north of L.A. was pleading with me to see her mother, who had very little time left. 'I can't,' I told her. 'I must be on a plane in a few hours for Europe. There is no time.'*

*"This woman pleaded and begged. I told her to put her mother on the phone and I would talk to her for a few minutes.*

*"'My mother can barely talk. Every day she becomes more paralyzed, and now she is losing her abilities to control her mouth.'*

*"'I am going to start driving north. You start driving south and we should meet,' and I told them approximately where. What kind of car should I look for? A van. Okay "Start driving. I should have about a half-hour to spend with your mother.'*

*"An hour later I was stepping into a white van parked on the side of the freeway. Lying on a cot was a dying woman, and by her side was a baby wrapped in a blanket, propped in the old woman's lifeless arm. The driver, the woman I had talked to on the phone, introduced me to her mother and her baby. Both the dying woman and her grand-daughter were drooling. I said to her, 'You know both of you are drooling?'*

*"She started laughing, and in a very garbled speech told me that had started only that morning. Each day the par-alyzing disease had moved up her body, and over the last*

*few months it had become apparent that her loved ones were watching her die inch by inch.*

*"I said, 'That sounds terrible.' And there were tears in my eyes for this poor soul.*

*"'Yes. It's my worst nightmare. I have wanted it to be over for so long, but a few months ago this child was born, and at least by holding on I have been able to know her for a brief while. A few weeks ago she discovered her hand. It was the same day I lost movement in mine. So I lay there paralyzed and watched her move her hand in front of her face. She is so fascinated by her little fingers.'*

*"'But you have lost yours. How does that make you feel?*

*"'This child is a gift. If I wake up blind tomorrow, I will listen to her baby talk all day. Each day is a gift until I die. I needed to tell you that. I knew you would understand.'*

*"I did, as I stood there with her daughter in the van, crying. I thanked these women for meeting me, for including me in this important moment. And I didn't miss my plane. This dying woman, her daughter, and her granddaughter gave me the strength I needed for my next talk and for many talks to come."*

*Elisabeth took a ten-minute break, and when she returned went on and on spinning one tale after another. She talked for two and a half hours, finally saying we were the healers of our time: "That's why you have gathered here. Now learn everything you can. Be sponges!"*

*And she was gone. The stage was empty. All of us filed out filled with Elisabeth Kubler-Ross.*

*I felt unable to talk but I didn't want to go up to my room, even though it was past one A.M. First I bought a tape of Elisabeth's talk. Then, the Sufis had reserved a room for meditation. Some new friends invited me to go there and meditate. We sat for about a half-hour. It was the first time*

*I officially "meditated." Then we said good night at the elevators and I got on. I was looking down at the floor but the corner of my eye picked up the hands of the other person on the elevator, and those hands were holding zinnias like those on the table next to Elisabeth.*

*I looked up to ask the person if Elisabeth had given him the flowers—and it was Elisabeth. I was alone on the elevator with her. I don't remember asking, I was so stunned, but she autographed the tape of her talk. The next thing I remember, we were standing outside her hotel-room door. I stood there stuttering and stammering. Somehow I managed to tell her I had been in a Circle Bed.*

*"Wait a minute," she said. "Very few people are walking around that have been in one of those beds." And then I was in her room, still stuttering, trying to tell her that everything she had said that night was what I had been feeling for the six years since my experience in the Circle Bed, but I could never find the words, much less say the words, to explain it. Even though she was visibly exhausted, her incredible power still came through.*

*"Young lady," she boomed at me, "just what did I say tonight? Just what do you feel?"*

*"That we're full of love. That healers are full of love for their fellowman. I have so much to give but I don't know what to do with it. It's love, but not like before. This is different and I'm afraid that people don't understand."*

*Elisabeth put her hand on my arm, looked me straight in the eye and said, "Nonsense. You go and spread it," and then she shouted at me, "Go and spread it." The next thing I knew, I found myself out in the hall again, alone. Her voice still echoed in my ears: "Go and spread it!" I can still hear her saying it as powerfully today, and every time, I feel that someone needs it. From that moment on, I never hesitated to help anyone.*

*The next morning, going down to breakfast, I met Elmer and Alyce Green, who were going to lecture on biofeedback. I was amazed that I had just read their book and now I was meeting them. Actually, I met almost all the speakers, including Olga Worrell, a famous faith healer, Robert Becker, M.D., who has since written* The Body Electric, *and Dolores Krieger, Ph.D., who ran a workshop about her master's-degree program at New York University for Nurses called Therapeutic Touch. At that time she had already trained four thousand nurses in the art of healing, or "helping," as she called it.*

*I came down in the elevator for the afternoon session with Himayat Inayati on the way to his workshop. He was a young Sufi who had talked to the entire gathering the day before. I enjoyed his talk about intuition so much that I was now going to do his workshop on meditation, called The Energy of the Holy Spirit. I told him I really had never meditated and wasn't quite sure what the name of the workshop meant, but I wanted to try it. He looked at me as though I were odd, but that was okay with me. Certainly I wasn't the only one at this meeting who hadn't put "it" all together yet. We really were a strange mixture of people from all walks of life.*

*I sat down in a large room. There were at least two hundred people sitting on folding chairs facing the front. Inayati came in and sat on a wood stool on a small stage. Behind him were closed curtains. Overall, I felt it was an old, rather shabby room. He started talking about Sufi customs aimed at purification, first of the body, then the emotions, mind, and heart. He talked about healing and how it all tied in to these levels, and he told us that this type of meditation involved the Holy Spirit, as did everything. He said some people had warned him that the Kundalini breath-*

*ing he was about to lead us in could be dangerous, that it could rupture the energy channels, as had happened to Gopi Krishna. Then he reassured us that the body was a transformer of energy to consciousness, and consciousness to energy, and as long as we moved from one level to the next, then the energy would continue to transform, and it was safe. I didn't understand much of what he was saying, but I was also getting tired of lectures and really was waiting for something experiential. As long as he said it wasn't dangerous, I would try it.*

*Most of what he did with us contained visualizations. He had us see ourselves rooted to the earth, and we breathed in and out to the earth. Then we did visualizations and breathing for fire, water, and air. Then we breathed in and out, up our spines, to the seven energy centers he called "chakras." This went on for a long time. I opened my eyes briefly in the middle, and the curtains behind him had turned to light. They were dazzling. I just closed my eyes again and continued. We breathed love into the room. We breathed love into the hotel. We breathed love into Washington, D.C. And then we breathed love to our country, our hemisphere, and all over the world. Sitting in a room with that many people and breathing in and out at the same time while visualizing love surrounding the planet Earth gave me the same sense of peace that I had had in the tunnel with my grandmother.*

*When I realized it was over, I opened my eyes and he was gone. So were most of the people in the room. Maybe thirty people were left. There was someone playing wonderful classical music at a grand piano I hadn't noticed before in the front of the room. There were crystal chandeliers, and some of them were reflecting from huge panels of mirrors on the walls. The walls were also covered in faded old brocade wallpaper. It was a beautiful room. The piano music was perfect. I just sat there for a while. No one else moved. Then I saw there was an open door behind the piano to the outside. I walked out into bright warm sunshine. I hadn't been outside in three days. I walked through the patios to where there were huge pine trees lining the bank of a creek. I could still hear the music coming from the hotel, distant but there. I suddenly had so much love for the person playing the piano. I picked up a pine cone and walked back to the hotel to give it to him. I walked back into the room, and there were fifteen or twenty people still sitting. I put the pine cone on the bench next to the man playing. He smiled and kept on playing.*

*Next I went up to my room and fell fast asleep. I opened my eyes in the darkness, hours later, and observed a gaseous blue ball shoot through the room, only to be replaced by a purple one. Then several streaks of color, collages of color, were in my vision. "What is this?" I thought quite calmly. I tried to count my breaths. My respiration was about four breaths a minute. It didn't make sense, but I really didn't care. I hung out like that for a long time; how long, I have no idea. Eventually I noticed it seemed that I had ceased breathing altogether, and realized this wasn't going to be good for me if I continued, so I just pulled myself out of it. The colors were gone from the room, but it seemed as though whatever it was, was still there. I slept better than I had slept in years.*

*When I awoke the next day, I felt great. I was glad I had elected to stay this extra day. There was space for only two hundred of us to stay for an extra meeting. And several of the main presenters were staying to discuss in greater detail their research and technology, including a Japanese doctor, Hiroshi Motoyama, who had dedicated his life's work to studying Kundalini energy.*

*I was sitting in the lecture hall next to two M.D.'s and we started talking before the morning session started. I asked them if they had attended the meditation workshop the day before with Inayati, and they had. I was concerned with what had happened to me in the middle of the night, and I explained it to them. In fact, I was still high. They both started laughing, and moved around so I was sitting in the middle between the two of them. Then they explained to me that I was really quite fortunate and that "seekers" meditate and pray for what happened to me and yet it may never happen for them. We had been in a workshop with Kundalini breathing and they said I had had a Kundalini experience. And then they wondered how many others in the room had had one. I wondered too.*

*We had a great day together. Israel Topel is a psychiatrist and Walt Stoll an internist in Lexington, Kentucky. At lunch, we ran across the street from the hotel to a fruit market and bought apples, bananas, and nuts and then we walked along the river behind the Shoreham and shared our experiences. When they moved away from their orthodox medical practices, they also moved away from their own ulcers, slipped disks, and a never-ending list of unhappiness. Walt was explaining the workshops he gives all over the country on holistic medicine.*

*A Russian healer was the first lecturer that afternoon. His name was Karamazov and he was a Russian Jew who had just moved to the U.S. He was hard to understand but his story was fascinating and we all struggled with his accent, especially after he had all two hundred of us hold our hands up—palms toward him—and he "splashed" us* with the energy he shook from his hands. Every one of us felt a tingling sensation. We all listened. He had injured his legs earlier and would have been crippled, but he worked on himself with massage and was now healed. And even more exciting, he was telling us that he now had healing abilities that could help other people. All this healing talk was beginning to sink in. As Elisabeth Kubler-Ross had demanded, I was now beginning to feel like a sponge.

After the last lecture was over, Walt and Israel told me more about their clinic and healing in general. Then they left to catch their plane.

My back had bothered me that day, more than it had in a long time. It felt hot, burning, not painful, but I was ignoring it until Walt and Israel left. I took a long soothing bath and ordered dinner up to the room and crawled into bed.

There was a knock at my door and a girl I had met the first day who was staying at a hostel across town was standing there. She had stayed to type for Motoyama. She had just had dinner with all the speakers and wanted to know if she could spend the night in my room. I was happy for the company. And as I told her that, I also said, "I am so jealous that you had dinner with all those amazing people. I really want to meet that Russian healer and ask him about my back. It is more tender now than it has been since a car accident a year ago. It feels hot. Do you think he would try to help me?"

She quickly left the room and went down to the dining room, where he was still sitting, and asked him to come up.

Five minutes later Karamazov was standing over me. He made several passes over the trunk of my body without ever touching me, and I could feel it. I could also feel that same

87

*wonderful feeling I had had in the breathing workshop the day before. I knew it was unbelievable, but I felt it.*

*At seven o'clock the next morning I checked out of the hotel. My back was still hot and I realized something that shocked me: I could feel the surface skin on my lower back. It had been numb since the surgery, and suddenly I had all my sensation back. I flew home and was free of pain.*

# 10

## Psychics and NDEs

"Above everything else, I wanted to make clear in my letters to Kenneth Ring the fact that the near-death experience was more common than previously believed," Barbara said. "I told him that a lot of my patients had reported experiences similar to mine. I was sure it was widespread."

"Dr. Ring's interest in what I had to say was piqued by the possibility that NDEs weren't isolated incidents, and he asked me to give him specific details. He sent me a copy of his first book, *Life at Death;* I wrote him long letters telling him about specific patients, and I also began giving him more details about my experience in the tunnel.

"Just before Christmas 1981, Ken said he was planning to be in Hollywood, Florida, for a conference on paranormal and psychic abilities. The two-day conference was sponsored by the Psychical Research Foundation."

When Barbara got there, she found Ken Ring surrounded by people who had come to Florida from all over the country. Some were people who openly said they had had near-death experiences like Barbara's, and they were all as anxious as she had been to share their stories with him. When he spoke, she just sat there in total amazement, because he was talking about the increase in psychic abilities reported by near-death experiencers.

When he talked about value changes in the lives of other NDErs, he was talking about her. When he talked about family members having difficulties understanding the need of an NDEr to help others—complete strangers sometimes—he was talking about her.

"I knew all of these things but had never put them together as this professor from Connecticut was doing now in front of me and a room full of people." Her near-death experience had been pushed to the back of her mind and had lodged itself somewhere deep in her unconsciousness. Now it was coming to the surface again. The memory of being in that tunnel, that feeling of total peace and serenity, had always been with her.

Although Barbara had never talked publicly, in fact, had never even verbalized her near-death experience, doing so that day seemed as natural as the NDE itself. When Ken finished talking, she began to ask questions. He then asked her to talk about her own near-death experience. In the past, she had talked to groups about altered states of consciousness. She had read stream-of-consciousness papers on the critically ill patient many times, but her role had been that of a clinician, not the survivor of an NDE. Suddenly, without warning, that era was behind her and she was able to talk freely about her experience for the first time in that room full of people. As she spoke, telling intimate details of leaving her body, her tunnel experience, and being with her grandmother, a sudden rush of relief came over Barbara.

*I was about ten rows back. All heads turned toward me as Ken, still standing in the front of the group, asked me to talk about my NDE. Suddenly everyone was staring at me and I felt as though I had never talked in front of a group before. I felt a lump in my throat. My heart was thumping fast. This was so private. But Ken Ring understood; he had to, from the beautiful way he had described experiences in his book and the way he had just talked to this audience, and no one had laughed or argued with him. He was looking at me intently. I took a deep breath and rushed through a medical explanation of what was wrong. That was easy, and it got me started. Then I told them about waking up out in the hall, and as I said it, I saw it! As I went on, all the scenes were in front of my eyes, all the feelings were rushing up. My grandmother's love first, the awesomeness of the tunnel. I had never really thought of it as a tunnel until recently, when I started reading all the new literature on NDEs, but I knew that was a good word for it. I could hear the sounds, feel the breeze, see my life. I was trembling inside, praying no one knew how I was shaking. I was getting in touch with that force—the energy of the universe—again, not like I had before, but enough that my body was reacting. I couldn't stop until it was over and I was back in my bed—I mean, back in the room at the meeting.*

*No one was laughing, but I felt somewhat foolish. My awareness was back in the room and I saw respect or at least questioning on everyone's face. I looked at Ken Ring and I knew that it was all right. That I was okay. And then he smiled at me and I tried to smile back.*

\* \* \*

At the same conference, Barbara had another experience she couldn't explain. A woman named Anne Gehman was speaking, talking about her work as a psychic. Anne worked for four police departments around the country as a consultant. She was called in on difficult cases and was asked to provide clues. She said she could connect with crime victims by simply holding something that belonged to them. "I found this interesting, but part of me still considered this sort of thing over the edge."

During her talk, however, Anne Gehman made direct eye contact with Barbara, who felt something physically change in her.

"I have a message for you from the other side," Anne said, talking about relatives who had died in separate incidents several years earlier. Ordinarily, Barbara would have ignored what she was saying, but Anne was able to describe accurately two of Barbara's dead relatives and knew how each had died.

First she described Barbara's Aunt Sylvia, saying that at death she had had trouble breathing. Aunt Sylvia had died of breast cancer, and near the end, the disease had invaded her lungs. Her lung tissue had deteriorated badly, so badly that breathing was almost impossible for her. Ann accurately described this condition during her reading.

"She wants you to know that she is all right and with a short plumpish woman with a big chest," she said. Anne knew that the short woman was Aunt Sylvia's mother. Barbara stood there listening but was stunned knowing that Anne was describing her grandmother, Bubbie.

"There is also a young man who wants you to know that he is at peace now," Anne said. "He wants you to stop grieving about his death. She was now talking about Barbara's cousin Stevie, who at seventeen had joined the Army and died in Vietnam. Barbara still felt a lot of pain over his death. "I was angry with him for getting killed. He had volunteered for Vietnam and then volunteered to be a door gunner in a helicopter gunship. He was killed just eleven days after he got to Vietnam." Anne had described details of his life and death that morning, and her reading dumbfounded Barbara.

"Then Anne told me that I too was psychic but had been afraid to use my gift. It had never occurred to me that I had any real psychic abilities, and even if it had, I would have dismissed it—just as she was suggesting that morning. I knew my intuition with the sick and dying was sharp, but the word 'psychic' had seemed too extreme."

"You have a very exciting life ahead of you if you are willing to embrace this gift and use it," Anne told me. "It was an eerie moment."

Ken Ring had talked about the fact that there was a detectable increase in psychic abilities among people who had had near-death experiences. Barbara had had out-of-body experiences since the NDE; she also felt things about people, without really knowing how she knew. Now this woman was saying it was a gift. Anne used terms Barbara didn't understand in describing this gift; even the word "psychic" still frightened her.

At the end of the day Barbara went home and prepared dinner just like any other night, intent on forgetting what had happened at the conference. Although the conference would resume the next morning, Ken Ring wasn't going to stay over, and he was really Barbara's only reason for attending. She thought about not going back, but found herself there the next day anyway.

She met Bill Roll, research director of the Psychical Research Foundation a parapsychology institute based near

93

Duke University in Chapel Hill, North Carolina. They had lunch and he encouraged Barbara to use her psychic gifts. She told him she was terrified by this awareness. She told him about her neighbor in Michigan, Don Madigan, and about Bernie Hirsch, the lawyer she'd found critically ill outside her respiratory-therapy school.

*"I trust that God wants me to do something for these people. I've overcome my fear of death and that's why I like working with dying patients,"* I told him, sitting in a restaurant at the hotel where the conference was being held. *"When I share those moments with other people, I consider it a privilege.*

*"Strange things happen to me all the time,"* I said. *"This conference is one of them. I stumbled across an article about Ken Ring's work. We started corresponding and three months later he just happened to come to Florida for a conference on paranormal phenomena."*

*"That's called synchronicity,"* Bill said. *"It's a concept popularized by Carl Jung and refers to a pattern of meaningful 'coincidences' that take place with no apparent causal link among them. It's a mistake to think that these things are coincidence, because they are meant to happen."*

*"Last month I went to a conference where Elisabeth Kubler-Ross was speaking, and there were thousands of people there,"* I told him. *"I bumped into her in the elevator and wound up in her room."*

*"Synchronicity,"* Bill said, smiling.

*"I read* Beyond Biofeedback, *by Elmer and Alyce Green, and within months I met them!"*

*"Synchronicity!"* Bill said, laughing.

*I told him about seeing balls of colors shooting through a dark room one night in Washington. His face became animated. "Have you ever heard of Kundalini?"* he asked.

*I had forgotten the word as soon as I returned home from Washington.*

*Bill said that there were many books referring to Kundalini, from an Eastern philosophical standpoint, and that it would be good for me to start exploring them. He tried to explain some of the structure to me, but it was so foreign to anything I had ever studied. Nothing in my respiratory training, the anatomy and physiology of the human body, could relate to this vague energy system he was talking about.*

*I listened but didn't understand anything he was saying. But on another level, I intuitively understood everything.*

*I drove Bill to the Fort Lauderdale airport, then drove home. When I got there, Sherwin had already started dinner, so I just pitched in and helped. My enthusiasm over meeting Ken, Ann, and Bill spilled out and Sherwin's reaction was the same as always.*

*"I understand that you enjoyed yourself this weekend,"* Sherwin said, *"but it doesn't make any sense. Let's not talk about it anymore."*

*I immediately forgot about Ken Ring, Ann Gehman, Bill Roll, and psychic research. I suppressed everything I had learned and went back to being Sherwin's wife. We spent Christmas as we had always spent the holiday since moving to Florida—entertaining our friends from Michigan at our house.*

Even though Barbara forgot about Ken, Ann, and Bill, they didn't forget about her. A month later, she began a series of trips that would have a major impact on her life.

It began with a call from Bill Roll. He invited her to meet him in early January in a place called Cassadaga, a town in northern Florida about a half-hour ride from Orlando.

*Bill was going to spend a week there with other parapsychologists from Duke.*

"The group is meeting there," he said, talking about scientists, academics, and medical professionals interested in psychic phenomena. The group included Anne Gehman, the woman who had given Barbara a psychic reading at the conference. Barbara lived six hours from Cassadaga and agreed to go. When she arrived, she had expected to find a luxury-resort-hotel complex. What she found was closer to the set of a Disney haunted-house movie combined with scenes from a Stephen King novel. It was community-owned and run by psychics and spiritualists from all over the United States.

Bill told her that Cassadaga was a very special place. It seemed odd to her, but she listened as he explained to her, "Don't think and don't feel. Eliminate any inside observations and try to sense what is going on here."

The events that followed will always remain burned in her mind.

*Anne joined us and asked me to accompany her to nearby Deland, where she wanted to visit her mentor and friend in the hospital. The man was dying and Anne wanted to say good-bye, something I had become accustomed to doing in my own work, so it was perfectly natural for me to go along. While Anne went upstairs, I stayed in the hospital chapel and prayed for her dying friend.*

*She stayed only a short time, and on the way back to Cassadaga, she complained about an awful taste in her mouth. It happened, she said, whenever she visited this man. The man was on a respirator and I knew from my own experience and as a respiratory therapist that the taste she was describing came from the secretions that occur when* a patient is on a respirator. She obviously was so connected with this man that she began to feel some of the things he was feeling while she was with him.

Afterward we went to Anne's small apartment. Bill met us there. Anne lit some candles and we talked.

Anne gave us both psychic readings, and in mine she said she sensed illness in me. She said it was located in my lower trunk and was related to either female or urinary problems.

I don't know if it was psychosomatic or what, but an hour later I began to suffer from shooting pains and knew I had either kidney problems or a bladder infection.

I called home every day that week. During one of those calls, Sherwin told me my mother had been hospitalized during a vacation in Hawaii. Doctors said she had pneumonia. Six weeks later she was hospitalized again because her kidneys were failing.

Throughout the week, I suffered from constant pain. When I got home, I went to my doctor, who ordered a series of tests. Nothing showed up. Anne had apparently picked up my mother's illness, not mine. Just as Anne had picked up the awful taste in her mouth when visiting a sick friend on a respirator, I had been exhibiting my mother's symptoms during her reading. Another psychic at Cassadaga, whom I always referred to as the woman with "Bette Davis eyes," told me that week that I was sensitive and a mystic. Anne called me a psychic. When I was finally able to unravel the details of my mother's illness and her subsequent diagnosis, I began to believe what they had been saying about me might be true.

About a month after we had all met in Cassadaga, Bill Roll had open-heart surgery for a faulty valve. I had prayed for him many times during his ordeal, as had Anne Gehman.

*We had both promised him we would. He had called me
once he could talk again, about three or four days after
surgery. I felt especially close to this researcher who had
helped me with my "psychic abilities," and had wished
many times over the summer that I could see him again.
One hot evening in August, Sherwin and I and another
couple went to a local movie, and as we walked through
the double doors into the dark theater, I looked up on the
screen and was practically thrown backward from the shock
of seeing Bill's face twenty feet high on the big screen. I
stuttered and stammered as I said, "Oh, my goodness!
Sherwin, look! That's Bill Roll on the screen." Sherwin
knew I had wanted to see Bill again, but this was too amazing. As we stood there trying to get our bearings, we realized
that we were watching a preview of the new movie* Poltergeist, *and Bill was being interviewed as a scientist on
the subject as part of the preview. Bill had written a book
in 1972 called* The Poltergeist. *It was a scientific review of
his research into the subject. Now I was seeing him on the
local movie screen. The coincidence was wonderful, and
all I could hear was my friend Bill Roll saying to me,
"Synchronicity, Barbara. They call it synchronicity."*

*I called him the next day and told him, and we both
laughed.*

*A few weeks after the Cassadaga trip, I took my son
Steven and my niece Brenda on a driving trip to Michigan.
We rode in my father-in-law's vintage Lincoln Continental,
a gas guzzler Sherwin and I had since his father died. The
trip up and the visit were routine. On our way south again,
I planned to stop in Kentucky. Steven was sixteen and I
wanted him to meet Israel Topel and Walt Stoll, the doctors
I had met in Washington.*

*At the conference, Walt and Israel had told me to buy*

*three books:* The Aquarian Conspiracy, *by Marylin Ferguson,* Joy's Way, *by Dr. Brugh Joy, a medical doctor, and* Stranger in a Strange Land, *by Robert Heinlein. They said these books were about and for people like me. After reading them, I too had willingly joined this so-called Aquarian conspiracy and I wanted Steven to meet Walt and Israel, leaders in holistic medicine. They both lived in Lexington, Kentucky, and that's where I was heading.*

*Lexington is a small town near the foothills of the Blue Ridge Mountains. When we arrived, Walt took us on a tour of a holistic clinic they ran. Unlike anything I had ever seen before, this clinic offered patients biofeedback sessions, training them to use relaxation techniques to release pain. The doctors at the clinic never called their patients "patients." Instead, they were either "clients" or "friends." Every morning at about seven-thirty, Walt said, the staff meditated with the clients in a sort of partnership in which the clients took an active role in their own treatment. Both Walt and Israel had given up their practices in large cities, trading high salaries for this rural life. The medicine I saw them practicing here was a radical departure from the medical practices I had seen previously, and it was refreshing.*

*Israel lived in a crumbling mountain cabin in the foothills, but he was building a house on his farmland that would have both solar and windmill sources of power. Walt and other people who worked at the clinic were helping him build it.*

*When we got to Israel's, he immediately made fun of my car, which could go only seven miles on a gallon of gasoline. I guess I had always accepted it as a symbol of the way I had lived. Sitting in it now on this farm where Israel planned to use only natural sources of power, I could clearly see my old life-style in stark contrast.*

*Israel had given up working with psychotic patients and now chose to work with people who were healthy but in search of their creative side. He was helping them realize their full potential. He believed that biofeedback was one way to do it at the clinic. Israel took us hiking in the foothills. He and Steven imagined scenes of Indians in the caves we explored. Then we sat for hours talking about all of this.*

*When we returned to the farmhouse, my musings were interrupted by a telephone call.*

*"There's a forest fire," Israel shouted. "If you want to help, get in my truck," he said as he dashed out the door. He tossed some tools in the back of his truck. We climbed in and he sped off, racing along a mountain road. A nurse and a young English physician who had been helping build Israel's house were with us. We drove to another valley where the air was filled with smoke. We pulled up to a farmhouse and a man came running to us. He had been burning trash when the fire started.*

*The scene was the most frightening I've ever witnessed. Fire engulfed whole trees, and we could see the fire spreading in the distance. My first impulse was to gag. My second impulse was to run. I imagined seeing frightened animals on fire. Even worse, I imagined my lungs filling with smoke. Even worse, I imagined Steven or Brenda getting crushed by a falling tree, getting trapped by the flames.*

*This same fear was on everyone's face. Nevertheless, when Israel started battling nearby flames, tossing shovels of dirt on them, we all pitched in to help. Everyone grabbed tools from the truck, blankets, and old jackets. Someone had filled an old garbage can with water and dragged it to the edge of the fire. We soaked the blankets and jackets in water, then laid them over patches of fire that ringed small trees.*

*I grabbed a rake and started to beat out flames that had engulfed a nearby bush. The fire was winning. One minute the wind would be coming from behind me; in an instant, it changed direction and the fire shot directly toward me.*

*My clothing could have easily caught fire, but somehow I managed to stay safe. Steven and the English doctor worked side by side. There was swirling black smoke everywhere, and every time the wind shifted, they'd lose sight of each other. When that happened, they called out each other's names loudly so they could be heard over the fire. My heart swelled with pride as I looked at sixteen-year-old Steven. Standing there bare-chested, working feverishly, I saw my son as a man for the first time. We kept driving back and forth from the farmhouse to get the garbage cans that Brenda was filling with water, then returned to the fire. We kept soaking the blankets and jackets and dousing the flames with them. Israel saw me put a blanket around a big stump.*

*"Forget those," he yelled. "Save the young trees." I did as I was told, and turned my attention to the saplings all around us. Each time I tended to one of them, a feeling rushed through me like shivers. What I was feeling was overwhelming compassion for these young trees and for all the natural beauty around me. Without thinking, I started putting my hands on the trunk of each tree, and knew that I was communicating some sort of comfort to it. I felt love, almost unimagined love for these trees, and somehow it wasn't unrequited. We worked for six hours, until the fire was out. Like a scene from an old Keystone Cops silent movie, just as the fire went out, a forest ranger pulled up and started unloading rakes and shovels from her truck. If we hadn't been so exhausted, we might have seen the humor in the situation.*

*"You're entitled to be paid an hourly wage for the work you've done," she told us.*

*"Use the money to buy more trees," one of us said, and we drove off.*

*When we got back to Israel's house there were people waiting for us. Neighbors had heard that we'd gone to fight a fire in a neighboring valley. The local women had gotten together and cooked dinner. When we walked in, the smell of freshly baked bread, cooked vegetables, and cakes greeted us. Israel and I were grateful. Steven and Brenda had never eaten the kinds of food Israel survived on—vegetables, fruits, grains, and nuts. Sensing their discomfort, he tossed Steven the keys to his truck, and the kids drove out of the valley to the nearest McDonald's for burgers and fries.*

*When they got back, I had massaged everyone's arms and shoulders. We listened to classical music for a time; then everyone went to bed exhausted. The next morning, I woke Steven and Brenda early and we left quickly. I dreaded leaving Israel and his mountain. Everything there was so clean. Even the sky seemed cleaner than any sky I had ever seen. This was the cutting edge of the future. I knew I had to leave right then or I'd never leave.*

When Barbara got home, a message from Ken Ring was waiting. He was coming down to Palm Beach to meet with a group of wealthy patrons who were interested in funding his research. He was going to speak to them at one of the mansions Palm Beach is famous for—and he wanted to see her. She was delighted.

The following Saturday she drove Sherwin's convertible over to Ken's hotel, hoping to give him a guided tour of Palm Beach. When he heard what she had planned, he balked, saying, "Please, that's all I've done since I got here. I'd rather just sit for an hour and talk."

When she took a closer look at him, his face was drawn and she realized he looked quite tired.

"Listen," she said, "why don't we skip it. You look tired. What you need is sleep."

He insisted that they talk for a few minutes. As they sat in the lounge of the hotel, Barbara put her hands on Ken's shoulders and started kneading the tension away. As she felt the tightness ease out of his back and shoulder muscles, he turned around and looked at her with a puzzled expression on his face.

"Are you aware of the energy coming from your hands?" he asked.

"I know that my patients feel better after I massage them," she said. "There is heat that comes from my palms when I do it, but I never thought of it as energy."

"I can feel energy coming from your hands," he said. "Have you ever heard the term Kundalini?"

"Yes," she said, "but I'm not sure what it is."

"It's a form of bio-energy," he said. It was the same thing Bill Roll had talked to her about.

"Different cultures call it by different names," Ken said. Whatever it was called, Ken Ring, a noted author, researcher, and doctor, was saying that he could feel energy of some kind coming from Barbara's hands.

In fact, he said, she was a good example of people who have activated this energy. He told her to read books about Kundalini and tell him what she thought.

In a nutshell, he explained Kundalini this way later on in his book *Heading Toward Omega:*

In Sanskrit, Kundalini means "coiled up." The term represents a postulated, subtle form of bio-energy said to lie latent, like a sleeping serpent, at the base of the spine. Under certain circumstances, however, this energy can be activated, and when it is, it is said to travel upward through the spine in a special channel. As it travels, it affects certain energy centers called chakras in the yogic tradition and may induce explosive and destabilizing energy transformations that are experienced both psychologically and physically. The way this energy is experienced by the individual varies, but typically its manifestations are extremely disruptive to one's equilibrium, even when the initial experience is itself one of supreme rapture.

In many instances, the physical and psychological concomitants of this awakening are very unpleasant and frightening.

Nevertheless, however, the actual process of Kundalini arousal may be experienced, it is held that this energy it draws upon has the capacity to catapult the individual into a higher state of consciousness. In full awakenings, a state of cosmic consciousness can be attained and, under certain circumstances, maintained.

The flow of energy is said to transform the nervous system and the brain to enable them to operate at an entirely new and higher level of functioning.

Metaphorically speaking, Kundalini appears to throw the nervous system into overdrive, activating its latent potentials and permitting the individual to experience the world and perform in it in extraordinary fashion.

Thus, Kundalini theorists (who usually have had profound Kundalini awakenings themselves) argue that the activation of this energy is responsible for genius, psychic abilities of various kinds, and have been reported throughout the ages. The idea that this energy, which is held to be both divine and divinizing, is responsible for humanity's evolution toward higher consciousness is called the Kundalini hypothesis.

Barbara chatted with Ken for a few more minutes in Palm Beach, then went home and didn't think about what he had said again until a month later.

*I drove up to Gainesville to pick Beth up from the University of Florida and found a book at the university bookstore called* Kundalini, Evolution, and Enlightenment, *by John White. It was a collection of papers written by yogi masters who had all experienced what they termed Kundalini awakenings. In each instance, they developed abilities like clairvoyance, telepathic insights, and other paranormal talents. I had experienced pockets of heat in different parts of my body. These were called symptoms of a Kundalini experience, and the yogi masters in White's book had all exhibited the same symptoms as I. I had seen colored lights in a darkened room. So had they, according to White.*

*One paper in White's book was particularly intriguing to me. It was by a man named Itzak Bentov, who wrote about something he termed the Physio-Kundalini Syndrome. Ken and I continued to write letters back and forth, exploring these exotic ideas I was reading. In one telephone conversation in July I told him I wanted to come to Connecticut to talk to him about the mystical things that were still happening to me.*

*"I wrote you two days ago, Barbara," he said, laughing, "inviting you to come to the university in the fall."*

# 11

## Going Public

Barbara went to Connecticut in the fall, and Ken Ring interviewed her as part of his research for *Heading Toward Omega*. For four days Ken interviewed Barbara for his book, a landmark piece of work based on extensive research into this relatively new science. While there, she began to understand that the work Ken was doing at the University of Connecticut and what Bill Roll was doing at the Psychical Research Foundation marked a significant watershed in the investigation of paranormal sciences. Ken, Bill, and dozens of others were in search of hard-core scientific explanations that could possibly explain mystical phenomena. All this held an even greater meaning for Barbara.

Repeatedly, throughout her stay, Ken gently affirmed her feelings about the psychic abilities she had become aware of. He said the experiences she was having weren't as dramatic as the NDE because the NDE had been the first and therefore the most intense. The NDE, however, was a seed, the beginning of a lifelong transformation.

As Ken explains in *Heading Toward Omega*, "The NDE is like a seed. It is, more precisely, a seed experience. As an experience, it is very beautiful and may seem complete within itself. In one sense it is, but it is a seed's nature to grow. It has the potential to grow, at least, but whether it does and at what rate depends on many factors. If it grows, you can see what kind of plant fulfills the promise of the seed—'by their fruits ye shall know them.'"

Ken Ring appointed Barbara the southeastern coordinator for IANDS, the International Association for Near-Death Studies, Ken's Connecticut-based organization. He encouraged her to start support groups and to promote understanding of the NDE.

*Every evening that I was there, Ken, Norma, and I would sit around the dining table in their two-hundred-year-old home—dubbed The Near-Death Hotel because so many near-death experiencers had visited there. We would talk for hours about the NDE and Ken's theories.*

*"If this is sought after by yogis and priests, why do so many NDErs now resist believing or telling their experiences?" I asked, remembering that I didn't tell anyone my experience for fear of being labeled crazy or depressed.*

*Ken said that NDErs don't go looking for the experience. It comes to them unannounced. In other words, we have no previous knowledge to prepare us. But yogis, priests, and holy leaders in every culture have prepared and prayed for this experience.*

*I was still having trouble with the "psychic gifts-abilities label." It seemed like a trap. Too many people were becoming so enthralled with it that they were losing the main point—or what I thought was the main point: service to our fellowman. "You can get lost in the psychic stuff," I told Ken and Norma. "Love is what it's about. Spirituality is the meaning. Taking the love that you felt in your NDE and giving it to people here. I feel very lucky to have received a spiritual seed, but the only way to have it continue to grow is to give it away."*

Back in Florida, Barbara began to solicit publicity for IANDS. In the spring she wrote to the Public Broadcasting System, hoping to be interviewed on Dennis Wholey's "Late Night" talk show. It was a national call-in show based in Detroit and aired at eleven o'clock five nights a week. She had planned to be in Michigan by the middle of April anyway to celebrate her fortieth birthday: "My friends in Flint were throwing me a party and I thought it would be an excellent opportunity to do some media work for IANDS."

Barbara told the producer that she was the southeastern regional coordinator for IANDS and could make herself available around April 15. Surprisingly, the producer called Barbara back and wanted her to appear on the show April 1. At first Barbara thought it was a joke. The producer was serious and offered to pay her expenses to fly in and put her up in the Pontchartrain, one of the most beautiful hotels in Detroit. She jumped at the chance, but not because she was anxious to be on a call-in talk show. The idea of answering questions on an open mike scared her. What convinced her was the fact that she'd appear on the show with Dr. Bruce Greyson, head of research for IANDS. Ken Ring had told this doctor Barbara's story. After Ken had met Barbara, Bruce Greyson and Barbara started corresponding.

Until now, Bruce was someone Barbara knew of only

through his letters. "Now I was going to meet with him face-to-face before the show. I relaxed and began to feel better about appearing on network TV." Although it had been her idea to do "Late Night," the speed with which they had accepted her offer, then insisted she appear earlier than she had planned, shook her a little. Knowing she'd be on the show with Bruce Greyson, a psychiatry professor from the University of Michigan, made her confident that it would go well.

She flew to Michigan on April Fool's Day. Dr. Greyson called to let her know that he would meet her at the hotel for dinner before the show. When he arrived, she could tell he was surprised at her appearance. From their letters and what he knew about her accident, he had expected to meet someone confined to a wheelchair.

Barbara talked nonstop through dinner about her paranormal experiences, Ken's next book, and the therapy she had recently become involved in with Dr. Stanley Dean, a psychoanalyst at the University of Miami.

"Stanley has studied the primitive culture in Bali, examining their ancient mysticism, healing ritual, and bioenergy theories," she told Bruce. "He's written extensively on psychiatry and mysticism and something he calls UltraConsciousness. Stanley believes that some people are capable of achieving higher levels of consciousness than psychiatry has studied, and is using his research from Bali to confirm it," she said.

Bruce said he was familiar with Stanley Dean's work. He told her: "Dean became a public figure in the middle and late 1970s, when he appealed to a U.S. congressional committee to fund psychical research. And Stanley was one of the founders of the American Association for Social Psychiatry."

"Stanley has been working with me in an attempt to prove or disprove Ken's somewhat radical theories about something he calls the Kundalini hypothesis," Barbara said. "I've been in sessions with Stanley for about four months and he's helped me become more accepting and aware of the psychic level and more in touch with myself than I've ever been. Stanley believes a Kundalini experience is the path to UltraConsciousness. He told me if I exhibited the aftereffects of UltraConsciousness, then Ken's theory was correct," she said. "Stanley and I had completed our sessions, and he had just given Ken permission to use his research on the character traits of UltraConsciousness in *Heading Toward Omega.*"

As director of research for IANDS, Bruce had been doing some fascinating research of his own, and they talked about it that night.

Bruce was collecting research data from near-death experiencers all over the country. At the time, he was conducting a survey of over three hundred participants. In that group, one hundred had reported near-death experiences, one hundred had come close to death without having an NDE, and one hundred subjects had not had a near-death experience or been close to death. The last group, necessary in any scientific study, was the control group.

"Is any of your research going to be part of Ken's book?" she asked.

"I've collected data on an increased incidence for virtually all of the psychic and psychic-related phenomena after a near-death experience," Bruce said. "In my study, the overall increase in psychic abilities was highly significant. I believe Ken is using my statistics in the book to reinforce his own research on psychic ability among NDErs."

Barbara told him some stories about her own psychic experiences.

"I was standing by my swimming pool one day, cleaning it with a long brush, when I got a sharp piercing pain in my right hip. It shot down my leg, and at the same time I felt some force push me into the pool," she said, excited that she was talking to a researcher who had investigated similar experiences. "A maintenance man hired to do work around the house had watched the whole thing happen."

"What happened then?"

"The man pulled me out of the pool. I was embarrassed and scared that my back was acting up, so I went to bed." My mother was in the hospital in Michigan while all this was happening. I called her the next day in the hospital to ask her how she felt, and she told me that two doctors had come into her room at precisely ten-thirty the morning before and one of them picked her up and put her in the bed. She lay on her belly, and they did a bone-marrow biopsy on her right hip. They had to push really hard, and the pain shot down her right leg. It happened at exactly the same time I felt pain in my right hip and leg and was pushed into the pool. That happened fifteen hundred miles away." Barbara was laughing. "Now, do you think my mother and I are connected?"

"That's a wonderful story," Bruce said. Barbara thought it was so refreshing to be able to say whatever she wanted without worrying that she might sound mad.

"I wrote it up and Bill Roll, head of the Psychical Research Foundation, told me to send it to the American Society for Psychical Research in New York. The editor of their journal, Rhea White, wrote back and wants more details," she said.

"I just wrote a paper that will be published in the *Theta Journal*, a publication of the Psychical Research Foundation, showing that statistically, near-death experiencers' self-reports show an impressive increase in out-of-body experiences," Bruce said.

"Rhea told me that my experience was a transcendence of space. Is that the same thing you're talking about in your paper?"

"In a way," he said. "In an altered state of consciousness, perception may seem haphazard and uncontrollable. Then it's brought back in language to be described here. Our language doesn't contain words for these altered states; therefore definitions overlap and become confusing."

"Does that mean I was in some sort of altered state of consciousness when I felt the pain?"

"Can you remember what you felt like before the experience actually happened?"

"Yes, the sun was shining brightly, the lake was like a mirror behind me. The sunlight was dancing underwater on the walls of the pool, and my eyes were focused on the pool. I felt peaceful, and now that I think about it, I was kind of mesmerized. It was hypnotic. I had never thought about it before."

Their segment of the TV show started at eleven-thirty. Promptly at eleven P.M., a limo driver was waiting for them outside the hotel. It was just a short drive to the studio near the famous Fisher Building, one of the city's landmark gold-domed skyscrapers. Bruce and Barbara were ushered into the green room, where guests wait to be called. Someone fixed Barbara's hair and makeup and then they went on the air. Barbara was nervous.

Dennis Wholey was on vacation and the show was being hosted by Steve Fox, a reporter for the "20/20" news show. It had been Fox who wanted them on PBS, not Wholey, as Barbara had earlier believed. After Fox introduced the subject, they switched to the phones and started answering callers' questions. Barbara was intimidated, feeling that Fox was slightly skeptical. The third call came from Miami, and she relaxed immediately because she heard Stanley Dean's voice boom across the studio.

"This is Dr. Stanley Dean," he said. "I am a professor of psychiatry and I want to compliment this young doctor, Bruce Greyson, on his most important research and Barbara Harris on her courage for telling her experiences to a television audience!" She could feel the tension melt from her body, and she was thankful Stanley had called.

When she arrived back at the hotel, the red light on her telephone was flashing to tell her she had a message. She called the hotel operator.

"I have a message from your friends Cookie and Gary Frenkel."

"What is it?" Barbara asked.

"You were *wonderful*," the operator said, screaming into the phone. She was bellowing. When she finished screaming in Barbara's ear, she apologized, saying Cookie and Gary had insisted that she deliver their message just as they had given it to her. Apparently they wanted their enthusiasm passed on, and it had been. On her bed, Barbara found a box of Godiva chocolates, a present from the owners of the hotel, and a card from them, thanking her for doing PBS "Late Night."

The next morning, Barbara's parents picked her up and they headed straight for a Big Boy restaurant, a highway landmark in the Midwest.

"We want the table with the best view," her mother told the hostess, "because my daughter was on television last night and now she's a star!"

"Thanks, Mom!" she mumbled with an incredibly red face. Her father was laughing. After she had her fill there, they headed for Lafayette Boulevard and the Coney Island Restaurant, another must-see Detroit institution. They ordered a dozen Coney Islands, a Detroit specialty—a hot dog smothered in chili—which Barbara was taking back to Florida. Their next stop was Olga's Souvlaki, a Greek chain, and she picked up a dozen souvlaki sandwiches there. On the way to the airport, they stopped in Farmington for three dozen Greene's hamburgers. Greene's is famous for postage-stamp-size hamburgers topped with grilled onions. Detroiters believe they are the best hamburgers in the world. So does Barbara.

She landed back home at Fort Lauderdale International Airport with a suitcase filled with this food from back home for Sherwin and her three children.

# 12

## Bigger than EST

As part of her media work for IANDS, Barbara also did a cable TV interview in Fort Lauderdale for a local station. With the local publicity, she began planning a local support group called "Friends of IANDS." While IANDS had an impressive name and a serious intent—to support research—the organization was still in its infancy. A few days after the show, Barbara got a telephone call from Bradley Forest, a wealthy inventor who wanted to help.

"I'm going to put IANDS on the map!" he told her, boasting that he could make the near-death movement bigger than EST. He was referring to Werner Erhard's pop consciousness group that pervaded the scene in the late 1970s with weekend seminars aimed at opening people up to higher consciousness.

Barbara passed Forest's offer on to Ken Ring and other IANDS board members, who took the news somewhat cautiously. Bruce Greyson, who was now president of the board, was wary but still curious. Forest was a man of action, and immediately offered to fly board members to Connecticut, where they could evaluate his offer during face-to-face meetings. Everyone accepted. Although Barbara wasn't a board member, she flew to the University of Connecticut with Forest and his wife, Betty. Bruce came in from Michigan.

During the flight, Betty Forest told Barbara that they were just recently married and that her new husband was secretly afraid that Bruce and Ken would think he was crazy. In passing, she also told her that Bradley was a manic-depressive. Barbara thought it promised to be an interesting four days.

Everyone converged on the Storrs campus of the University of Connecticut, where IANDS had a three-room office in the psychology building. They all met for the next four days in marathon meetings at which the fate of IANDS was discussed in great detail. In a conference room in the Graduate Center, Nancy Bush, executive director of IANDS, gave an overview of IANDS assets. The presentation was well-organized and enlightening. The only real asset the organization owned was its affiliation with the University of Connecticut and the office space they occupied. Traditional sources for grants had failed to come through, and IANDS was supported solely by membership dues and an occasional donation, including many made by Ken. They knew that Ken had a following from his first book, *Life at Death*, which had been reviewed by leading magazines and television networks. The publicity created a painful paradox. While the organization needed the publicity, it created a flood of mail and telephone calls that IANDS wasn't equipped to handle. There was part-time help who often worked without paychecks because IANDS was financially strapped.

None of this seemed to dampen Bradley's enthusiasm.

"This is an idea whose time has come," he said. "We can't sit here in our ivory towers anymore. It's time to hit the mainstream. The trouble with this world, the source for all wars, is fear of death. Eradicate that fear and you'll have a beautiful, loving world. It's time to take the leap and meet the people on a grass-roots level," he said. "We'll put an IANDS chapter in every major city in this country, then in Europe, and finally everywhere."

"How do you handle something of that magnitude?" Nancy asked. "There are real kooks out there who will try to take over the vulnerable people who come to us for help. It's not that easy," she said. "You don't understand that people that have just had NDEs are extremely open. We've had reports of new experiencers giving everything away. These people are kind and loving, but so vulnerable."

"Ken has already started a system by appointing regional coordinators," Bradley countered. "The individual chapters run by coordinators will raise their own funds. The regional coordinators' travel expenses will be paid by the charters, and they can visit U Conn several times a year for advanced training. Also, individual chapters will support the mother ship—this office at U Conn. In return, they will get directives, publications, and support from us."

The word "us" echoed throughout the room. This flamboyant stranger had come out of nowhere and suddenly seemed to be positioning himself to become their Messiah, promising to lead them to the Promised Land. The problem with all of this was the fact that no one at IANDS was in search of a Moses.

Bradley's plans were grand, elaborate ideas that lacked

details. Nevertheless, those meetings helped the board focus by defining the organization's weaknesses. The board needed specialists in scientific and management disciplines. Its needs were not clearly defined. Publicity seemed to be easy to obtain, but this caused more problems. In addition to the interest generated by Ken's book, Ray Moody's book *Life After Life* had taken off and become a best-seller since its publication in 1975.

On the final day, Bradley nervously summed up what he believed would solve all of these problems. He offered to help the board "get the ball rolling" by becoming a general promoter and fund-raiser. The meetings were adjourned and everyone flew home. The next afternoon, a Saturday, Barbara got a telephone call from Bruce.

"Bradley has had some sort of experience," he said. "Betty Forest called me twice. Bradley had a seizure last night about midnight. She called Emergency, and paramedics treated him for a seizure."

Bruce, who had questioned Betty thoroughly, believed that Bradley had had a Kundalini experience, not a seizure. Ken agreed, saying, "Bradley was drawn to the subject of Kundalini and near-death experiences from watching Barbara on television." The group had discussed the Kundalini phenomenon often during the four days and had had several emotional discussions on death, a subject Bradley seemed afraid of. Those things together could have triggered something—possibly a Kundalini awakening. A near-death experience was one way to trigger this experience. Intense emotions were another.

Some time later, Barbara got another call from Bradley. He had forgotten about IANDS. He was now booking people on exotic charters. He had chartered two sailing schooners and was taking about fifty people to South America.

They were climbing a mountain to meet a tribe of people who all claimed to be over one hundred years old. Bradley said he was intent on learning their secret. He wanted to know how these people had escaped death, and he wanted Barbara to go with him.

''Together,'' he said, ''we can guide and rule.''

She declined, and never heard from Bradley Forest again.

# 13

## The Road Well-Traveled

Bradley Forest might have disappeared, but he had left an indelible impression on those who had met him. The International Association for Near-Death Studies needed to build a strong network of satellite groups to support the "mother ship," and it needed to become financially solvent. This point was stressed at the summer board meeting in 1983, and Ken Ring dramatized the point by writing out a personal check during the meeting. Board members got the message. While Barbara still wasn't on the board, she returned to Connecticut for the meeting to help.

John Migliaccio, the only near-death experiencer on the board, said a few local chapters had already been formed around the country. Barbara was starting one in Florida.

Bruce Greyson and Nancy Bush drove Barbara to the airport after the meeting and gave her a surprise before she boarded her plane. The three of them would plan an IANDS research conference on clinical approaches for the near-death experiencer.

"Hopefully, we'll emerge from the conference with strong guidelines that health professionals can use to recognize a patient who has had an NDE, and give them ways to help their patients cope with the experience," Nancy said.

Barbara was moved beyond words.

*My heart leapt and lodged itself in my throat. I held back tears. For seven years, I couldn't talk abut my experience because I was afraid people would dismiss me, calling what happened a hallucination. Even my psychiatrist didn't understand. I remembered a patient I'd met in an intensive-care unit who'd had an NDE. His experience was similar to my own NDE and he shared it with me. I knew that being able to talk with someone who understood, helped. Two hours later, he died peacefully, knowing that he was returning to that beautiful light.*

*Now we were going to hold the definitive conference that would make that kind of communication between a dying patient and his doctors or nurse possible everywhere. A conference like this would define ways to help patients like me and thousands of others affirm the near-death experience. How wonderful and compassionate it would be for all health-care professionals to have an understanding of the NDE so that a patient's confusion could be replaced by some understanding.*

Barbara spent the summer at home, surrounded by new books and enthusiasm for all the new discoveries they brought. The pool and the lake beyond her backyard were especially attractive to her that summer. The more involved she became with IANDS and the near-death-experience research, the more estranged she felt from Sherwin. Her life had become a paradox, both fulfilling and painful at the same time.

"I wanted to share all this with Sherwin, but it was like we were talking two different languages," Barbara recalls. "I certainly never blamed him for not having any interest in medicine. But I began to realize that we only had the kids in common. Oh, how that hit me. A quiet voice inside kept whispering to me, saying this paradise I called home wouldn't be home to me forever."

Barbara spent most of that summer alone. Her sons were away touring with a drum corps. Her daughter, Beth, still lived in Gainesville, where she was a student at the University of Florida. Steven would be moving to Gainesville in the fall to begin college, leaving only Gary at home. Sherwin and Barbara had just bought a beautiful town house in Gainesville for the two children to share.

The clinical conference was planned for February. In the fall, Barbara made reservations for it at two conference centers in south Florida. Bruce was trying to get a grant to pay for it. If the funding didn't materialize, the conference would be canceled. "We had no idea how much money we'd get, so I made reservations at a Holiday Inn with meeting rooms, and another reservation at the Bonaventure, a luxurious hotel, spa, and conference center. A modest grant would pay for the Holiday Inn; a generous donation would land us at the Bonaventure," she said.

Meanwhile, she and Sherwin spent weekends wandering on the beach where he wanted to buy a house. "The sense I had of impending change stayed with me all summer and through the fall," Barbara said. "I dismissed it, saying Sherwin was planning to buy a house on the coast and that was the change I was sensing. We vacationed on Marco Island and fought the whole time. We never fought at home. At home, we barely spoke," she said.

In the fall of 1983, she resumed traveling on IANDS business. First she went to the University of Michigan, where Bruce Greyson was holding an informal workshop for near-death survivors. It was historic for Barbara because it was the first time she had met a group of other people who had had NDEs.

*I wasn't going up to Michigan specifically to go to Greyson's. Actually, one of my teeth had crumbled, and I was still having my dental work done in Michigan. I called Bill Hande in Flint, and he said, "Sure, come on up. My lab can make the crown while you stay and visit with us. It won't take more than a few days. Jeanine and I really miss you. It'll be great having you around. And I have some new records I want you to hear."*

*I told Sherwin I wanted to drive, not fly. I needed the time to be alone. It was apparent to both of us that we were strained, and it would be good to be apart for a while. I ached for our son Gary. I knew he was picking up more than we dared to share with him. From a family of five, he was down to the only child, and his parents weren't getting along.*

*It took three days to drive up, two peaceful nights in motel rooms and three days on the road with my favorite tapes, classical and light rock, my new Saab, and me.*

*I settled in with Bill and Jeanine. Staying with them was always fun. We had been friends through the pregnancy and baby years. We knew each other's children well and talked endlessly about our kids. The Handes had full-time help in this huge house. I never had to lift a finger except in the greenhouse, where Jeanine and I would putter. They had a hot tub, sauna, and full gym in the basement, and we would spend hours down there.*

*Bruce Greyson called from the University of Michigan, only an hour away, to tell me that everything had fallen into place for the workshop he wanted to have in his home the following weekend. Tom Sawyer was driving in from New York State. I wanted to meet him. I knew he too had been interviewed by Ken Ring for* Heading Toward Omega. *And Bruce said three other near-death experiencers would be there. He had also invited his coworkers from the psychiatry department at the University of Michigan to attend. It sounded really good. None of us had experienced five NDErs together at the same time. So Friday, late afternoon, I kissed Bill and Jeanine good-bye for the weekend and drove the forty-some miles to Ann Arbor, home of the University of Michigan and of Bruce and Jenny Greyson.*

*The University of Michigan Hospital is massive. There had already been many times in my life, living so close for thirty-five years, that I had visited this highly respected institution. My father had surgery there twice when I was a child. My mother had been there too. I could still feel my grandmother's hand in my life review leading me through the maze of corridors. Our friends who had become M.D.'s had all trained there, and we had spent many weekends in our late teens and twenties socializing on this campus. Bill and Jeanine Hande had lived here when he was going to dental school. Detroit had its wonderful moments, but it could never compete with the culture of Ann Arbor. As I parked my car in the middle of this rich atmosphere, I remembered how happy I had always felt in this town.*

*Bruce Greyson was waiting for me near the bank of elevators I was to take. How can I explain feeling like an old friend of Bruce's when we had met only that year, but seeing him again at the university felt as natural as seeing old friends—as if it had always been this way.*

*I couldn't wait to see his office. As I scanned it for the first time, the giggles were bubbling up. It was just as I had pictured it. The window was a little higher than I had imagined, but the desk, the sofa, and even the shelves were in the right place. We were talking when Bruce was called for an emergency, a new patient just brought in by ambulance. He quickly told me how I could find him if I wanted to, and left. I wanted to meditate, so I put my feet up on the sofa and closed my eyes. Some time passed and then I decided to take the plunge—follow Bruce's directions down the stairs and see if I could at least find some coffee.*

*There were several women in an office at the bottom of the stairs, and I asked for some coffee. One of the women talked to Nancy Bush from IANDS often when she called, and recognized my name. She was coming Sunday for the meeting and said she was looking forward to it. She thought the subject was fascinating.*

*As I left their office I glanced down the corridor and caught my first glimpse of "Dr. Greyson" in action with a badly agitated woman who had been picked up on the streets of Ann Arbor.*

*We were able to leave a short time later, and I followed Bruce to a pretty center-entrance two-story colonial. Marigolds were still blooming everywhere, and a three-year-old blond boy named Eric was at the door, waiting impatiently for his daddy. He leapt up into Bruce's arms, staying only long enough for a fast hug, and then was off into action somewhere else in the house. Devon was right behind her father and babbling with a rather worried look about her day's happenings. Standing in the kitchen door-*

*way, hands clasped, was Jenny Greyson. Taller than I would have guessed, she had the most beautiful deep-set blue eyes, straight honey-colored hair parted in the middle and tucked neatly behind her ears. She smiled nervously at me and said hello. I instantly liked her.*

*Devon showed me to her room, which was to be my room for the next two nights. Then she showed me family pictures hanging in the hall. There was a group picture of the four of them recently taken, and next to it, at the same ages and sitting in the same positions, were Bruce, his sister, and their parents. He and Eric looked identical.*

*Eric was wild, the two cats were circling, dinner was almost ready, Tom Sawyer was there and talking, and Jenny was chilling the bottle of Piesporter I had brought. She said it was her favorite wine. I had loved it for years. Dinner was lively. Then Jenny and Bruce and I did the dishes, and by the time the last glass was in the dishwasher, Jenny and I had finished the wine.*

*While the Greysons were putting the children to bed, Tom Sawyer told me what had happened to him. He told me his story just the way he had told it to Kenneth King for* Heading Toward Omega *and then I did the same.*

As a boy growing up near Rochester, New York, Tom made fun of his name to escape ridicule. A good-natured kid, he was well-liked in school because of his athletic abilities and was generally thought of as friendly and outgoing. However, he was never able to live up to the literary image his famous name implied. Mark Twain, who authored those famous tales about an adventurous boy who hustled his friends and relatives on the banks of the Mississippi, might never have written those classic stories had he met this Tom Sawyer.

The only similarity between the literary Tom Sawyer and his New York namesake might have been their mutual dislike of school and academic learning. In fact, the real Tom Sawyer managed to get through high school without reading.

"I hated books. I stopped reading books in the seventh grade, and until I was thirty-three, I read nothing," he said. As an adult, Sawyer earned his living as a part-time auto mechanic and snowplow operator. He had worked as a garbage man and once worked as a carpenter, all manual-labor jobs. His life was predictable. In 1967 he married his childhood sweetheart, and he and Elaine had two sons. In short, Tom Sawyer's life had been uneventful.

The only unpredictable thing in Tom Sawyer's life was his athletic prowess. A year after he married Elaine, he qualified for the U.S. Olympic bicycle-racing team. The only other unusual thing that shaded Sawyer's life, that separated him from others, was his religious beliefs. Tom Sawyer had none. In fact, he was a self-styled agnostic. The existence of God, some higher power who dwelled in a heavenly landscape, was just religious myth to him, as it had been for Barbara.

"I believed that religion didn't do any harm, but I wasn't convinced that it did any good either," he often said. "I thought religion was just a bunch of foolishness. I believed that when you die, you die. Everything goes black, and that's it."

In 1978, however, Sawyer suddenly knew that there was a God.

His conversion began in an odd place—under a pickup truck in his yard. One morning he decided to do some work on his truck. He enlisted the help of his nine-year-old son, Todd. They jacked up the front wheels of the truck and Sawyer slid under it, lying on his back. Suddenly, without warning, the jack slipped and the truck slammed down on his chest, pinning him under it. By conventional medical standards, Sawyer started to die the second he stopped breathing.

Todd raced inside and dialed 911.

"My father's been pinned under our pickup truck," he told the emergency operator. He gave their address, then raced back outside, screaming for help. Neighbors arrived and tried frantically to free Sawyer. Minutes raced by and their efforts to lift the heavy pickup truck proved fruitless. Minutes raced by and Tom Sawyer was no longer breathing. Although he appeared lifeless during the emergency, something odd was happening that he was able to explain only months after the accident.

"When Todd made the phone call, I heard it very clearly and vividly," he said. "There were other things I was able to hear that were impossible for me to hear with my normal hearing; I heard the conversation of the paramedics getting into the ambulance three and a half miles away.

"As I went unconscious, I experienced a sensation of waking up. It wasn't like waking up from a sleep state," he said. "It was like being unconscious or absolutely asleep, and at the click of a fingernail, I was absolutely awake. The only problem with this feeling of waking up was the fact that I saw only darkness.

"The darkness gradually took the shape of a tunnel, and way off in infinity appeared a speck of white light. It was the most beautiful thing I ever experienced in my life.

"All the pressure of the truck being on me, and the horrendous pain were gone," he said, "and I felt very comfortable. I was motionless. Then I felt myself moving faster and faster, going forward toward the light. At the end of the tunnel I was confronted by the light of God, and that light included absolutely everything.

"It was absolute, total knowledge. I had direct communication with that light in a telepathic way. I had the opportunity to ask questions, and the absolute, unequivocal answer would be emanated to me instantly," he said. "Needless to say, I had many questions answered and many pieces of information given to me, some of which was very personal, some of which was religiously oriented. One of the religious questions was in regard to an afterlife, and this was definitely answered through the experience itself. There was absolutely no question in my mind that the light was the answer. The atmosphere, the energy, was total knowledge, total, pure love; everything about it was definitely the afterlife.

"I then experienced a total life review. Every event, every moment, every second of my life came before me, my Olympic trials, my marriage, everything came to me and it was a complete life review. It was every day, every second of my life all there at the same time.

"I was given a choice. I could return to normal life or become part of this light," he said. "I chose to stay and become part of that light. I then had the feeling of going through the tunnel in reverse, and I slammed back down into my body. I am the only person you'll meet who can say he was kicked out of heaven."

Meanwhile, his neighbors wedged a four-by-four piece of lumber under the truck and used another piece of wood as a fulcrum, still trying to free him. Straining, they lifted the truck off his chest and pulled him out. The ambulance rushed him to a nearby hospital in Rochester, where he was treated in the emergency room. Tom Sawyer had been without oxygen for fifteen to twenty minutes. Nevertheless, doctors found no broken bones. He suffered from internal bleeding, but was treated and released hours after the accident.

Elaine drove Tom home in the back seat of their car. The pain in his chest was overwhelming. In his mind he kept replaying the scenes he had experienced while he was pinned under the truck. The one thought that kept popping up was how beautiful, how peaceful the landscape he had seen had been.

"I kept blurting out things like, 'It's so wonderful, so beautiful,' during the ride home," he said. He was troubled by the experience too. "I chose to stay and become part of the light. I believed it was heaven, and without explanation, I got kicked out for some reason.

"I vaguely recall the ride home. I was alone in the back seat, groaning from the pain, but I remember blurting things out and moaning."

He had no idea what had just happened to him just hours before. Elaine, however, had a vague recollection of reading about such things and believed that night that Tom had survived a near-death experience. Her suspicion was confirmed on the ride home, when Tom mumbled something about seeing the light.

"Don't you know what that was?" she asked her now-drug-dazed husband. "That's called a near-death experience."

"I don't believe in that hocus-pocus baloney," Tom told her.

She drove him home and put him to bed. It took weeks for him to recover. A short time after he began to feel better physically, like Barbara, Tom too began behaving strangely.

"I started saying things I didn't understand and Elaine didn't understand either," he said. "Lying in bed one morning, I blurted out the word 'quantum.'"

"What?" Elaine asked.

"Quantum," Tom said. "Quantum."

"What are you talking about, Tom?" Elaine asked.

"I don't know."

About two weeks later, Tom and Elaine were watching television when Tom blurted out the name "Max Planck."

"Do you know who Max Planck is?" Tom asked her.

"No," Elaine said.

"Neither do I," Tom said, "but you'll be hearing more about him in the near future." Tom had no idea what he meant, but says he knew he was speaking the truth intuitively. Elaine encouraged her husband to write down his thoughts.

What he wrote surprised them even more than his random quotations.

He began writing down fragments of equations and mathematical symbols. One of the recurring symbols he wrote in his notes was the Greek letter psi. It is widely used in psychology, parapsychology, and physics, and usually denotes "the unknown." Tom knew none of this when he began keeping a journal. A friend told him that psi was also the symbol for the number seven hundred.

During this period, passages from books Tom had never read began to appear to him. He showed these passages to Kenneth Ring, and Ring identified them as passages from *Scientific Autobiography* of Max Planck. When Tom wrote down those passages, however, he still did not know that Max Planck was one of the originators of a science known as quantum physics.

For a man who had shunned books most of his life, Tom now did something even stranger. He went to the Rochester library in an attempt to piece together what he was now writing and thinking. He went to a librarian and simply said he wanted to learn something about quantum. "Is there anything about quantum energy?"

A little confused, the librarian wasn't sure herself at first. Then she suggested he look in a physics book in their science section. When he got there, however, Tom was just as confused as when he had first walked into the library. He saw a stranger looking at books and asked him for help.

"Excuse me, sir," Tom said. "I want to learn what the quantum theory is, and I only have a high-school education."

"Well, I'm afraid what you've done, young man, is pick a subject that requires a college education just to understand it."

With that said, however, he showed Tom a few books that might offer him some introductory material. One of the books Tom found immediately answered some of his questions.

"When I opened it, there were two things that stood out on one of the pages. I saw the symbol psi I had written in my notes, and a title under the picture of a man. It said 'Max Planck.' Planck was called "the father of quantum theory." Tom began to devour books on the theory, a scientific explanation for mystical happenings. Although the jargon was unfamiliar, he seemed to understand it intuitively. How he found the books he read and learned more about this science is as strange as his as sudden uncharacteristic interest in quantum theory itself.

Once while in a bookstore to buy a particular book for his son's birthday, Tom found a book on quantum physics directly under the book he had planned to buy for Todd. When he saw it, he knew he was supposed to buy it, so he did, and took it home. Like Barbara, Tom felt compelled to enroll in college. He met a professor and explained his sudden interest in quantum theory. The skeptical professor gave him a list of four books to read. The list contained the only four books on the subject Tom Sawyer had already read, books he had found himself.

Tom contacted Ken Ring at the University of Connecticut and, like Barbara, was invited to become one of Ring's research subjects for *Heading Toward Omega*. In a letter to Dr. Ring during this period, Tom's son Todd told Dr. Ring that his father was "starting to talk more like Einstein" after the accident. It was a telling observation.

Elaine too wrote to Ring:

> *Many times he says a word he has never heard before in our reality—it might be a foreign word of a different language—but he learns it in relationship to the "light" theory. He talks about things faster than the speed of light and it's hard for me to understand . . .*

Tom became an avid reader of parapsychology, metaphysics, and books dealing with higher consciousness. He was able to have long and precise discourses on cosmology, religion, and ancient history, all subjects he says he learned during his experience "in the light." By all accounts of friends and relatives, he remained the boyish man he had always been. Despite the fact that he gradually became familiar with the works of such science luminaries as Einstein and Planck, he kept his job driving a snowplow for the city.

In *Heading Toward Omega*, Dr. Ring ends the section about Tom by saying, "It seems safe to say that this unusual young man is certainly worthy in his own right of the name that his fictional counterpart made famous." Barbara agreed after hearing his story that evening at the Greysons'.

On Saturday the Greysons, Tom, and Barbara went to

the Detroit zoo. Barbara loved walking around the zoo. It was close to Oak Park and her first house where her children were born. She had spent many days with her toddlers at this zoo and now it brought back beautiful memories.

*Sleeping in Devon's bed was not easy that second night. Being with Tom had brought up so many new feelings for me. I had listened to my patients' experiences many times, but had never sat with another healthy human being and talked this way. Now, in a matter of hours, three more who had "been there" would be here, and I didn't know what more I could expect. Being at the Detroit zoo with Devon and Eric had brought back so many memories of my own children and me when they were little and I had been on only this side of reality. There was sadness or longing for that old way again. Something had gotten in the way of me and my family. Was that it? I don't know. Things had changed for me so much. It was a fitful night.*

*We were all up early. Bruce and I drove to the bakery for fresh bagels. Jenny set up a brunch in the dining room and soon the living room was filled with people. Bruce and Jenny sat together in front of the windows. It was hard to see their faces with the light behind them. The NDErs formed an inner circle in the middle of the room, and behind us were medical students, psychiatry residents, and some of the department secretaries. None of the other physicians from the department were there. Bruce Greyson's research on NDEs was not well-received at the University of Michigan, an exceptionally conservative institution that encouraged only "hard scientific research."*

*We started a discussion among the experiencers, with everyone else listening. As I got a grasp on what was happening, I realized that Bruce was remaining quiet. I was*

*the one that was facilitating the group. This was sponta-
neous, and although I was surprised that he, Dr. Greyson,
wasn't leading the group, I was doing all right. I was just
glad I hadn't known this in advance, or I would have been
a wreck.*

*The five of us were taking turns telling our experiences.
After Tom, Audrey Harris, a black woman who had driven
in from Southfield, told hers. At age sixty she had just
completed her second master's degree at U. of M. Her first
one was in public health, and now she had completed her
second one in social work. She had also been working as
a volunteer with the dying for ten years, since her mother
died in 1973. She started off by saying she needed to help
dying people.*

*Her experience happened in childbirth in 1948. She was
twenty-five. She told about being in labor for nineteen hours,
and when she was taken into delivery her foot was injured
in the stirrups and a doctor was touching her head and
soothing her when the room disappeared and she was suddenly in a beautiful wooded area. She could smell the earth.
There was a damp feeling of being in a dense forest. The
flowers had an incredible color, and the grass and earth.
There were animals gathered around a figure that she knew
to be the child Jesus. She remembered cherubs gently flying
around him. Also lions and lambs peacefully rested in the
scene. She could hear the cherubs' trumpets and the lambs'
bleating. A peace moved through her that she could still
feel.*

*When she woke up after the delivery, she didn't remember
anything about it. However, a week later, at home, her
beautiful new baby made a bleating sound just as the lambs
had, and it all came back. Now as she told the story, filled
with the emotion we could all feel, she told us that even*

*though it had been thirty-five years ago, she could still see it brightly, and as she finished, she said she could smell the smells and feel the moisture at this moment. And that wonderful peace she had felt then was still there.*

*Another black social worker from Ann Arbor told her NDE, which had happened to her as a small child. Audrey Harris and she, who had known about each other, were joyful that they had finally met.*

*A young man, a grad student from U. of M., talked about his NDE next, and then I told mine. We stopped for brunch.*

*I walked up to the grad student, who was shy, and I don't know why, but I started telling him while we were getting our food about the time I heard voices while driving alone in my car. He turned pale and started speaking rapidly to me. He remembered how, while taking a tour of the concentration camps in Germany recently, he had heard the screaming and crying of the tormented souls, and he was still terrified. He said that he had started seeing Dr. Greyson on his return and had told no one else. This was happening to me a lot lately. I would make a comment about a past experience and the comment would jolt someone else.*

*We went back to the living room, and what started out as a two-hour sharing ran for five and a half hours. This young man opened up. He told of strange things beyond this reality that had happened to him since his NDE five years earlier. And so did all the other NDErs. We were all feeling a catharsis as we heard each other's tales. I had teased Audrey Harris by saying that she, a black woman, was my sister, and she said, "Well, we are all sisters after all!" And then she told us about what a privilege it was to help people die. I was so happy to hear someone else talk that way. Even her two master's degrees had been linked through the concept of the hospice movement. She worked* for the Comprehensive Health Planning Council of South-eastern Michigan as a senior health planner. Her actual position was to analyze projects in health services for the community, and she was trying to focus the area on a five-year plan to create the hospice concept there.

Over and over, with passion and with compassion, Audrey used the word "privilege." It was such a privilege to work with dying people and bring the hospice concept to the community. I suddenly felt a powerful kinship with her.

There was a tremendous amount of emotion filling the room. Some of the medical students and residents had to leave, but everyone else stayed until we were through.

When it ended, everyone was hugging. I felt high. Spacey. I went into the kitchen alone and started washing dishes. I needed to keep my hands in water. It grounded me. I needed to leave, get into my car, and contemplate during the forty-mile trip back to Bill and Jeanine.

Jenny came in and asked me not to do the dishes, but I had to. So more people came in, and we were busy doing things. The atmosphere was electric.

I eventually got thrown out of my position at the sink and went and sat down in the now-empty living room. Bruce came in with his children and cats, who had been away for the whole time and were now clinging to him.

I said my good-byes and got back on the road. About ten miles away I saw a McDonald's and pulled in for a cup of coffee and french fries. Many NDErs agree that when you need to get grounded—if you're feeling high and need to come down—McDonald's french fries bring you down. It could be the salt. I'm not sure. But it works.

This face-to-face meeting with other experiencers was a first for me, but I'll never forget it because of the rush of emotions that swept through me.

*At first, I felt exuberant, elated. Through them, I could affirm my own feelings, my own experience. Over the years, though, I have learned to expect a kind of withdrawal, a sense of crashing after these encounters with other NDErs. The high we get from sharing our common experience is too intense to be sustained for long periods of time. Everything surfaces at these meetings. Each time, emotions that have been buried surface, and there is a feeling of bursting forth.*

*These meetings satisfy a longing to find others like yourself. After the meeting, all kinds of fears can take over. To the casual observer, we experiencers appear able to "get high from life," passionately, quickly, and intensely. However, a sort of grieving process always follows, grief over the loss of a time when we knew eternal peace and happiness. It is sobering to realize that we all still have to "chop wood and carry water" here in our present reality."*

Four days later, Barbara returned to the Greysons'. Bruce and Barbara drove to Chicago. All Barbara could think about as they drove west was how far she had come in just eight years. Eight years ago she was seeing a psychiatrist who had given her antidepressants after she finally found the courage to talk about her experience in the Circle Bed. NDEs hadn't been officially acknowledged by anyone that Barbara knew back then. Now, however, she found herself traveling with a scientist who had published articles in several prestigious medical journals on the near-death experience and was the editor of *The Journal of Near-Death Studies*.

Bruce had written that NDEs occurred in normal people. If the experience could be integrated, he'd written, it could be a powerful tool for personal growth. Barbara was traveling with him to do a television show on NDEs that would be seen by millions of people in the greater Chicago area. The show was called "Common Ground," a popular late-night talk show hosted by Derek Hill.

They arrived at the studio early, so Bruce and Barbara took a walk down to the Navy Pier just a few blocks away. It was on Lake Michigan and had beautiful huge round fountains shooting water high into the air.

On the set, they were talking about the show's format when a cameraman came up and told them the taping would have to be canceled because the cameras they were planning to use had just broken down.

"I'm sure it's my fault," Barbara told Derek, laughing as she spoke. "All kinds of electronic equipment breaks around me." Derek looked puzzled, so she explained. "My bio-energy field, the result of the NDE, affects electronic equipment. The energy affects anything that uses micro-chips, including computers and photocopy machines. Ordinary car batteries are sometimes drained when I'm around them," Barbara said. "The up side is that burned-out light bulbs sometimes work again around me. The down side is that streetlamps sometimes blow out as I walk past them."

"You've graduated from streetlamps," Bruce said, teasing her about their current dilemma.

"I've given up going to the bank because their computers don't work around me," Barbara said, "and I can't get near a computerized cash register in a department store because they go haywire." The taping was canceled until the next day.

Meanwhile, Derek offered to take Bruce and Barbara out to dinner. They went to the top floor of the tallest building in Chicago. The maître d' showed them into a circular dining room, an elaborately decorated place that resembled a movie set. There were huge crystal chandeliers and the waiters wore tuxedos. A baby grand piano sat in the center of the room and a man played classical music on it as the whole restaurant revolved slowly, giving them a panoramic view of Chicago.

After the taping the next day, while driving back to Michigan, Bruce told Barbara that his mother would be visiting the next weekend. The show would be shown then, and perhaps he and his mother would drive into the area that received Chicago television and check into a motel and watch it there. It would be a nice opportunity to visit with his mother and see the broadcast.

When she arrived back in Florida, Barbara found a message waiting for her from one of the people she counseled.

"This client was referred to me by Bill Roll because his psychic abilities frightened him. The client was a young man from north Florida with whom I had been working for only a short time over the phone." she said. "He had been troubled lately by bad dreams, he said, and was having waking visions of airplane crashes and explosions. I imagined he'd dreamed of another catastrophe and thought that was why he was calling. When I reached him, he said the mood and content of his dreams had changed."

"In the dream," he said, "I was with my mother in a bedroom with a big-screen TV. We were watching people near a huge body of water. There were round areas in the dream, with water shooting up. Then I saw TV cameras. Abruptly the scene changed and I saw men in tuxedos, a piano, and overhead, there were crystal chandeliers everywhere."

For Barbara, being tracked by one of her clients who had paranormal abilities now seemed almost explainable. Research into psychic abilities had become a hot topic as early as 1976. By the early 1980's, even the government was interested in delving into it. Barbara found this out during the next IANDS meeting, held in November 1983.

The meeting was held at the home of an Army officer in Washington, D.C. Lieutenant Colonel John Alexander had a doctorate in thanatology, the study of death and dying. He had worked with Elisabeth Kubler-Ross and now worked at the Pentagon in a division called, oddly enough, the Human Technologies Task Force. The unit had been set up to study psychokinesis and enhancing human performance. Both the U.S. and Soviet governments had been doing extensive research. Spy-novel stuff had become real.

*The November board meeting was especially significant for me because I was elected to the board, becoming the second member who was also a near-death experiencer. My first assignment was to continue planning the upcoming February conference. So far, Bruce had gotten fifty-four clinicians—clinical psychologists, psychiatrists, social workers, nurses, and five people who were near-death experiencers—to come if we had a grant to help cover expenses.*

*Sherwin said he wanted to take a vacation. We both knew our marriage was sick. It had soured and was dying. This trip together was a "last-fling" attempt to save it. We used to love museums. I wanted to see London, a city of museums. He wanted to take a cruise. I hated cruises. Two years earlier, we had taken a cruise to celebrate our twentieth wedding anniversary. I would have had more fun on the Titanic. Sherwin spent hours in the casino. I didn't gamble and found sleep impossible in a cabin without windows. This time, he promised accommodations that included a porthole, so I gave in and we cruised to Mexico, Jamaica, and the Cayman Islands. The ports were wonderfully refreshing. Unfortunately, there were no special moments of reconciliation for Sherwin and me. He played blackjack. I wrote poetry.*

*Beth and Steven came home for Christmas. Our Michigan friends made their annual trek south to our house for the holiday too. I cooked Christmas dinner for twenty-five. Every year it was the same. After dinner, people would lounge in the pool or hot tub. We'd talk endlessly about the folks back home, about divorces, infidelities, and money. After dinner, Beth pulled me into my bedroom, and she was furious.*

*"We aren't like these people anymore," she complained. "Listen to what they value—cars, money. Listen to them," she said. "That's not us anymore."*

*That night I couldn't sleep. Beth had struck a nerve, a feeling I'd been trying to come to terms with for years now. My children and I no longer clung to the same values as these friends we'd known for decades. We had remained friends, careful never to talk about real issues in our lives unless they were upbeat reflections of our respective wealth and stature.*

*Unable to sleep, I played classical music.*

*I spent many hours that Christmas week writing poetry about my changing world. I wrote angry poems about materialism, and sad poetry because it was me that didn't fit in anymore with the values around me. Beth could see some of it, but not the repercussions between her father and me.*

# II

## THE BEGINNING

I sit patiently, now
in my solitude.
Awaiting the dawn
of my release . . .
Knowing a death has
  occurred.
Too cautious still
to announce my rebirth.
But starting to sense my need
for lessons in crawling,
then walking.
So I may eventually Skip
and Dance
and Live
To my Heart's Own Content.

—Barbara Harris,
August, 1984

# 14

## The IANDS Conference

By early January it was clear there wouldn't be any grant money for the conference. Without it, the group couldn't afford to help participants with their travel expenses and couldn't afford accommodations at a conference center. Barbara decided they could hold the conference at her house. It was large enough, with over three thousand square feet of living space and a screened-in terrace that measured thirty-five by forty feet.

Bruce Greyson wrote to everyone about the financial dilemma. Twenty-two participants had to drop out. He received firm commitments, however, from the remaining thirty-two clinicians, M.D.'s Ph.D.'s, R.N.'s, and social workers, plus a few other interested academics, and of course several near-death experiencers who had been active in IANDS.

Barbara bartered with a local health-food restaurant,

which agreed to cater the meals in exchange for a new sofa from Sherwin's factory. Sherwin graciously agreed to donate the sofa to their cause, although he wasn't happy with Barbara's new plan to bring thirty-two strangers into his house for a four-day conference and a board meeting before. Barbara rented tables and chairs for the terrace, plus a huge coffeepot and a classroom-size blackboard on a stand. Then she bought paper products, coffee, and other supplies for thirty-two people. Every time she got nervous about the conference, she'd bake another double batch of chocolate-chip cookies and put them in the freezer for her guests.

Sherwin reasoned with Barbara, saying their privacy was being invaded. When he couldn't get her to change her mind, he offered to visit relatives in California. She encouraged him to leave, but instead of going to California for the entire period of time, he took the van and drove to Gainesville and stayed with Beth and Steven for the two days of board meetings, coming home and going to work each day during the conference.

The week before the conference, the tension between them rose to an all-time high.

Then Gary got sick. The doctor said he had mononucleosis and would need bed rest for weeks. Barbara's resolve to have the conference, no matter what, started to crumble. She called Bruce, voicing her concern to him long-distance.

"Gary's only fifteen," she said. "Maybe he's too young to hear about all this at his age. I'm afraid."

"I think this will be good for Gary and you," he countered, putting on his therapist's hat for her benefit. "He's old enough and should be exposed to what has become your world. Let him understand, Barbara. He sounds bright, and from what you've told me, he's sensitive."

"I'll believe you, but I'm still concerned because he's never been around anything like this before," Barbara said.

146

Things smoothed out temporarily between Sherwin and Barbara. He was polite to her guests, but left for Gainesville as planned. Gary stayed home.

*People started arriving that Friday for the board meeting on Saturday. Friday evening I ordered pizza for twenty-five. A forty-cup coffeepot was going around the clock next to the six long rented tables and chairs out on the terrace. The pool and hot tub were full of happy people who had just escaped from winter scenes up north. Eleven people stayed at our house; the others were at hotels or with friends. Raymond Moody, sometimes called the father of the near-death movement because of his best-selling book, Life After Life, arrived early on Friday and threatened to move in permanently. Immediately, Gary attached himself to this jovial southerner and followed him around for the rest of the week.*

On Saturday they held a board meeting. IANDS' financial status remained about the same—dismal. Kim Clark, an NDEr, had already started two successful Friends of IANDS chapters in Washington State. She told the board the need for more chapters was crucial.

"I know IANDS has been a research organization up to now," she said. "No one appreciates that more than me. For those of you who don't know me, I'm a social worker in a large hospital in Seattle. I work on a trauma unit that handles emergencies for a five-state area. We see a lot of near-death events. Being a near-death experiencer myself, and being exposed to them constantly, has put me in a unique situation. I have talked at professional conferences on the NDE. Many nursing and respiratory-therapy conventions have sponsored me to speak on clinical approaches to the NDE.

"Naturally, I appreciate the encouragement and support I have received from IANDS, but now, as a rapidly growing organization, we need to develop at a grass-roots level," she said. "More people are having this experience than we even begin to realize. I see·it all the time. IANDS needs to focus on service to the community."

Everyone agreed; then they adjourned to enjoy the pool and the Florida sunshine.

Sunday they had a schedule of arriving flights into Fort Lauderdale and Miami International and set up a pool of drivers, who began shuttling people as their flights arrived.

Months earlier, Barbara had called Israel Topel, the psychiatrist from Kentucky, and he agreed to come. "Does this mean I have to get a haircut?" he asked, joking with Barbara during the phone conversation. She picked him up at the airport. She spotted him coming down an escalator, but she wasn't sure he was the same man. Israel had shaved, and his hair was short.

"Is this okay, friend?" he asked, modeling his new look for her. Israel was an M.D. who still traveled with his belongings in a knapsack.

Back at the house, people had been drifting in all day. Most of the time was spent lounging and getting acquainted. An impressive group of intellectuals, leaders in their respective fields, had gathered here, chosen by Bruce Greyson and Ken Ring because they had been published professionally on the near-death experience, or had had an NDE, or were professionally interested in the research. By late Sunday night, even Raymond Moody was impressed.

He called his wife, Louise, who had stayed home in Georgia with their two young sons and urged her to come. "I want you to see this!" he told her. And then he proclaimed in his southern drawl, "We've just moved near-death studies to a new level. There's a wonderful group of people here with big hearts, honey. They know there's a lot more work to be done than we've covered this far in telling about the experience. They have patients who have needed help coping with NDEs. These people that are here are willing to sit down and hammer out techniques to help people who up to now most everyone in the medical field would have labeled 'psychotic.' This is a rare group of brave clinicians and academics, and I want you here to witness what we started grow into something so much bigger than we ever dreamed.''

Louise arrived on Monday, the first official day of the conference.

''Looking back on my memories of the thirty-two people,'' Barbara recalls, ''I am sure that each one would tell a different story about that IANDS conference. There wasn't one reality. There were thirty-two unique realities.''

Bruce opened the first session Monday evening in Barbara and Sherwin's living room. People she had never met sat on the sofa or on rented chairs in the entry hall and dining room, unable to get any closer to the blackboard Bruce had set up.

Just before Bruce started, he wrote many phrases on the board, including ''Near-Death Experiencer.'' A wave of anger shot through Barbara, and she couldn't control herself.

''That's one of the big problems right there!'' she said to Bruce. He stopped writing, giving her his full attention.

''I resent being labeled,'' she said. She was shocked at her own words. Bruce was her friend and a doctor, and she resented being labeled by him or any other doctor. She was shocked because a few days earlier Bruce had specifically asked her if near-death experiencers harbored any anger against doctors who didn't understand their experiences and instead encouraged patients to ignore them. Barbara had told him that she didn't feel anger toward anyone. Now she was plainly exhibiting her anger at being labeled.

Barbara recovered from her outburst. Bruce remained calm as always. A few minutes later he introduced himself and started the conference. He talked briefly about the problems they had encountered setting up the conference. He asked the participants to introduce themselves by describing their backgrounds, their interest in near-death experiences, and anything else they wanted to share with the group.

Nancy Bush started by introducing herself as the executive director of IANDS. Leslee Morabito was next. She assisted Nancy in the office.

Israel introduced himself as a "New Age psychiatrist" interested in any spiritual experience that could help a person grow.

"I had two experiences that have drastically altered my sense of reality," Barbara said when it was her turn to speak. "They changed my relationship with my family and to the planet. My new sense of oneness with and love for the planet became a wall in my marriage. I've spent the last nine years trying to understand what happened to me," she said. "Until just a few minutes ago, I denied being angry at the people who took care of me when I was sick, but now I can say there's probably a lot of anger and frustration among near-death experiencers."

Chuck Flynn was next. He was a sociology professor from Miami University in Ohio and was writing a book about the NDE. He talked about being fascinated by the love the NDEr talks about and displays after the experience. He had created a new course for his students that he called the Love Project. He showed the class videotapes of NDErs talking about the light, about love, and he used a lot of material from Leo Buscaglia. Then, as their term projects, the students had to choose other students on campus that they didn't necessarily get along with and give them "total acceptance," as the NDErs and Buscaglia talked about. As their semester projects, the students kept journals and used class time to discuss the difficulties that surrounded "unconditional love."

Two therapists then introduced themselves. A clinical psychologist came next. He started off by giving an impressive list of academic and professional credentials. In the middle of what he was saying, he stopped abruptly and began to shake. In a trembling voice he said, "A few years ago I had an experience that wasn't of this reality. It wasn't a near-death experience, but something similar. I've never told anyone because I know it was a break from this reality and I was pretty sure it was a psychotic break. I haven't felt the same since it happened," he said to a room full of strangers. He turned bright red, obviously embarrassed, and stopped, unable to say anything else.

There was a deafening pause after he finished. The next clinician gave her credentials and then with a shaky voice told of seeing her life flash in front of her after the impact of an auto accident, although she was in no way hurt. She had no way of explaining it.

John Mig told a little of his near-death experience. He said it had totally changed his life at the age of eighteen. John said it was important for him to be on the IANDS board. He said that he was uncomfortable with the labels that divided experiencers and clinicians at this conference, and he hoped they could transcend them.

Next Raymond, in his slow southern accent, told everyone that he had been dubbed. "Dr. Death" since his book *Life After Life* had been published in 1975. Almost immediately it had become a best-seller, and still sells two hundred thousand copies a year and has been translated into thirty languages. Dr. George Ritchie had shared his personal experience with Raymond while a student at the University of Virginia in the early 1970s. Not yet ready to process the information, Raymond admitted it had lain pregnant within his mind until he was teaching a philosophy class and a student began to share a similar story. This piqued his interest and he began to keep notes of such phenomena. Finally he wrote the book, and NDEs were out of the closet.

He told them that the divergent makeup of the group was the key to how effective they were going to be. Their different backgrounds—psychiatrists, psychologists, mental-health professionals, nurses, counselors, and the experiencers—had all been carefully picked by Bruce Greyson and Ken Ring. Raymond thanked these two for their hard work.

When the participants had started, they seemed cautious of professional images, sharing bits of background with an occasional, "I'm an experiencer!" By the time they had shared; warmth and understanding, tears and anxiety had diluted the caution, and a roomful of people entered into a group process that had never been tried before. Instead of observing subjects, as is usually done in science, some of these brave clinicians had actually become the subjects. Up until then they had attended conferences where they sat in an audience taking notes as they were lectured to by an expert. Now there were no experts and no separate observers. These thirty-two brave people were subjects and observers together in uncharted territory.

\* \* \*

*As each person talked, more emotion was poured into the room. Almost everyone had a personal reason, not just a professional one, for being there.*

*Bruce Greyson charged us with the task at hand. He explained the process we would be using. We would divide into four groups, which he had already created, each with a psychiatrist and an equal makeup of people by profession and an equal number of near-death experiencers. Of course, at that point he didn't know how many of the clinicians were also experiencers. That was still to unfold. He also had placed Nancy Bush, Leslee Morabito, the IANDS office assistant, himself, and me in individual groups so we could check back with each other and know where we stood. We would have morning and afternoon sessions at which we would be given tasks, and before the next session each group would report to the whole group. Evenings would be spent unstructured as long as the focus was on the issues of the conference, until nine p.m., and then we were free to relax until breakfast at eight-thirty the next morning. The conference that had begun on Monday evening would run through Thursday noon.*

*By the time Bruce ended that first session the first evening, we were all open, heart-felt, feeling as one group. And then it happened. Several small groups formed to chat.*

*Several near-death experiencers formed a group hug. We felt so overjoyed with what had just happened. We put our arms around each other all at once and squeezed, all laughing and saying things like, "Finally!" and "Thank God!" Chuck Flynn and a few others were standing nearby, and I tried to pull them in, but there was resistance. We were a group of experiencers and they felt they didn't belong. The resistance bounced around my house until four the next morning. That hug had divided everyone again. I don't remember any resolution. We just identified the absolute fact that emotions were hot and high about everything. I crawled into bed a little past four.*

Barbara and Sherwin's alarm went off abruptly at seven in the morning. He left for work and she dragged herself out to start breakfast. In the hallway she saw Louise Moody.

"Girl, my husband is the father of all this," she said. "These are my children. Go back to your room and rest, and I'll get breakfast started. You don't need to be out here until eight-thirty. Let me tend to breakfast!"

"We need to buy bagels," Barbara said. "Bruce knows where to get them."

"Okay," Louise said, pushing Barbara in the direction of her room and telling her, "It's going to be a long day."

At eight-thirty everyone had assembled for a breakfast of juice, bagels, and coffee, the same breakfast that was served each morning. Bruce, Nancy, Leslee, and Barbara met for about fifteen minutes before the morning session in an attempt to gain an overview. Nancy was unaware of the emotional outburst after the group hug the night before. She was in Beth's room all night with a therapist from Wisconsin who had started falling apart during the meeting and needed to talk, and did so most of the night. The three of them tried explaining to Nancy what had happened the night before, the division, the resistance. When they heard each other's accounts, they realized that they didn't agree on what had happened.

*Bruce said we needed to stay in the big group for the morning. I said I wanted an hour to talk, and then I knew John Mig wanted an hour too. We agreed, and just as we were about to call the morning meeting, I panicked quietly to Bruce.*

*"Gary,"* I said. *"What about Gary? I don't know what I'm going to say, but if he's listening, I'll be inhibited. He's too young to hear this. He doesn't know what's going on with his father and me. Oh, God! I don't want to expose him to this!"*

*"Okay, Barbara,"* Bruce agreed, *"if that's what you really are feeling about him hearing this particular talk, then tell him. And tell him why, what you are feeling right now. And he'll respect your wishes. Besides, it's obvious that he's not feeling well, and this will be a good opportunity for him to get some rest."*

*"Thanks, Bruce!"* I said, and went off to find Gary and talk to him before we began. I found him out on the back terrace. I told him I needed to talk to him.

*"Gary, I'm going to be talking to the group for an hour, and then John Mig is. We're each going to be talking about personal problems—psychiatric-type problems that we've had since our NDEs, and . . . well, I'm sorry, but I need some privacy. I mean, there are thirty-two people listening—that's not privacy—but I mean I'm the only one here with a relative!"*

*"Okay, Mom, I understand."*

I smiled, relieved. *"Thank you, Gary. Thank you, honey."*

We began five minutes later. Bruce announced that we were going to stay in the big group for the morning and that I was going to present first, followed by John Mig.

I quickly said a prayer, pleading for my ego to get out of the way so I could be a clear instrument for the light, for God. Please let what we need come through, I said. I started to tell about my injury, what had led up to my NDE. I heard myself talking about Valium, Percodan, pleading for sur-

*gery because I didn't want to go on the way I was anymore.
I remembered the chaplain who came in to see me. I identified myself as an atheist before my experience. I described
my condition clinically, using the language of a respiratory
therapist, so I owned my training too. I tried to give every
detail I remembered of my experiences. That took me back,
deeper into my memories than I had ever gone before. I
looked at everyone as I heard myself say I returned to my
body in the Circle Bed and then realized where I was.*

*I was wide open. I told them about being told I had
hallucinated, and then the feeling of indignity when I would
be sedated for protesting or pleading for help. I had asked
to see a psychiatrist several times. It had felt like I was
being sedated for trying to make people understand that I
had left that bed.*

*Then I plunged into how my family didn't understand, or
at least didn't understand me. It was a paradox to me that
I was open and vulnerable to everyone that crossed my path,
yet totally shut out from my own family. I talked about going
to see the psychiatrist, about being given antidepressants,
how I didn't blame him. Raymond Moody's book hadn't
even come out yet. But I asked the group several times if
life would have been different for me if some professional
had understood. Would my marriage still be intact? Would
Sherwin have been helped to understand why I needed to
change? Would he accept my need to work with the dying?*

*Finally I pleaded with the group to work together as one,
to stop the individual responses to imaginary barriers and
create clinical approaches to the near-death experience.*

*The only thing I realized when I finished was that my
appeal had been extremely emotional.*

*John's talk was similar to mine, only John has a special
presence about him. He's a strong, intelligent Italian and*

*I could admire his emotion as he showed it. He had drowned at eighteen. John said no one had understood. He still felt different, and had accepted that difference, but wanted so much to change things.*

They broke up into small groups after lunch. Raymond Moody led Barbara's group. Bruce had asked each group to deal with problems in personal relationships that occur after any NDE. He asked them to identify the biggest problems they faced. He also asked them to identify their hopes for the outcome of this conference. And finally, what did they personally hope to take home with them? When Barbara's turn came, she talked about relating to her children. She was worried about Gary.

"He'll be okay, Barbara. He understands a lot more than you think," said Raymond, who had been friends with Gary for five days now.

After dinner, people chatted at the pool or sat in small, informal groups and continued to talk about all they had experienced earlier in the day. Beth's bedroom became the emotional emergency room. It was removed from the activity, and people felt comfortable in that room when they were having a crisis. A lot of heavy-duty therapy took place in there. Someone would start talking and suddenly find himself letting go about a hidden memory he had repressed. Bruce was often called in to rescue someone. People just kept taking turns.

The second night, things got even more emotional than the first. Throughout the house, people were giving out impromptu hugs or telling intimate stories.

*I knew that some sort of group dynamics had swept us all into a powerful state, but I couldn't identify it any further.*

*Sherwin was already home and in bed for the night. I was wandering around out by the lake, voices floating out from my house. It was late and there were probably fifteen or twenty people still up in the house. Leslee came out, finding me in the dark. The two of us were strongly connected and we knew it. She asked me what was up.*

*"I don't know. It feels like the doctors want to diagnose and the experiencers are clinging to their sacred moment, protecting it from the doctors. And some of these clinicians are experiencers one minute and doctors the next. I can't keep track! I thought they were experts on the NDE. That they were prepared to share their abilities to handle all this."*

*Leslee had thought that too. But she had given up that impression when she gave up trying to "keep track." She was trusting the group process, and when she started getting upset, would pray, turning it all over to the Universe.*

*I told Leslee that I felt so much pain in the room when we gathered in the big group that a few times I had to walk out. I knew a lot of it was my own, but everyone else was hurting too. She softly said she knew and that I had to remember that it was good for them to get in touch with their pain and that we had created a safe atmosphere for that.*

*She told me that I had to remember that most of the group were fearful of giving up their rational approach to life and switching to an experiential mode. There was a lot of risk involved, and people were battling their own fears about risking a whole new way of perceiving. And then she reminded me that having an NDE is one of many ways to open up to all of this. Slowly but surely, these brave people in my house were admitting to the manner in which they had stepped, for a brief moment, into a way beyond the rational.*

*Maybe that was why they had chosen their professions, just as I had chosen respiratory therapy. Only now they were coming to terms with all their buried fears.*

*After we hugged, I went to my room. In the dark I got ready for bed and crawled in next to Sherwin. He was fast asleep. I don't think I ever fell asleep. I lay there for the few hours left until the sun came up, praying, pleading, hoping that everyone would be all right.*

When they met on Wednesday morning, the divisions were less important, and those who had proclaimed "It can't be analyzed!" were reconciled to sensitivity being an approach. The most analytical of the psychologists confessed, "There have to be right-brain approaches." By Wednesday afternoon individuals were using words like "psychic," "sensitivity," "intuition," "synchronicity," "grounding," "telepathic," "sacred," and "the Universe" with great respect.

By Wednesday evening Chuck Flynn had recovered from that group hug the first evening of the conference. He put his hands on Barbara's shoulders and lightened her mood a little with, "Just wait until you see this in your next life review! You're going to love it! So many people are getting help here. I promise you, you're going to love it, honey," he said, laughing.

Barbara was so deeply involved in her own problems, she couldn't understand what Chuck could see, but she filed away his words very carefully, hoping that someday she could understand.

*Thursday morning, we sat in a big circle in my living room. Louise Moody was at the blackboard all morning.*

*Each point, reported from each group, seemed to be at least a paragraph long. Bruce would translate each point into a phrase or, at most, a sentence. Then Louise would write it.*

*There were ways to approach identifying an experience and helping the person integrate it. Then we were listing the other ways to have an experience—during great emotion, in meditation, during intense prayer, spontaneously, or through this new way of perceiving, gently, through synchronicity. The group defined "synchronicity" as becoming aware of linking coincidences; being aware of life being woven from some higher point of awareness. This point more than any other seemed to make an impact on the group and turn thirty-two separate individuals into one entity.*

*The four groups suggested clinical approaches for every time period during and after a near-death experience. From the emergency room and intensive-care unit, as Bruce, Kim, and I had professionally experienced, through old age to the moment of dying, we had suggested ways for clinicians to listen and encourage their patients.*

*Louise wrote visual techniques on the blackboard. At the end of this long list that filled the board, we all decided that our work as clinicians was finished when the experiencer could take the love that he or she felt in the experience and share it with others personally and professionally or through volunteer work.*

*Bruce reminded us that these approaches filling the blackboard had not been tried, tested, and proved. That was now up to everyone in the room.*

*"Take these suggestions back to your practices. Try them out. Publish on the ones that work, and please tell me about the ones that don't," Bruce said.*

*We stood in a circle and held each other's shoulders in*

*a huge group hug. Israel said a wonderful prayer. We hugged and kissed good-bye.*

*Some left for the airport. The group that remained waiting for later flights walked to McDonald's about five blocks away, for lunch. We laughed as we all ate french fries to get grounded.\**

---

*See Appendix: ''Clinical Approaches to the NDEr'' by Bruce Greyson, M.D. for the strategies and techniques that resulted from this conference. The general principles discussed are for relatives and friends of experiencers, as well as professionals. In general, this paper can be helpful not only for NDEs but also for anyone in close contact with someone in transformational crisis.

# 15

---

# Synchronicity

Barbara's relationship with Sherwin deteriorated even further after the conference. The days which followed it, however, still loom with significance in her mind even now, because they marked the beginning of the end of a long marriage.

*We went for marriage counseling for three months. Sherwin kept saying that he wanted me to go back to the way I was when we first met. Or he said he wanted me to be the way I was when we first married. I couldn't. I knew it. I knew our marriage was over. I knew we still loved each other and always would, but I couldn't contract back down to the way I was when we met. That was twenty-six years ago. I couldn't blame him. I was the one who had changed.*

*About the only thing we had left to share was late-night shopping at the supermarket. We would buy cups of coffee, then stroll through the aisles filling our cart. We especially liked the Grand Union store near our house because it was open all night. One night, soon after the conference, we pulled into the parking lot and, to our dismay, found the store had gone out of business. The sign said, "Grand Union has moved out of Florida." We looked at each other, knowing that the moment was significant and we had our last laugh together. We couldn't even share these shopping trips anymore. There was nothing left of our marriage, our Grand Union!*

On April 12, 1984, Barbara's birthday, Sherwin took her to lunch and gave her a gift with a card that said he still loved her. Looking each other straight in the eye, they agreed they could no longer live together and began the first steps toward ending a twenty-two-year marriage.

It took a month to work out the details, but Sherwin moved out in May 1984. While he was moving, Barbara took a trip to Connecticut for a board meeting.

*I stayed with Nancy Bush, and the first night in Connecticut she and Leslee took me to the Friends of IANDS support group they were the coordinators of at Manchester Community College near the Storrs campus of the University of Connecticut. They told me on the way over that the group had met several times, and although the nonexperiencers had enthusiastically discussed the NDE and its meanings, the near-death experiencers themselves had said almost nothing: there was little reporting of experiences, no sharing of what they had learned. They seemed to be afraid to talk about it.*

*We walked in, and while Nancy introduced me, I said a prayer asking to help. I told my experience and then de-*

scribed the difficulties I had had in adjusting after my medical recovery. Then I asked the other NDErs what it was like for them now. As Nancy said, "I might as well have opened the valves of Hoover Dam!" They couldn't talk fast enough. We heard anger at being "taken back" from the light, frustration with families and friends who did not understand, and confusion about the lives to which they had been abruptly returned. As the outpouring continued, another member of the group, who was not an experiencer, cried, "But you shouldn't feel this way! You have been to the light; tell us what to do!" Then there was only silence again. No one would talk. I ached for these people. This was one of the problems discussed at the conference. I had dubbed it the National Enquirer Syndrome. Many of the newspapers talk only of the saintly qualities of people who have had these experiences, putting them on a pedestal, which is a pretty lonely place to be. Near-death experiencers can tell us what the world needs to be peaceful, but they can't determine how to keep their own lives peaceful after they have been turned inside out by the experience. Not everyone has that problem, but for the ones who do, talking about it in a safe environment like a Friends of IANDS support group usually helps.

After the meeting, when we went back to Nancy's house, she handed me the galleys of Heading Toward Omega. I read for the next three days and cried off and on. My marriage had just ended and this book had just been born. In it were many quotes of mine. For the first time in my life I realized just how much I had changed: my outlook on life, my values, my very being. I was reading my "self" and saying, "No wonder, no wonder." I suddenly had an understanding of how and why I had changed, and felt so horrible because Sherwin and I really hadn't had a chance.

*But somewhere in the grieving for my lost marriage was relief that I was okay.*

Barbara went back to Florida and was alone for the first time in her life. Steven and Gary traveled all summer with their drum corps, riding around the country on a bus with a hundred other young musicians. At least she had the IANDS support group in Fort Lauderdale that she had helped start. There was now one in Palm Beach too, so she had two meetings to attend.

Nothing remained of the life Barbara had lived for twenty-two years that could help her maintain her equilibrium. Waking up to an empty house was one of the hardest adjustments she had to make in her life. Nothing had prepared her for this. Intellectually, she knew her marriage was over. While the death of Barbara's old life had come gradually over the years, she suddenly realized that without it, she didn't have much of a life at all. She grieved all summer for the loss of her relationship with Sherwin.

*I was married right after high school, and like many women, I moved from my parents' house into my husband's. Some women might have felt liberated over this new freedom. I was terrified and was crumbling under the weight of my new found solitude.*

*Sleeping became a problem. How I was going to take care of myself became a preoccupation. The only thing I feared more than being alone, however, was staying in a dead relationship. I knew there was no turning back. I just wasn't sure how I was going to carry on alone.*

*My emotions vacillated from tremendous fear to tremendous guilt. My routine was severely limited, and I realized I had to escape this luxurious prison, so I called Beth and asked if I could come for a short visit. Reluctantly she said okay, but reminded me that she was working and wouldn't be able to spend all her time with me.*

*Alas, I now had something concrete to do for the next six hours. Gainesville was a six-hour drive. I had a goal, a destination, some purpose for the first time in weeks. When I arrived, I would have gladly changed roles with Beth. I badly wanted to tell her to take care of me, but the mother in me knew better, so I kept my needs to myself.*

All of this quickly evaporated, however, because it was obvious shortly after Barbara arrived that Beth was having some problems of her own. "We were polite but careful not to invade one another's space," Barbara said, knowing that Beth too had been hurt by the divorce. "I wanted to rescue her somehow. But how? I was lost, unable to help myself. How could I rescue Beth?"

Barbara lay down on the sofa after Beth left for work and began praying. "God help me," she said, trying to clear her head, and then she began sinking into a deep meditation.

*Instantly I was immersed in clear nothingness, falling deeper and deeper into a meditative trance. I drifted to a place where there was no feeling, no fear, no pain, nothing. Then I began to sense the feeling of falling, descending at an accelerating speed. Suddenly I was gripped by terror, and something inside me called out to God for help. It was similar to a scene I had seen in the movie* Star Wars *when the main character, Luke Skywalker, realized he must leave his mentor, Yoda, to enter the Cave of Fear. In the film, Luke had been brave. I was falling out of control into my own Cave of Fear and trying to be brave about it.*

*At the same time, I somehow began to touch Leslee's mind. We had felt so connected at the IANDS conference, and I needed her kind of strength and wisdom now. Some-*

*thing was about to happen to me and I wanted Leslee's help. My soul was screaming and I suddenly saw beautiful rolling green hills. Connecticut was seventeen hundred miles away and I could see the area where Leslee lived. Then I was moving through darkness. I felt Leslee and also realized that in that moment I had become all that I feared. The murky blackness I was moving through now was my own poisons. The instant this occurred to me, the darkness was transcended and I became one with it as it was moving upward. I felt the sensation of being lifted; I was rapidly moving away from this cave of darkness, speeding toward a cathedral of light above.*

*When I opened my eyes, back on the sofa, I was looking up the stairs ahead of me, and above them sunlight flooded in through the skylight.*

Barbara drove home the next morning, still a little shaky. Luba and David Aaronson, friends who knew she was having a hard time, called and invited her to lunch.

"In my car, I was waiting at a stop sign about to make a left turn when I saw a small car stop at the intersection across the street," Barbara said. "There was a small box sitting on top of the car. I honked my horn, trying to get the driver's attention. She ignored me, so I pulled out into the intersection, stopped, and got out. I could see the car was filled in back with gift boxes. As I walked toward the car, the driver pulled off, turning sharply, leaving me standing alone in the middle of the street. The box on the roof was airborne, and as the car speeded past, the box hit me in the chest and then fell to the pavement. I picked it up with the contents spilling out and waved to the car, but the driver was long gone.

"The box was in one hand, and in the other I was holding

a frilly white garment. It was trimmed in beautiful eyelet lace and satin ribbon. It was a baby's christening gown and bonnet. I chuckled and wondered if it was really intended for me. I knew I was dying; maybe the Universe was also telling me to stop being fearful: after death, you're born again! I got back into my car and drove to the restaurant."

Barbara telephoned Leslee.

"I knew something was going on," Leslee said after Barbara had told her about the afternoon two days earlier when she had pleaded telepathically with Leslee to help her.

"I didn't know what or who was involved, but I was sitting on my couch doing needlepoint when this wave of energy moved through me, and I knew someone or something was trying to connect with me."

"We were over a thousand miles apart but we connected. I wasn't really alone, and I felt better than I had felt in weeks. What happened next confirmed just how connected we really were," Barbara said.

"My sister is arranging for a christening for her new baby. Did I tell you she had her baby?" Leslee asked.

"Has she bought a gown for the baby yet?" Barbara asked.

"No, I know they haven't," Leslee answered.

"Well, they have one now," Barbara said, then told her about the christening gown she had "acquired" just a few hours earlier.

# 16

## Take Care of Your Baby

In the fall, Steven moved into the town house in Gainesville with Beth. Gary started tenth grade and Barbara realized that she had some serious personal and financial decisions to make. With Sherwin gone, keeping up the house physically and financially would be impossible, even though she had already accepted a job at a nearby hospital as a respiratory therapist. Gary had announced that he wanted to stay with whichever parent kept the house. "I was relieved that he was picking a situation—a place to live—not a parent," Barbara said. "I pictured myself living in an apartment in the area, working and being near Gary. Sherwin had a steady girlfriend and they had continued seeing all of our married friends, so my social circle was gone too.

"There was an IANDS board meeting coming up in Connecticut, and everything fell into place for me to lecture in several places in New England and at a big near-death-studies conference in Charlottesville, Virginia. I could go to the board, have my travel expenses taken care of, and start earning money. I asked Sherwin to move back into the house with Gary for three weeks, got in my car, and drove to New England, hoping I could sort out what I was going to do.''

Ironically, Bruce Greyson had been offered a position in the department of psychiatry at the University of Connecticut Medical School and had already moved his family to West Hartford over the summer. He became chief of the inpatient psychiatric unit at John Dempsey Hospital, which is part of the University of Connecticut Health Center. The massive complex contains a medical and dental school. Bruce also continued teaching and was encouraged to continue his research in near-death experiences. The University of Connecticut, unlike the University of Michigan, recognized the need for near-death studies.

*Ken Ring was less than an hour away at the Storrs campus. So was the IANDS office, with Nancy, Leslee, and Jim, the office manager. I had recently been elected treasurer of IANDS. This group felt like my family now.*

*I wanted so much to raise the necessary funds to get IANDS moving. I knew I could do that if I lived near the office, but that would have to be as a volunteer. We could barely afford Nancy, Leslee, and Jim's salaries. I could work at a nearby hospital to support myself and throw myself into fund-raising for IANDS. I thought about it, but in October I wasn't ready to make that decision. Every time I started to think about moving to Connecticut, I would also start to cry. Gary was still a child, only fifteen. I couldn't handle the thought of leaving him. I was just going for a brief visit, and saw it as an opportunity to sort things out. I needed help from my friends in Connecticut to figure out what I could do. I had been told four years earlier, "No direct patient care"—because of my back being reinjured—but now I knew I had to work in respiratory therapy to support myself. Could I maintain the house so Gary and I could live there? I didn't know what Sherwin's obligations would be. I still hadn't talked to a lawyer. I had become a recluse in the last few months. The only ones that called to keep checking up on me were Ken, Nancy, Bruce, and Leslee. This was my first venture out in a long time.*

*Heading north in my car, I stopped in Gainesville to visit Beth and Steven. Beth looked awful. She had seen a doctor a few days earlier and he suspected she might have a serious problem. She admitted that much to me, but she really didn't want to talk about it. I knew by the way she looked that she felt much worse than she was admitting to. Beth had always felt responsible for everyone, her younger brothers especially. When she was small we used to call her "Steven's little mother." Now she was trying to protect me by saying it was probably nothing.*

*That night I slept fitfully with Beth in her double bed; it felt as though I was out only long enough to have this lucid dream. (We call these dreams "lucid" because they are very clear and there is a part of the dreamer that knows it's a dream and this part actually feels awake and watching.)*

*A tall, strong woman in a dark suit and white blouse carried a baby into Beth's room and put the infant down on the bed. Then I heard my voice saying, "Take care of your baby!"*

*"She's your baby!" the woman said to me in a powerful voice. "You take care of her!"*

"The next morning, I was sure of what to do," Barbara recalls. "I ran downstairs and called Bruce Greyson on the kitchen phone. I gave him Beth's symptoms."

"Get her back to the doctor now," Bruce said. "That dream told you to, and now I am. Do it now and then call me and tell me what he says!"

When Beth came down, Barbara told her she was taking her to a doctor. Beth didn't protest, saying she felt worse. She was examined at the university clinic and the doctor said there could be several possible reasons she felt the way she did. Some of them were awful. Some of them weren't. Barbara and Beth filled a variety of prescriptions and went home. "I grocery-shopped and cooked several meals and put them in the freezer. The next day Beth promised me she'd follow her doctor's advice, so I packed my car and continued north toward Connecticut," Barbara said.

*The IANDS board meeting was held at the Greysons' new home in West Hartford. Actually, their new home was over a hundred and fifty years old. It was wonderful, real New England, a former schoolhouse. During the lunch break, Leslee and I left to attend her little nephew's christening. Even though the baby and his parents lived an hour away, the parish they had chosen was in West Hartford, only five minutes away. And coincidentally, it just happened to be the day of the board meeting and during our lunch hour. Leslee and I laughed and thanked the Universe for such wonderful synchronicity. This time we even had to call it "grace"! We walked into the church and saw this beautiful infant wearing the gown and bonnet that had hit me in the chest only two months earlier!*

That week Barbara gave a lecture for an evening adult-education class at a West Hartford high school. The class was simply called Love and she was asked to talk about the type of love felt in an NDE.

"I was reluctant to go, feeling tired from all the traveling I had been doing and feeling depressed from all my problems, but I had promised, so I went. I began by describing my NDE. As I spoke, two more women came in and sat down. Time passed quickly, as it usually does during one of these talks. I was flush with that kind of spiritual love that always seems to fill the room once an NDEr talks about their experience," Barbara said.

"One of the women who had come in late asked me a question after I mentioned the possibility of moving to Connecticut to fund-raise for IANDS."

"How do you feel about leaving your children?" she asked. Barbara felt her heart sink, and a lump swelled up in her throat. She looked directly into the woman's face, and everything around her seemed blurred.

"I can't answer that," Barbara finally said, "because that's such a painful thing for me right now . . . I can't answer that." Nothing had prepared Barbara for that question.

"During an NDE—over there—things seem so clear," she continued. "But you return to your body and this reality and try to live what you've learned during your experience, but it's not as easy as it sounds. I'm really sorry, but I can't answer your question. It's very painful!" she repeated.

When the questions and answers were over, the same woman approached Barbara and handed her a piece of paper. On it was her name, Mary Ellen Layden, and her address and phone number.

Mary Ellen said to her, "If and when you do move up here, come and stay with me for as long as you like. Stay a day, a week, a month, until you get settled in your own place. My children are grown and have moved out. I have a four-bedroom home and you are more than welcome to stay with me."

Then she just walked away, leaving Barbara with the piece of paper. Barbara spent the next few days working on IANDS business in Bruce Greyson's office. On her last day in Connecticut she had lunch with Ken Ring and Bruce, who had good news. He had applied for a grant to study the near-death experiences of suicidal patients admitted to the psychiatric unit of John Dempsey Hospital. The grant included funds for a research assistant, and he offered the position to Barbara. It meant she could move to Connecticut and be totally involved with near-death studies.

Ken was supposed to drive Barbara to her car after lunch so she could leave for Virginia and then home. "He had heard about Mary Ellen handing me that piece of paper that night at the high school. He asked to see it, and after I got into his car, he drove away from the University of Connecticut Health Center in Farmington and ten minutes later we were driving down a beautiful suburban street in West Hartford."

"Typical New England street," he said, stopping the car in front of a yellow colonial surrounded by huge old trees. "This is Mary Ellen Layden's house," he said. "This is where you're going to be living. When things get rough enough in Florida, think about all of us here and picture pulling up to this house."

That weekend, Barbara went to Charlottesville, Virginia, to speak at a conference given by the Quest Institute. Ken Ring, Bruce Greyson, Raymond Moody, and a physician from Finland were also going to talk.

The doctor from Finland was a woman named Rauni Luukenen. When Barbara saw her, she was immediately struck by the clothing this woman wore. She was dressed in a dark suit and a white blouse, the same clothing of the woman in the dream Barbara had had at Beth's house two weeks earlier. "When she spoke, the voice was identical to the voice in my dream and I could clearly hear her saying, 'Take care of your baby, she's your baby!'" Reacting visibly, Barbara bolted backward in her chair and said "That's her. That's the woman in my dream," to Bruce and Ken.

Officially, Rauni was a medical doctor and chief medical officer for twenty-two hospitals in Lapland, Finland. She was also the author of a best-selling book in Europe called *There Is No Death*. Spiritually, she had become Barbara's dream friend and Barbara convinced her to go home with her. Rauni gladly accepted. She had become fascinated by the fact that parapsychology was rapidly gaining respectability in U.S. circles. She was bolstered by the fact that mainstream scientists like Ken, Bruce, and others were conducting research in their fields. Rauni was determined to make the medical establishment in Europe view parapsychology as an acceptable science.

*We drove south, stopping first for a few days with Beth, where Rauni spent a long time talking to her about her health. Then we stopped at Disney World and Dr. Rauni Luukenen became Rauni the tourist, replete with a Mickey Mouse T-shirt. She stayed with me for four days, long enough for me to introduce her to some of the American research I had collected over the years. I gave her copies of Bruce's papers that had been published in medical journals. I showed her Stanley Dean's work. Stanley was a local phone call away. I called him for her and they talked and talked. Rauni seemed to be increasingly overwhelmed by the fact that a large number of American doctors were taking mysticism and parapsychology seriously enough to document and publish their research.*

# 17

## Strangers in a Strange Land

Christmas 1984, Sherwin took Beth, Steve, and Gary to visit relatives in California for two weeks. Barbara spent the holidays alone. The day after Christmas, she called Mary Ellen Layden, the woman who had offered her a place to live in Connecticut.

"Hello, this is Barbara Harris," she said when Mary Ellen answered.

"I had a dream about you last night," Mary Ellen said. "When are you coming?"

"Right after the New Year," Barbara said, trying her best to sound calm and thinking she could see her kids when they returned and before Beth and Steven left for Gainesville.

They chatted a little while longer and after they hung up, Barbara broke into sobs that lasted for hours.

\* \* \*

*On January 2, Steven helped me pack my clothes and stereo in my car, wrapping my speakers carefully so they wouldn't be damaged during the long ride north. Gary had already left that morning for school. Steven stood on the front porch waving good-bye. I couldn't look back at him; the pain was welling up harder than I had ever felt pain in my life. I felt I was doing the worst thing a woman could do—I was leaving my children.*

*That ride up was the hardest time in my life. What should have been a three-day trip took me two weeks. I stayed with Beth for two days in Gainesville, and even though she was her usual sweet self, I was terrified that she and her brothers might never forgive me for leaving. I was pulled over in Georgia for speeding and received a hefty fine. I became sick in Charlottesville, Virginia, when I stopped to visit Kay Allison at the Quest Institute. She took care of me for days.*

*I arrived on January 16 and moved in with Mary Ellen, living off my savings until April 1985, when the research grant at the U Conn Health Center came through. Then I moved into an apartment in nearby Hartford.*

*My work with Bruce Greyson and the suicidal patients immediately gave me direction and purpose, and I jumped headlong into my work. We interviewed patients that were admitted through the emergency room of the John Dempsey Hospital at the Health Center. Over the year-long grant, twenty patients were accepted to the study, first in the emergency room and then as patients in the inpatient psych unit at Dempsey. They usually stayed for a month. The office Bruce shared with me was right off the unit, so I was in close proximity to these people. We put them through several long psychological tests, including the ones I had taken for Ken Ring and Bruce. They also took many more lengthy tests dealing with suicidal tendencies. And we would sit and talk for at least an hour at a time, getting to know them well. There had already been two other projects like this, but not controlled in a hospital setting like this one. The other two, one by Ken Ring and Stephen Franklin and the other by psychiatrist David Rosen, were based on anecdotal self-reports, possibly years after the attempt. Their results were the same as ours. People having a near-death experience during a suicide attempt usually don't attempt again, a remarkable finding. Up until now, the literature on suicide has taught psychotherapists to teach coping skills to alleviate suicidal ideation (that is, "suicidal thoughts"). In other words, help a patient work out his problems. The method hasn't been all that successful.*

*Rosen, who lives in San Francisco, went through twelve years of records of jumps from the Golden Gate Bridge. He was able to find and interview seven people from that time period who survived. All seven reported near-death experiences, and only one had attempted suicide again, and only once. The survivors talked about a sense of "God," or as they called it, "the Universe" or "Cosmic Unity." They also talked about meetings with dead relatives who told them they wouldn't be allowed to stay. They said they were told they had to go back and face their problems. Ring and Franklin's anecdotal work revealed the same type of results.*

*All twenty of our patients returned monthly after discharge for the year of the grant. The follow-up visits took from one to two hours. We tried to keep track of everyone even after the funding ran out. Four of the twenty had near-death experiences. In one case, an intentional overdose, the patient told us that he was definitely hallucinating from all the drugs when he was suddenly watching himself from ceiling height during the hallucinations. He said there was a huge difference between the hallucinations and the out-of-body and near-death experience that followed.*

*As far as we know, the four who had near-death experiences have not attempted suicide again. They hadn't willingly told us about their experiences either because they were afraid we would label the experiences negatively or because they really hadn't thought about talking about their experiences yet. It was profound for us to hear these experiences so fresh in their minds. All four said they experienced what we have referred to as "Cosmic Unity," and all four felt differently about this reality and doubted if they would try again.*

*The last time we had information on the other sixteen, we knew that two had taken their lives, one had disappeared, and several others had made a variety of suicide attempts.*

*During my travels as a lecturer, I am repeatedly asked about suicide. Logically, people assume that since the NDE is such a peaceful, pleasant experience for most who have them, why don't more NDErs take their own lives to get back there?*

*The NDErs we have talked with said they wouldn't attempt to take their own lives again even though NDEs do romanticize death, because the NDE also romanticizes life. Living becomes more meaningful. We have been told, "Taking your own life is like throwing God's gift back in his face!"*

*Over and over again, in analyzing the research, we are confronted with a paradox. Almost all the experiencers we have interviewed aren't afraid to die, but what we also hear over and over is: When you're not afraid to die life becomes much more meaningful. Or to quote the song "The Rose": "It's the soul afraid of dying that never learns to live."*

Unfortunately, the research grant ended in April 1986. The lease on Barbara's apartment was also over, so she put all her belongings in storage and took the opportunity to travel. But first she participated in an experiential workshop with Stan and Christina Grof. Stan Grof, M.D., was the scholar-in-residence at Esalen Institute in Big Sur, California, overlooking the Pacific Ocean. It's a wonderful meeting place for scientists both to conduct and to participate in psychospiritual workshops and scientific meetings. Stan and Christina had founded the Spiritual Emergency Network. There are now ten thousand therapists all over the world who belong to this network. It is a referral service for people in crisis, aimed at more appropriate methods of what may appear to be a psychotic break but could be a spiritual breakthrough.

The workshop, "Working with Kundalini Energy," was five days of lectures, visualizations, and relaxation exercises, followed by a unique breathing technique that induces altered states of consciousness similar to, but less dramatic than, the NDE. Barbara was amazed and relieved to realize that these states of consciousness are available to everyone, without using drugs or coming close to death. Many people had tried to convince her that certain drugs would induce the same experience, but she had never witnessed anywhere near the same long-lasting positive aftereffects from drug-induced experiences that she saw in an NDE. And now the Grofs had developed a safe way to induce the process slowly.

Ken Ring arrived at Esalen after Barbara experienced the Grof workshop, and they attended a three-day meeting with a group of scientists. Barbara and Ken explained the spiritual aftereffects of the NDE, and what they said was well-received. From there, Barbara went to Los Angeles to celebrate her parents' fiftieth wedding anniversary, and then was again meeting Ken in Seattle for Kim Clark's wedding. She and Kim had remained in phone contact, and Kim had come east several times to visit Barbara since the IANDS conference at Barbara's house. Whenever they were together, they laughed about life and talked about the Universe.

# 18

## Good Company

As the plane descended, Barbara could see a majestic, almost regal view of Seattle. The mountains were surrounded by thick green forests and the landscape was dotted with sprawling lakes. She kept trying to get a glimpse of Mount Rainier, the icon of American filmmaking. A thick cloud covering hid it from view, even from this vantage point. Kim met Barbara at the airport and reassured her Mount Rainier was still there, all 14,410 feet of it.

Kim was getting married in another week, and while Barbara was in town for the wedding, the trip also gave her an opportunity to meet with local chapters of IANDS and do some media work. She was also scheduled to give a lecture at Children's Orthopedic Hospital while she was there.

Kim was the only person on the planet who still called Barbara "Barbie." When they got to Kim's house, Mary

Fielder, another bridesmaid, was waiting, and the three of them got into Mary's fifteen-year-old VW Beetle convertible and tooled through the mountains, top down and sixties music blaring. At breakneck speed they made their rounds. First, they went for their fittings at the dressmaker's.

In her gown, standing in front of huge mirrors, the tall, slim, blond Kim, now covered in yards of white lace and pearls, looked stunning. Mary and Barbara tried on their strapless red satin gowns. The dresses were pulled tightly around the waist, and yards of fabric billowed to the floor. They paraded in front of the mirror and started clowning around.

"Okay, Bride," Barbara said to Kim, "we all know who you are, but what are we supposed to be?"

"French whores!" Kim said, sending them into fits of laughter.

Secretly Barbara was worried about wearing a dress like that to church. She had only been to weddings held in synagogues or temples, where the women were always covered, often wearing high-necked dresses. In that red dress, she didn't feel like a bridesmaid.

The next morning, Kim took Barbara to a local television station to do a half-hour interview on a talk show called "Good Company." Barbara had been interviewed on many talk shows before, but always as an experiencer. This was the first time she was on television as a researcher and NDEr. It was also the first time Ken Ring was in her audience. He was sitting next to Kim. The local Friends of IANDS was there too, so the audience was filled with NDErs. They hoped that the TV publicity would draw a big crowd for the hospital talk too.

At first Barbara was nervous, because years earlier, it

had been she who sat in the audience while Ken lectured on NDEs. Now he was sitting and listening to her. She had truly come full circle after years of struggling to find answers.

Shortly after she arrived, the show went on the air.

"Today's guest will be discussing the whole issue of near-death experiences," the interviewer said, opening the show. "A lot of us hope that the experience has the answer for what happens to all of us or to the soul after death. I had a friend who had two near-death experiences and she did not want to come back. People were yelling at her to come back, and they made her come back. She did not want to; she was very peaceful and happy," the interviewer said, and then introduced Barbara.

"Eleven years ago you were very happily married, a very content mother of three, and the wife of a successful businessman," the interviewer said. "You injured your back, which resulted in two years of pain and agony, which ultimately resulted in an operation. You had surgery, and the day after surgery, what occurred for you?"

"The day after surgery, complications set in, not from the actual surgery but from the shock of what my body had been through. I started moving toward death," Barbara said.

"How did you know that?" the woman asked.

"Well, I didn't know that. I didn't know anything at the time. I was suspended in a Stryker Frame Circle Bed, a bed that's used for totally immobilized patients," Barbara said. "The bed moves, the patient doesn't. And I remember waking up and looking at this tremendous abdomen and then starting to scream." And then Barbara told of her near-death experience.

"How did you feel after?" the interviewer asked.

"Well, the first thing I realized immediately was that my

eyes were more sensitive to light and my hearing was painfully acute. Then, a week later, after the life review, all my feelings inside were changing about my family, about my memories of my childhood. I suddenly knew that the pain we had created wasn't the truth; under the actions that created the pain, there was confusion, but certainly not intentional cruelty, and underneath our confusion there was love. I suddenly felt that everything was built on love, and that somehow had gotten twisted.''

"What brought you back?" the interviewer said. "My friend had risen out of her body over the operating table, the first time. She was very peaceful, an extraordinary peace, a peace that she had never experienced at any time during her life. I think she mentioned gray, or clouds, and a kind of floating feeling. Then everyone in the operating room started to scream at her, 'Eva, come back, come back. Eva, don't leave!' She really didn't want to come back, but they were so insistent that she went back.''

"I've had a lot of people tell me that," Barbara said. "I went on to become a respiratory therapist, and I became one of the people screaming to bring others back. A lot of times, they'll tell us that our voices calling their names do bring them back into their bodies. I had no choice. I was just back.''

"Do many people have these kinds of experiences?" the interviewer asked.

"Our statistics so far have shown anywhere from one-third to forty percent of the people that come close to death report this experience," Barbara said.

"Now, there are different stages, and I'm sure we'll get into those as the morning progresses, but you wrote someplace here that the 'experience stripped away all the scars that I had collected and gave me all the tools that I needed to be who I am now,'" the hostess said. "I understand that this experience is transformational for people. How is it transformational?"

"Well, it just doesn't happen. It is a seed experience," Barbara said. "It is planted in you, and after that, some people are compelled to search for something unknown, like the characters in the movie *Close Encounters of the Third Kind*, where people were drawn to something beyond what they knew. We are compelled to find answers that will explain our experience," Barbara said. "I became a seeker. I started to read all kinds of books on quantum physics, Buddhism, all the major religions, psychology, and finally psychiatry. I was given information about myself during my NDE that I couldn't integrate," she said. "It took me years of looking and searching. I don't want to give the impression that all the work is over once you've had an NDE. The work is just beginning after the NDE. What I learned in that life review was all about the unhappiness I lived through as a child. I was a lonely child. I was extremely sensitive when I was little. Maybe intellectually I could have told you that before, but I didn't know what that really felt like until I went back and felt it again. But at the same time, I had this all-encompassing sense that everything was okay," she said. "That everything was perfect the way it was. That this was part of a 'cosmic setup,' so to speak, and that there were lessons to be learned from everything that happened. And everything was really okay," she explained.

"I'm wondering if you can't reach that conclusion, though, just by living a long time," the hostess said. "You don't need a near-death experience to get to that point."

"I'm beginning to believe that people who 'get a near-death experience' do so because it is exactly what they need. I certainly did," Barbara said.

"What separates this experience for you from an extremely vivid dream or hallucination?" the interviewer said. "Can you tell us this difference?"

"As a researcher, I would say that the big difference is in the aftereffects," Barbara said. "Hallucinations will cause some sort of aftereffect, and so will dreams, especially when they're quite vivid. But what we have found in doing interviews with hundreds of people is that a near-death experience has a lot more impact in terms of aftereffects. The experience seems to get stronger, more vivid over time. A dream or hallucination fades. A near-death experience seems to grow in depth."

"Do these people reorder their priorities and have a less materialistic outlook in their lives?" the interviewer asked. "Are there changes in their relationships?"

"I couldn't go back to the way I was. I was the proper mother, the proper wife, an active member of many, many community organizations. These things are important and I am not putting them down, but they couldn't take up all my time anymore. I needed to be with sick people, I wanted to be with dying people. I went back to school and became a respiratory therapist. And then, as this evolution of my own being became stronger and stronger, it did not fit into my marriage anymore, so it had to end," she said.

"But, Barbara, isn't this something that could also be described as a result of mid-life crisis?" the interviewer asked, leaning forward to emphasize her skepticism.

"I'm sure I would have gone through mid-life crisis, but this is different. There is an impact that goes far beyond mid-life crisis. It's as if I got a glimpse of pages in a book, and the book was my life. The author lifts you out of the pages and you find yourself up there," Barbara said, pointing to the studio lights, "up there with the author looking down at your own story. After this communion between the two of you, you are put back down to live the rest of your life. From that point on, things look a lot different," Barbara said.

"We asked the audience, before the program, how many had had a near-death experience, and I was surprised at how many here have had one. Statistically, it seems that one in twenty Americans, eight million adults, have had the experience," the interviewer said, and then asked the audience, "Carol, you think you had one?"

"About twenty years ago, I saw myself on the ceiling, and it wasn't in relation to an illness or serious trauma," Carol said, "but it had a powerful impact on me and I never forgot it. And as time passed, I never thought about it again, but it wasn't a dream and it wasn't a hallucination."

"Being close to death is a reliable trigger for this kind of experience, but there are many other triggers besides being close to death," Barbara said.

"Elaine has also had a near-death experience?" the interviewer said.

"It changed my life completely!" Elaine said. "You're kind of drafted into this. It's not something that you ask for. All at once you're picked up and put into an experience and brought back to life. It changes your whole perspective."

"You had a brain tumor and then brain seizures?" the interviewer asked.

"A tumor triggered a stroke, and with the stroke, I had multiple seizures," Elaine said. "My heart couldn't keep up with the seizures. It was a strain."

"And you're currently having marital difficulty?" the interviewer asked.

"It's very difficult for your partner to understand that

you become a very giving individual. Your partner is usually still in a very materialistic realm, and materialistic things just don't matter to you," she said.

"If you feel that you are much closer to God, couldn't your attitude be almost condescending after you've gone through this experience?" the interviewer asked.

"We were afraid of that," Barbara said. "We were also afraid that people who experienced death as so pleasant would want to die. We had all of those fears. But the more people we interviewed, the more we realized that this whole thing is a paradox. It isn't that you feel above anybody else or different, as much as you feel so close to them. It leaves you with an overwhelming good feeling for yourself and the people around you. We know that our selves don't end with our skin. It's an illusion that we end at our skin. We're really not separate. We're really all one, together, and that becomes the difficult part. Everybody is somebody that you love," Barbara said.

"Rick, you've had a near-death experience?" the interviewer asked.

"It was twenty-five years ago tonight, as a matter of fact!" Rick said.

"You walked around thinking that you were going out of your mind for a while?"

"My family denied that I was ill," Rick said. "They said just get on with your life, everything's okay. So I went back to college and did try to live a normal life, but I walked around for twenty-two years thinking secretly that I was crazy."

"What should people do who have gone through this and are reluctant to tell somebody about it?" the interviewer asked.

"If you tell somebody and they don't listen, find somebody else," Rick said.

"And just telling the experience really helps ease this disquieting feeling for you?"

"Yes, particularly if there is any kind of acceptance or credence given to what you're saying. But if people just tell you to get on with your life, it forces you to stuff it into the back of your mind, and you try to get on with your life," Rick said.

"Is there life after death?" the interviewer asked Rick.

"Yes!" Rick said, smiling as he looked around the studio, and the audience applauded.

"You're convinced of it now as a result of this experience?" the interviewer said.

"I think death is just a transition between this body and whatever is coming next," Rick said.

"Isn't that a kind of Oriental philosophy as well?" the interviewer asked. "Couldn't a skeptic say you didn't have a flat EEG? You still had some brain activity, so your brain was conjuring all this up? We'll never know what lies after death until we can bring somebody back who was totally brain dead . . . and that's not possible," the interviewer said.

"That's one way of looking at it. Another way is first to tell the skeptics they'll find out soon," Rick said, and the audience erupted into laughter.

"Barbara, you are at the University of Connecticut doing research on the near-death experience. What are you finding?" the interviewer asked.

"What we're finding is that too many people are dwelling on the question. 'Is there life after death?' What we're finding is incredible new information on how to live," Barbara said. "Everybody who's had this experience agrees that they aren't afraid to die. And what that does is give you all kinds of new ways of living!"

"Do you have extrasensory perception when you come out of this?" the interviewer asked.

"We have found a great many people telling us that all of a sudden after the experience they have greater intuitive powers, to the point of even being psychic," Barbara said.

"I have been aware of things that are about to happen in my children's lives and things that I feel very fearful about and things that I feel very excited about, and these things seem to transpire," said Evon, a member of the audience.

"Any other life changes you can tell us about?" she was asked.

"Things that were very important to me. . . . My classic statement is that I really enjoyed driving a Lincoln Continental, but now it has become a source of transportation for hospice patients," Evon said. "I spend a great deal of time with them."

Another woman in the audience, Tina, was questioned about the aftereffects of her near-death experience.

"I was in a very high-pressure, fast-moving world, looking for the almighty buck. That is important now as a means to an end, but it's not the only thing. It's as though someone took me by the shoulder straps and said, 'Hey! What are you doing?'" Tina said.

"What about those people who are suicidal? Doesn't that bother you?" Barbara was asked.

"That was what my research was about for this last year, working with people who had made suicide attempts and finding the ones who had had near-death experiences. We followed up both groups," she said. "The ones who had NDEs still have the same problems when they come back, but they're more willing to deal with them," Barbara said. "They have a new sense of 'Cosmic Unity' or they tell us they saw dead relatives who told them that they won't be allowed to stay . . . they are told they have to go back and face their problems."

The interviewer asked, "Why the desire to be with people who are near death? Or are in a hospital?"

"You know, I didn't understand that at first either, and I still can't totally explain it, but death to me is not what I thought it was before my experience. It's not final. Death is a doorway to another reality," Barbara explained. "And when you can be with people who are dying, it's . . . you become their partner, their friend in this movement, this passage from this life to the next kind of life."

"So you make it easier for them?"

"Yes! And people who are dying—if you just give them the open listening and understanding that they need—want some honesty about what's going on. They want to be able to talk about it. Most of their relatives and friends are in too much pain, so it's a privilege for someone like me, or Elaine, who is doing this too. It's a privilege to just be able to listen."

"Do you find yourself, though, stopping, saying their names fifteen times, trying to bring them back?" Barbara was asked.

"No, no!"

"But you still want to bring them back?" the interviewer asked.

"No, no . . . you become their partner in that moment. It's amazing when people are dying—at the final ten minutes, their coloring comes back. They're relaxed. They have a healthier look than they've had for the whole time of their illness or whatever. And as they die, they're giving you comfort and you're giving them permission to go."

*As soon as they broke for a commercial I ran over to Ken Ring and said, "Well, how did I do?" He answered,*

192

*"Honey, you don't need me anymore. You did just fine!"*
*And he gave me a big hug.*

After Barbara's two-hour talk that evening at Children's Orthopedic Hospital, a social worker from the hospital spoke to her, identifying herself as Susan and asked Barbara to visit a dying child. Barbara agreed, but not without reservations. She had worked a little with sick kids but had never knowingly worked with terminally ill children. The thought of doing it made her shiver. She didn't feel capable. Nevertheless, she agreed to go back to the hospital the following morning.

Dave McDowell, a retired man from the Seattle IANDS chapter, had volunteered to drive her around while she was there. During these short trips, she usually chatted with Dave, a tall quiet man who listened intently as he drove. The day he took her to the hospital, she was unusually quiet. She didn't know what to expect and had the nagging feeling she wouldn't be able to help.

"You can stay here if you like," she told Dave as he pulled his Volkswagen van into the hospital parking lot. "I'd like it, though, if you'd come in with me and pray silently in the background. It'll help. The more connections we have, the better it will be."

Inside, the nurse told them the boy they were supposed to see was in a private room just behind the nurse's station. The chubby two-year-old from Latin America had suffered irreversible brain damage in a drowning accident, but physically he looked healthy. There were no obvious signs of recognition of Barbara's and Dave's presence as the boy's mother hovered over his bed. Her torture was immediately evident. In many respects, the situation was identical to others Barbara had seen with adults. Grieving family members, unable to let go, unable to realize how hopeless the situation was, can prolong dying for the patient. Even such a helpless baby might wait until his mother let go.

*I spoke to the mother, quietly asking her to tell what she knew about her son's condition. She got the medical facts straight, with one exception—she failed to tell me there was no hope of recovery. Her husband had gone back home to South America to care for their other children.*

*First I asked if we could form a healing circle. I drew the shade on a window that looked into the nurse's station. Susan left the room, leaving Dave and me alone with the mother and the boy. Just as the mother and I were about to lay our hands on the child, a man dressed in a white hospital coat walked in, nodded a greeting to us.*

*He looked around the room for a second, told us to "carry on," then left. I was told later that he was the head of the hospital. He carried the morning newspaper with him that contained an article about our research and a picture and quotes from me.*

*We touched the boy gently, laying our hands on him, palms-down. I opened my eyes once and saw a swollen face with a blank expression. The only sign of life was the sucking noises he made with his mouth. I closed my eyes again and we all prayed, staying in that position for some time. I very strongly felt Dave's presence and was grateful for the grounding he gave me. Finally I opened my eyes and waited for the others to follow.*

When the mother opened her eyes, Barbara looked directly at her and said, "When you are ready, you have to let him go."

"I know," she said, holding back the obvious tears welling in both eyes, "but I can't."

# 19

## Willie

On Sunday, July 13, 1986, Kimberly Clark and Donald Sharp were married. The front of the church was three stories of glass windows that overlooked a forest, a meandering stream, and a landscaped rock garden. It was an incredible background for an absolutely beautiful marriage ceremony. The aisle they walked down was the longest one Barbara had ever seen. She was relieved to have one of Don's ushers, a paramedic, like Don, to hold on to.

After the ceremony and reception, they took the three hundred pearl-white and pink helium balloons that had decorated the church reception hall outside. The two hundred guests lined the steps and sidewalk outside the church. "We each thought of a wish for the bride and groom and released the balloons as Kim and Don Sharp drove off with balloons filling the back seat of the car and hanging out the windows,'' Barbara said. ''The crowd looked up and watched the balloons as they floated off into the clouds. Mary Fielder and I stood there together looking up, surrounded by two hundred well-wishers and feeling great for the bride and groom. Susan, who was also a guest, walked up and asked if I'd visit the Latin child again and another child with leukemia at Ronald McDonald House the next morning. Again, shivers rippled through my body, and I am sure goose bumps were evident as I stood there in the July heat, wearing a strapless red satin gown.''

On Monday morning Dave McDowell pulled up in the van in front of Kim's house. Kim's parents put their arms around Barbara before she left, and the three of them prayed. Dave and Barbara drove in silence. They were going to visit the baby in the hospital first; then Barbara would visit the child at Ronald McDonald House.

*Ten minutes into the half-hour ride through town, Dave pointed out the window. Off in the distance, beaming at us, was the peak of Mount Rainier, floating in the blue sky to the north. I suddenly felt our day would be all right. I could feel my body relaxing. I heard myself release a deep sigh. Seeing this floating peak surrounded by a circle of white clouds suspended in the deep blue summer sky, so grand and mystical, I remembered that there is something much bigger than us running the show. That was the only time Mount Rainier appeared in the two weeks I was there.*

Susan was waiting for them in the lobby of the hospital. They visited the South American baby. The mother was there and greeted them as they walked into the room. The four of them prayed together around the baby, holding hands. ''We separated. I hugged the woman for the last time and left, feeling as connected to her, to Susan and

Dave, as if we all were still physically touching,'' Barbara said.

Ronald McDonald House is a nonprofit residence, set up by the McDonald Corporation to house sick children and their families while the children are being treated at a nearby hospital. On the ride over, Susan and Barbara talked about their lives. Both were care givers, both were single mothers. ''We connected like long-lost sisters even though we had only met days earlier,'' Barbara recalled. Dave pulled up to a rambling one-story redwood house. It was surrounded by a sprawling lawn and simple but well-landscaped gardens. Inside, they walked through a hall paneled in the same redwood as the exterior. On one wall there were windows that overlooked one of the gardens. On the opposite wall were clusters of plaques made to look like balloons, all painted bright, cheerful colors, with names printed on each one.

Beyond the hallway there was a corridor with small private bedrooms on each side. Nearby was a large living room. Thick redwood paneling covered every wall, giving the house a peaceful, natural look and absorbing sound.

They were coming to visit a six-year-old black child named Willie. Willie's leukemia had been diagnosed over two years ago and he had undergone a series of chemotherapy treatments. His disease had gone into remission, but was now active again. Willie refused further treatment, saying he just wanted to be left alone. Medically, doctors could do nothing for the boy but honor his wishes. Susan said Willie made his wishes clear, and they halted further treatment. His father, like the South American father of the two-year-old, had returned home to Alaska to care for another child. Willie was here with his mother.

*Susan led us to one of the bedrooms. The three of us, Susan, Dave, and I, made eye contact; then she opened the door and we walked in. As she greeted the mother, I looked around the room. It looked like a motel room, two twin beds, a dresser, a desk, and a single window. A bulletin board was covered with get-well cards. In the bed next to the window, a small child was curled up, lying on his side facing us. His normally dark skin and hair had been bleached yellow, apparently a side effect of his disease and the chemical therapies.*

The introductions were brief; then Barbara sat down next to Willie. When she slowly reached out to him with both hands, he yelled "No," knocking her arms away by swinging his little hands. Then he leapt up and dashed out of the room. Stunned, they all got up and followed him. Willie had gone into the living room. As they walked, his mother pointed to the balloons on the wall.

"They are bought by the parents," the mother told her. "They are little memorials to the children, and the parents donate five-hundred dollars to Ronald McDonald House for each balloon." She and her little boy had met some of the children whose names were now enshrined on the wall.

The living room was dominated by a huge stone fireplace. Adjacent to it was a large kitchen where families could prepare meals. Another family was using the kitchen, making their lunch. The four of them sat on two sofas in the living room. What had just happened in Willie's room had shaken Barbara. "Was I an intruder, interfering with these people's right to face death in their own way?" she wondered. She wanted to run, leave the house as fast as Willie had escaped her clutches. A glance at Willie's mother reinforced this feeling. She sat with her legs tightly crossed, arms folded equally tight across her chest. Her jaw was clenched shut; her body was stiff with tension.

Meanwhile, Willie was playing and running around the other side of the room. He was as active as any six-year-old, one minute playing contentedly with toys on the floor, the next, running around, almost skipping.

"Is there anything I can do?" Barbara asked sheepishly, talking to Willie's mother. It was a nervous question. Jumping to her feet suddenly, Susan said, "Elisabeth Kubler-Ross is going to be here in October."

Willie won't be here in October, Barbara thought. "Maybe she could visit Willie," she said, lying, trying to ease the tension in the room.

"I have a beautiful poster for you, a scene drawn by a sick child," Susan said nervously. "Dave, would you drive me back to the hospital, and I'll get it? We'll be right back," she said, turning to Barbara. Then she and Dave left them alone.

"Is there anything I can do?" Barbara again asked the woman.

"No," she said politely.

"Do you have anyone you can talk to here?" Barbara asked.

"No!"

"Don't you need to talk about this?" Barbara asked.

Before she could answer, Willie raced across the room and dived facefirst into his mother's lap. He crashed into her body, yelling "Yes" loudly. Both of Willie's hands pushed against her shoulders. His mother fell backward, her arms fell apart, and one of her shoulders now rested on the back of the sofa facing Barbara. She looked dazed and shocked. Her eyes moistened and she looked straight at

Barbara. Her pain, not evident on her face before, now distorted her expression and animated her face. Willie reached up and squeezed her cheeks with both hands for just an instant; then he bolted off again.

Her guard was down now.

"When I talked to my husband last night, I asked what clothes he wanted Willie to wear for the funeral," she said. "My husband was furious, telling me that he wouldn't talk about it until Willie was really gone. He told me I shouldn't talk that way until Willie is gone," she said.

"That must hurt," Barbara said. "He's so far away with your healthy child. Does he understand what you're facing alone here?"

"Willie can last a long time," she said. "Look at him. We could be here for a long time."

Barbara looked at the boy, now sitting alone at a miniature table-and-chair set. He acted like a healthy six-year-old. "Maybe it'll be a while," Barbara said, unsure whether this child was near death or could hold out a long time.

"Can Willie's father come back for another visit so you aren't alone?" Barbara asked.

"No," the woman said. "This is it." As she spoke, Barbara could see her withdraw again.

Willie now circled the room, yelling, trying to get their attention. Again he jumped onto his mother's lap and squeezed her face. Then it hit Barbara. This boy wasn't just running around, randomly playing a child's game. He was listening to every word they had been saying. He knew what was going on between his mother and her. He was reacting to her, responding to her responses, psychically connected to his mother.

"Willie needs to go soon," Barbara told her, picking

her words carefully. She was more sure of herself now. "Whether your husband will talk about it or not, Willie needs to know that you can let him go. He's very connected to you now. He can't go until you let him," Barbara told her.

"I know," she said softly, loosening her grip on the pain again. "What can I do? I don't know what to do!"

The image of the balloons floating up into the sky at the wedding flashed in Barbara's mind.

"Buy him a balloon plaque. Willie understands the meaning of the balloons. That'll be your way of letting him know that you'll be okay after he's gone."

"I'll ask my husband tonight on the phone if I can write a check as a deposit for one."

"Okay," Barbara answered. "And then tell Willie you're going to do it."

Susan and David returned. She held up a brightly colored poster of a scene a small child had done. The poster was advertising a lecture by Elisabeth Kubler-Ross. Barbara looked at it, then looked past it, scanning the room for the little six-year-old. Willie was gone.

Alone, Barbara went to his room and found him in bed.

*His eyes were closed and he looked peaceful. I tiptoed softly over to his bed and sat next to him.*

*"Willie," I said softly, "I want you to know that dying doesn't hurt. Honestly, honey, if there's one thing I can give you, it's the knowledge that dying doesn't hurt."*

*He opened his heavy brown eyes. A faint smile crossed his lips and he lifted his little hands and put them on my temples, holding my head in his small hands.*

*Suddenly I was transported back to all the sensations I had had during my own NDE. I felt the peace, the love, the warmth of that place again. His smile widened.*

*Willie had taken me back there again, only this time, here.*

We could have been like that a minute or an hour. Time had melted. I left him sleeping quietly. I went back and said good-bye to his mother. Dave dropped Susan off at the hospital. He took me back to Kim's. I don't remember the rest of the day.

*The gift that Willie had given me lasted until evening.*

# 20

## Melvin Morse, M.D.

Mel Morse, a pediatrician from Seattle, recently did a two-year study using the medical records of forty-two children between the ages of three and sixteen. All had been hospitalized in the pediatric intensive-care unit at Children's Orthopedic Hospital between 1978 and 1983. Half of the patients were critically ill with little chance of survival; the others were seriously ill with a good chance of survival. "Every child I've interviewed who has had a cardiac arrest has had one of these experiences," Mel said.

His first experience with a young child telling him of an NDE came in 1982 after she had been in a deep coma for several days. When she had been brought in, she hadn't been breathing for at least twenty minutes. Yet three days later when she awoke he said to her: "You don't know me, but I took care of you when you were first brought to the hospital." She surprised Morse and her parents by saying that she knew the doctor and could remember specific details about her treatment in the emergency room.

"I thought she was hallucinating," Morse said, "because of the stress of being so ill or because of the drugs we had given her." However, he quickly changed his mind when she told him details about her treatment that someone in a severe coma couldn't possibly have known unless she'd had an out-of-body experience and had also been conscious on some undefined level.

"What convinced me was how accurately she was able to describe elements of her treatment. She knew things like the fact that we were pushing on her chest, that we moved her from the emergency room into another room," he said.

"Then she told me she wasn't dead. She was still alive. She said there was a part of her that was still alive. Seven years later it is still very clear to her."

*For the last three years Mel Morse and I have corresponded and talked on the phone long-distance about NDE research. I met him recently. The findings of his recent study are really exciting. Small children don't have a cultural overlay to cloud their interpretation of their experience. In other words, they don't have all the same beliefs to wade through as we adults do. Every experience Mel told us about was pristine. Over and over we heard of light beings, of peace, rainbows, and returns. We were also moved by the fact that these kids had not told anyone, or rarely told anyone. They just accepted it and knew it. The pictures they drew gave more information than the words. Words can get in the way, trying to explain a realm that the English language still hasn't mapped out.*

*And Mel also said, in his wonderfully enthusiastic way, "You know, up until 1900 everyone died at home and all the relatives and friends heard these deathbed visions. When dying was done at home, these experiences were considered part of the dying process. It's only in the last eighty-nine years that people have died in hospitals, where nobody has the time to listen or patients are afraid to talk about what they're experiencing because we've all decided that these visions don't exist. I say these near-death experiences aren't paranormal. They're normal, and we as physicians have to learn more about them and the dying process.''*

*How true. The science of medicine until now has treated death as the enemy, and the goal is victory over death. Hospice, on the other hand, has recently started teaching the art of letting go, of surrendering to the inevitable. My experience with dying patients proves to me over and over that dying is a process in which unfinished business worked through can produce incredible growth, not only for the dying person but also for all the people involved. Recently, at a workshop I gave for Hospice in Bar Harbor, Maine, we shared stories of our dying patients, and I told the participants to have tape recorders with them and ask the dying persons to tell stories of anything they could remember or were now experiencing, for their children and their grandchildren and for future generations to come. I told them to coax their clients to have life reviews that can live on tape for their loved ones to cherish. At that workshop we also talked about and practiced simple touch techniques to help our dying patients relax. More than any other form of communication, touch is the easiest and most profound. We all agreed that even someone in a coma may still be able to hear and even feel someone touching him.*

# 21

## Three Other Stories

*When I returned from Seattle, Mary Ellen invited me to move in with her again, and I did it gladly, relieved that I wouldn't be alone. I kept my furniture in storage and was trying to figure out what to do next.*

*Funding was made available for me to return to the university as Bruce Greyson's research assistant part-time. I also started a program at a local accredited school to become a massage therapist, something I had always wanted to try. I had been working with touch for years; now I could learn technique. I didn't know where it would fit in, to be formally trained in massage, but I felt it was the next step.*

*Funding had dried up for the IANDS staff that had been at the U Conn Storrs campus, so we packed everything up there and brought it over to Bruce's and my office.*

*Except for money being tight, I was happy with what I was now doing. I spent as much time as I could in our office keeping up with the IANDS mail. And the media work was increasing all the time. We received a steady stream of calls from experiencers. We had constant requests from reporters and producers interested in doing stories on our work. Then there were postgrad students working on their master's and Ph.D.'s who were doing their research on the NDE. The rest of the time I devoted to going to school and studying. It took me two years to get through the one-year full-time program. During school breaks I would drive down to Florida to be with the kids and my parents.*

*Occasionally I would be asked to speak at local groups like Theos (widows and widowers) or Compassionate Friends (bereaved parents.) And of course, every month, Bruce and I facilitated the IANDS support group at the U Conn Health Center.*

*The three stories you are about to read are from people I met through all this activity. Sharon Keevers Grant heard about the IANDS support group and I met her there. We are now wonderful friends. Steve Price and I met at a Compassionate Friends meeting when he came to hear Ken Ring talk. I was substituting for Ken that particular night. Steve and I are close friends now too. I am so thankful I have these two people in my life. The third story is from Ron Chester, a convict serving a sentence for murder in an Australian jail. We have been corresponding for over a year.*

## SHARON KEEVERS GRANT

Twenty-three-year-old Sharon Keevers harbored a dormant loneliness back in the 1960s, a hopeful time when the youth of her generation mounted a vigorous antiwar movement against U.S. involvement in the Vietnam War. At the same time, it was a generation that also struggled to find meaning in their lives through drugs and political activism.

Sharon, however, had difficulty accepting some of the dogma of the times, especially the ideology of some factions of the student movement. She found no solace or meaning in the sexual revolution or violence of that decade. "The Students for a Democratic Society (SDS) were active," she said, referring to a movement punctuated by violent bombings of government buildings and offices by the group's radicals. "I knew instinctively that violence was not the way to create a better world," said Sharon, a petite woman with blond hair and a soft voice. Sharon's life was severely curtailed by illness in her family. First, when she was sixteen, her mother became critically ill. Sharon nursed her for six months until she died. A short time later, her father turned to alcohol, unable to cope with the grief and loneliness after his wife's death, and Sharon cared for him through a serious illness. Meanwhile, the few free hours she had were spent either reading or going out with friends.

"I was searching for answers," she said during an interview at Barbara Harris' house. The answer she sought, however, enveloped her without warning one morning in a hospital bed shortly after a routine appendectomy in 1963.

"I had an operation and was recovering from the surgery," she said. "The next day, I was sleeping and I had what I thought then was a dream. In the dream, I heard a voice telling me I had to wake up. I could see myself struggling to wake up," she said, adding that her body was surrounded by a soft white substance that resembled cotton. "I had to push through it to become conscious."

When she woke up, Sharon said, she sat up in the bed and told a patient in the room with her to call her doctor. "I felt myself fall backward onto the bed," she said, and felt herself continue to fall, although her body was reclined. She slipped into unconsciousness.

"The next thing I realized," she said, "I was very high up on the ceiling, looking down at myself. I looked very small. I seemed to be very high up, but I was still in the confines of the hospital room, looking down at my body."

Sharon's body had mysteriously shut down. There was no heartbeat, no pulse, no vital signs at all. A medical team rushed into her room and began working to revive her. As she watched all of this from her vantage point above her body, Sharon realized that she had either died or was dying.

"I had been a Catholic and I was taught to believe that death was to be feared," she said. " But I wasn't at all afraid. I just looked and wondered where the real me was— up on the ceiling or down there in the hospital bed."

Amazingly enough, she said, she felt indifferent about the whole scene she was watching, and stopped looking down. "I turned around and looked out, and everything opened up. I was out in space with no limits," she said, "and I saw a light that radiated. It was warm and bright and it was home to me," she said, "and very familiar. I could hear my mother's love. If you can imagine hearing an emotion, I was hearing my mother's love. She was in my head, in my heart, and her love surrounded me, and then she was just holding me," Sharon said.

In that moment, she felt an enormous burden lifted from her, the burden of grief she had lived with since her mother's death several years earlier. "My mother died before I could tell her things I wanted her to know. Now I could feel her joy."

At the same time, she said, she was aware of the presence of other people, although she saw no one. "I sense my hands and my feet, but I can't see them. I am still whole, but not the way I am whole in this dimension.

"From the light," she said, "I got a lot of information about things I had always wondered about, like: Is there a God? Why are we here?"

And then the light began to move toward her and she toward it. Through the light she could see a being, arms outstretched, reaching out to her, moving toward her. She began to move joyfully toward this being, aware that when their hands clasped, she would be truly "home."

"I knew what it was," she said. "The purest essence of love. It was beyond what we consider love. It was intelligence, compassion, and it was greeting me. This is where I am going," she thought. "I am going to blend into this light and become whole. I know that when I get there, I will be complete."

As she anticipated merging with the light, something happened. "Just as I reached the light, I was jerked backward, and at the same time back into my body," she said. "I could hear the doctor working on me. I could hear a nurse saying, 'There's no pulse, no blood pressure, nothing.'" When she opened her eyes, she saw a doctor over her chest, pounding on it.

"I just looked up at him, and the tears came. I was back. I didn't want to be there and it was heartbreaking," she said. She remembers getting a brief message from somewhere at that moment, a mysterious silent "ping" of awareness that told her to accept being back. "It's okay," was the message; "accept it."

"I accepted it immediately."

When her personal physician came to see her shortly after the incident, she told him that she had nearly died. Impossible, he said, because her chart indicated nothing unusual had happened to her.

A check of her medical records later showed no trace that

the incident ever occurred. The doctors who knew what had happened could not explain why she had started to die, and assured her over the next few days that she would survive.

After the initial conversation with her personal physician, Sharon never mentioned the incident again. "I just didn't talk, trying to figure out what had happened."

When she was released from the hospital, she had an immediate gut reaction against something that had always been an automatic part of her existence. "Life went on, but I never went back to church," said Sharon. "I had been taught if you didn't go to Mass every Sunday, you'd go to hell. I just woke up that first Sunday morning when I could go out and decided I wasn't going to church anymore. Somehow, I understood that organized religion had lost the essence of that incredible light and love I had encountered. I, we, all carried it within us."

In the ensuing years, Sharon Keevers married and became Sharon Grant. The couple had a son and moved to Massachusetts, where they bought a restaurant and motel. While her experience in the hospital always loomed large in the back of her mind, her life was hectic. The new business took enormous amounts of energy to run, and the demands of an infant son and husband left no free time for anything else. During this time, Sharon's ailing eighty-six-year-old grandmother moved in, adding another dimension of responsibility to an already stressful existence. After several years this stress took its toll on Sharon's marriage, compounded by her husband's increasing dependence on alcohol and resultant violence. Finally Sharon put her ninety-year-old grandmother and four-year-old son, Brian, in the car and drove away, determined to create a more peaceful, loving life.

A caring friend took Sharon and her family in temporarily.

Her immediate concern was to find a nursing home for her grandmother, who was now totally incapacitated, but they had absolutely no money. Sharon began the frustrating, backbreaking job of dealing with the state bureaucracy to find convalescent care for her grandmother. The overall advice was for Sharon to go on welfare, an abhorrent thought to her. Finally, after a month of fruitless phone calls, a warm, compassionate woman heard Sharon. "It took her two weeks, but she placed my grandmother in a nearby nursing home with full benefits from the state." During this time Sharon never gave up hope that God would help her grandmother. "I knew that the trust I had would be fulfilled; it was no surprise that the woman who helped me was named Grace."

All the while, Sharon read feverishly, trying to find answers for what happened to her that day in 1963. She read Greek philosophy, Eastern philosophy, Gandhi, and ancient wisdom in search of these answers. In 1976 she stumbled across *Life After Life*, Ray Moody's landmark book on near-death experiences. "I already knew that I had nearly died," Sharon said. "Now I learned that others had had the same experience and there was a name for it. It made understanding it a lot easier. There was a significant reason for the way I was feeling, and I wanted to tell somebody." She sought out people to talk to, and a friend gave her a pamphlet put out by IANDS, describing the organization. Sharon learned that the IANDS support group met every month at the University of Connecticut Health Center in Farmington, Connecticut. She was determined to meet these people, and went to the next meeting.

"I saw Barbara and immediately there was a connection," said Sharon, who found that meeting room filled with other NDErs willing to listen to her story. Unlike the alien in a novel both women had read, *Stranger in a Strange Land*, by Robert Heinlein, Sharon Keevers Grant was among friends for the first time in more than twenty years.

Ironically, Sharon had her NDE at the age of twenty-three. It took exactly twenty-three years for her to find Barbara Harris, now among her best friends and confidantes.

Some might call that coincidence. An NDEr might just shrug it off as the kind of routine synchronicity many of them experience all the time and think nothing of it.

## RON CHESTER

As convicts went, Ron Chester was probably a little different from the hundreds of inmates locked away in an Australian prison, where he was sentenced to serve a life term for killing another man.

Ron Chester, however, was also an enigma.

By all accounts, especially his own, Chester was considered a hardcase until he began to feel intense remorse for his victim, a man he had shot and killed at point-blank range with a shotgun. Sitting in a jail cell in Bathurst, New South Wales, he began thinking of ways to atone for his sins. He came up with a truly bizarre way of doing it. On the surface, it may sound like a cliché, but he decided to imagine what it must have been like to be a victim of his own violence. As he imagined himself as his own victim—the man he had brutally shot—he found himself journeying into another time, another place.

In a letter to Barbara in 1988, Chester described an experience that occurred seven years after the murder. It is included here because of the amazing transformation that he says followed the experience, a significant shift in perspective by an incorrigible career criminal that closely resembles the transformations reported by NDErs. The literature abounds with personality changes by NDErs, including the likes of a mob hit man who suddenly felt a need to help others. In one instance, a man with several killings to his credit began to counsel wife abusers following an NDE. Although Chester wasn't close to death, his experience resembles Barbara's NDE in part because he too was confronted with a new reality, presented to him in the form of bubbles. His transformation, by his own account, occurred afterward, when he got a glimpse of the pain, the suffering he had caused another human being. Whether or not it is truly a permanent transformation is a question that can only be answered by time.

The details of his experience closely resemble the experiences of others included in this book, despite the fact that Ron Chester had taken a life and was not in danger of losing his own. Here's his story in his own words.

"In my case, it was a total commitment to face with honesty what I had done, and even more to the point, to face why and put myself through the anguish this poor person must have experienced in those moments just before and while I was killing him," Chester said in an elaborate handwritten letter to Barbara.

"I had just been recaptured after ten months of being an escapee from a previous sentence. I was charged with murdering a man who was about to give me up to police if he wasn't paid money," said Chester, who had met his victim while he was a fugitive. After his capture, he began to wonder to himself why he had been able to murder with such ruthlessness. "Was it a subconscious desire just to kill someone?" he asked rhetorically. "Was it emotional baggage from my childhood, bursting out in aggression?

"I was filled with an anguish for the terror I had put the man through. I had not terrorized him in the normal sense. Instead, I had questioned calmly, coldly, then shot him cleanly when he finished answering my questions. I so wanted to put myself through what I had put him through, as a way of saying I was sorry to him and atoning," said Chester.

"I started focusing on the shooting scene and imagined it was I who faced the shotgun out in the forest. As the shot was felt entering 'me,' I felt something strange beginning to happen. I was experiencing sensations that were not in my control, and I stepped back a little with a conscious recognition that some unknown factor was now present. I could surrender myself to this 'unknown factor,'" Chester thought, "and learn something, or flee.

"I chose to go with it, and in total abandonment surrendered myself to what was still a 'tingling' feeling that was taking me to the edges of my consciousness. I began to meditate. The strange feelings resumed, and I was drawn into an amazing experience with my eyes closed, but filled with visions.

"A voice called, 'Watch and learn,' and my body began convulsing in death throes—no pain—just a sense of numb movement, and my body began shuddering. I went into a different state, where I knew there was only a rushing toward somewhere, a feeling of moving at great speed, like being sucked into the universe.

"I then moved into a state of floating peace where I could now see a universe filled with bubbles, and in one bubble I could see a nongender smooth-skinned being (like a gentle boyish alien stereotype) which I yearned to be one with. It looked like an innocent version of myself, and pressing my hands against the bubble I was floating in, I willed myself to move closer, so our bubbles could touch and melt into each other, forming a union. All the while, I was experiencing a oneness with the universe and interconnectedness and sense of purpose with the other bubbles, which were touching and melting into each other, with beings in some of them.

"Many things came to me in this period, a wonderful sense of wholeness, fulfillment, purpose, and a great love for all things, as I realized all things were of me, as I was of them.

"I had many insights. I felt a sense of anguish when I could not quite melt into this other being's bubble; we were just touching, but still the skin of our bubbles separated us. This, I felt, was a state of 'hell,' where a feeling of separateness still existed, where total union still was not achieved, to our perception.

"I then felt I was being drawn toward somewhere else. I began to lose sight of this vision, and then saw, below me, a small speck, and I was rushing toward it. It became clearer as I recognized it was a fetus which I 'knew' was three months old.

"Just as I was about to enter this fetus, I came out of the whole experience and was left sitting in my cell on my bed with the night quiet around me.

"I began to laugh with tears of joy in me, for I felt clean and purged, so in love with this being whose life I had taken and with a purpose and direction. Before, my life was without satisfaction or sense; I was trying to fit in, but lashing out in frustration when my emotional weakness and undeveloped character let me feel I was being unfairly ignored and not given love, support, or opportunity."

Chester believes the experience alone rehabilitated him, just as Barbara felt her two experiences were akin to having years of psychotherapy in an instant. Somehow, these two experiences—alike in so many ways, yet different—are linked in some cosmic way that both Barbara and Chester believe are a significant part of some universal order they were lucky enough to get a glimpse of during stressful periods of their lives. Barbara and Ron Chester continue to correspond between Connecticut and Australia. He hopes to be released in 1993. Then he and his wife will travel to the United States to meet Barbara.

## STEVE PRICE

Steven Price lived for the Corps. Even at the young age of nineteen, he was already a career soldier in the Marine Corps and had begun to cover his hulking 220-pound body with eighty tattoos. By the time Steve was twenty-one, he had already done two tours in Vietnam and won a Purple Heart for a near-fatal chest wound.

Standing six-feet two inches tall, Steve was what you might call a manly man, a genuine, authentic American hero from Connecticut. His lifelong dream to serve his country as a military man, however, began to unravel shortly after he was wounded in 1965. Arriving in South Vietnam in late August, Steve took a piece of shrapnel early in September during a mission near the Da Nang, a picturesque waterway called the River Tourane by the French. The experience that followed rendered Steve Price almost defunct as a soldier, because he could no longer fire a weapon, even under attack. It wasn't fear that prevented him from taking up arms against the so-called enemy. It was love, the same unconditional love which Steve found himself showered in a few days after he was wounded. The memory of that

217

feeling, a vivid remembrance of it, turned him into an unwilling pacifist armed with an automatic weapon he couldn't use—even if his life depended on it.

Steve had a near-death experience. Like the others whose stories we are retelling in this book, it made him no longer fear death. Unlike the others, however, death, for Steve, always loomed behind the next bend in the river or in the next bush.

Already wounded once, he always knew he could be hit again by a sniper's bullet or meet death at the hands of the many cleverly disguised booby traps the enemy was famous for setting. Something, however, kept him from firing another shot, despite the fact that he volunteered for a second tour of duty.

Stories abound about Vietnam veterans who had difficulty adjusting to civilian life after their war experiences, but Steve's story differs in both content and scope because of his near-death experience. Even his bouts with alcoholism and the haunting memories that kept Steve a little out of kilter for nearly twenty-three years after his experience in Vietnam are not typical.

In his own words, here is how Steve Price was transformed from a career soldier into what some now say is a gentle giant.

"When I got in country, there was a lot of turmoil in and around Da Nang," said Steve, who was a vehicle mechanic assigned to repair amphibious troop carriers that patrolled the river. Shortly after he arrived on August 28, 1965, Steve's unit was attached to Charlie Company, which spearheaded Operation Harvest Moon. The mission was a tactical one aimed at keeping the Vietcong from capturing the newly harvested rice crops in an area known as Marble Mountain a few miles outside of Da Nang.

"I don't think we were out more than two or three miles when we set up our night defenses, because it was already getting dark," he said. "I saw what looked like mortar pits already dug where we were making camp. Our people dug them out a little and we were settled in in less than fifteen minutes.

"The Vietcong had dug those pits, and we didn't find out until it was too late, but they had measured off the positions of those pits and began to lob mortar shells right on top of us that night," he said. The moonless night made seeing even a few feet impossible, and enemy troops lay in waiting. Suddenly, all hell broke loose.

"Short round, short round," people began yelling, meaning shells fired from American mortars were exploding shortly after they were fired. Steve doubted it. The enemy mortars were simply hitting the mortar positions of Charlie Company because they had accurately measured off these foxholes, originally dug by enemy soldiers.

"I was riding in a vehicle when those rounds started coming in," Steve said. "I knew we weren't hearing short rounds because one of those rounds went right down the barrel of one of our eighty-ones, [81-millimeter mortar cannon]. I decided to get under my vehicle, and started to jump off. Air-burst mortars were exploding about thirty feet overhead, showering Charlie Company with white-hot molten shrapnel.

"Holding my rifle in midair, I was about to jump when I saw what looked like a serrated coil spring. It was white-hot and coming right for me," he said.

Two slivers of metal sliced through his shirt, directly under the armpit, and entered his chest just above his flak jacket.

"I'm hit," Steve yelled to his buddies, who were still in the vehicle.

"Bullshit," someone yelled, "Get your ass back up here."

"Get me a corpsman," Steve said. "I'm hit." His body slumped over. His mind raced back to boot camp, back to the yells and taunts of his drill instructor at Camp Lejeune in North Carolina. "Always cover a chest wound," he heard, "to keep your lungs from collapsing." Steve covered the wound by clamping his arm down close to his side. A corpsman arrived and shot him up with a heavy dose of morphine. Although it dulled the pain, Steve's body was racked by sharp jolts and shivers.

"He's going into shock," the corpsman shouted.

"I knew that shock was the biggest killer on the battlefield, and I was determined not to pass out," said Steve, who began concentrating to stay alert. He yelled out his service number, B11–34–02, his address and post-office box number, anything to stay alert. He strained to hold on to consciousness and instantly slipped into a realm that would later be called a life review.

"I saw everything that had happened in my life. I saw myself as a baby, I saw the things my father did to me, and I saw a lot of things I really didn't want to remember," he said. Unconscious of time, unaware of his surroundings, and free of pain, Steve Price relived his life.

"The one thing I saw that horrified me was the sight of me stealing money from my grandfather. I saw it all over again. My grandfather was old, eighty-nine years old when he died, and he spent the last five years of his life bedridden," he said. "Even though he hadn't left that bed in five years, he kept his trousers at the foot of the bed and always had money in his pants.

"In that life review, I saw myself stealing twenty bucks from him. I was about eight years old, and in the review,

I was judging myself, saying, 'Steve, what are you doing?' I was lying wounded in Vietnam, feeling pretty bad about something I had done to my grandfather, and at that point I hated myself,'' he said. "I knew I wasn't dead, but I kept seeing these pictures of my life in my mind and thought I was about to die,'' he said. "I felt relieved when the life review ended, totally relieved, the way a child is relieved when he gets a spanking and it suddenly ends.''

"P.O. Box 762, Deep River, Connecticut,'' he heard himself saying. "B11–34–02,'' he said, trying to hold on to consciousness. A helicopter picked up eleven torn bodies that night, one of them Steve Price, and flew them to a nearby medical unit. Steve woke up in a medical tent and overheard someone say, "If he makes it through the night, he might make it.''

He awoke the next afternoon and was loaded aboard a C–141 medical transport plane and flown to Clark Air Base in the Philippines. When the plane touched down at Clark, ten patients were loaded aboard school buses. Steve was put into an ambulance and taken to the base hospital. A day or two later, doctors planned to operate on his chest to inflate his collapsed lung.

"A nurse gave me a pre-op injection that nearly put me to sleep,'' he remembered. "I was wheeled out into a hallway and was only semiconscious. The wall was red brick and I remember thinking how strange it looked. All of a sudden, I didn't feel bad anymore. My pain was gone and I could breathe easily. I had left my body and I was up on the ceiling looking down at myself, and I remember saying, 'Hey, what are you doing down there? It's time to go. Let's go.'

"I turned around to face the brick wall, and that wall turned into light and that light was God. It was a very intense

221

white light, but I saw everything very clearly. I felt what I can only describe as a mother's love, only it was a million times more intense. It was like floating inside a comfortable cloud. I was with God, and he didn't care that I had done all of this stuff, and was just going to hold me for a while. I don't ever remember being held in such a loving way," Steve said.

"After some time, I left the light and was in this place where there was a stream," he said. "On the other side of the stream I saw my grandfather standing there in his nightshirt, just as I remembered him in 1953 when he died. Behind him, I saw a wild yet orderly forest, and everything was perfect. There were trees and flowers, but the colors aren't in our color scheme. Everything glowed almost as if it was neon, and I think it was because everything was filled with God's light," he said. "My grandfather suddenly told me it wasn't my time.

" 'You've got to go back,' he said.

" 'I don't want to go back,' I said. 'All I have to do is jump over this stream.' "

He tried to jump and found himself back in his hospital bed. The operation was over, he had spent some time in the recovery room, and was once again back in bed.

Disillusioned, Steve started crying. He had wanted to stay, but had been made to return to his body and this reality, and he was sure he was being punished. When he got glimpses of his life review and again saw himself stealing money from his grandfather, he was sure he had been kept out of heaven for that sin. Confused and again in pain, he tried to tell a nurse about seeing the light and hovering above his own body before the operation.

"You're on a lot of drugs," she said. "You're having hallucinations." Steve shut up and never mentioned his experience again. However, he knew something unusual had occurred, and it hadn't been induced by the morphine he was on. "Whenever I got a shot of morphine, it dulled the pain, but I always knew it was there. When I was in the light, and I could still see it and feel it afterward, the pain was completely gone."

Weeks later, he was flown to St. Albans Hospital in Queens, New York, where he began to drink heavily.

"I was trying to block out the light," he said. "Part of me believed I had been punished, and seeing the light just reminded me of it, so I drank. Sometimes I just wanted to sleep."

In 1968 he returned to Vietnam as a staff sergeant. But he had changed. Although he carried an M–16 rifle, he didn't fire it once in the year he spent in combat during this second tour. He told the men under him how to protect themselves, he gave orders and carried out orders. Steve just couldn't use his own weapon.

"I did everything I was supposed to do, but I never fired that weapon, even though I was in heavy combat. I was a marine and marines are trained to shoot people. I was a staff sergeant, so I told people to keep their heads down, I taught people how to use their weapons, but I just couldn't fire my own," said Steve, who survived without incident and was rotated back to the States in 1969.

When he returned, despite the fact he was still on active duty, he was assigned to a Marine Corps reserve unit in Birmingham, Alabama. When he tried to explain to his wife, Claudia, whom he married one year before his first tour, what had happened to him both in Vietnam and later in the Philippines, she paid little attention to him, fobbing it off as a typical casualty of the war. She, too, thought he was having hallucinations.

Claudia was having her own difficulties coping with Steve, who now drank heavily. "I told her if she'd just leave me alone, I wouldn't drink," he said. After months of drinking fifths of Jim Beam bourbon from water glasses, one night he just stopped drinking. "I was a pretty nasty guy," he remembered. "I was pretty rotten to my wife. One night, as I was drinking, I realized I suddenly didn't like it anymore."

Much to Claudia's surprise, they received an invitation a few nights later from a neighbor to attend a church service, and Steve agreed to go.

"I really don't remember what the minister was saying, and after a little while I told Claudia I wanted to go home. I tried to walk down the steps, but something physically turned me around," he said. "I don't know what it was, but I couldn't leave that church. Claudia was ahead of me and kept telling me to come on, but I couldn't move. The preacher saw this and came over and asked if I wanted to talk. I really wanted to go home, but I stayed and talked to him about my life and my drinking. I went home that night and found every bottle of liquor I had in the house and poured it down the sink."

Thereafter, Steve joined the church and found himself surrounded by people. "I felt raised up, born again, and it was a turning point in my life," he said. "I wasn't religious, but I liked all the camaraderie at the church." Despite the closeness he felt, Steve never spoke about seeing the light or his experience in Vietnam.

In 1972 he was given a medical discharge from the Marine Corps because he could no longer do some of the physical exercises required, because of his wound. Returning to Deep River, Connecticut, he did odd jobs, including a stint as a gravedigger.

A noticeable change had come over him, something Claudia noticed only because, whatever it was, it kept Steve out of their home a lot.

"I had this overwhelming urge to help people," he said. Joining a nearby Connecticut National Guard unit, he was called out during emergencies and always threw himself into that work. "During the floods of 1983, I stayed away from home for three weeks helping other people while my family was stranded. I helped every Tom, Dick, and Harry, and Claudia almost left me. Our house was falling down, but I went and helped some guy build his house."

Meanwhile, Steve lived with a vivid memory of his light experience and often saw clear flashes of his life review. In the late 1970s someone told him about Raymond Moody and his book about near-death experiences.

"I went to a bookstore in Old Saybrook," he said, "and tried to find Moody's book. I was too embarrassed to ask anyone for it, so I spent a long time looking for it. I was about to walk out of the store when a book fell off a shelf and hit me on the head," he said. It was Moody's book *Life After Life*. Ten years later, a nurse Steve knew invited him to attend a meeting at which a professor from the University of Connecticut was speaking before a group of parents whose children had died.

"She knew about my experience, because after I read Moody's book and found out that hundreds of cases like mine had been documented, I could talk about it. Since she knew my story, she said I might find this professor interesting. The professor was Ken Ring."

When Steve arrived at the meeting of Compassionate Friends, he learned that Ring had sent a substitute—Barbara Harris, who talked about the research she and Bruce Greyson had been conducting.

"Barbara recounted her NDE at that meeting. The parents really needed to hear these kinds of stories."

"Many of them hadn't been with their children if they died suddenly, and they suffered from immense pain," he said. "It was soothing to know that dying wasn't what it appeared to be."

When the talk ended, Steve waited in line and merely asked when the next meeting of Friends of IANDS would be held.

Several weeks later, at that meeting, Steve arrived, unsure of what would happen.

When Barbara asked if anyone wanted to tell his story, Steve raised his hand and launched into it. "It was as if I belonged there. I felt euphoric and full of energy." Within eighteen months, Steve retold his story many times. He told it once on national television during a segment of the Phil Donahue show, he told it before cameras filming two separate documentaries for European audiences, and he has been interviewed numerous times by newspaper and magazine writers.

Steve's transformation took almost twenty-three years. He attributes his turbulent life after Vietnam, his rocky marriage and bouts with alcohol, to a misunderstanding that occurred after his NDE.

"All those years, I thought my grandfather had sent me back to this reality to punish me. I stole money from him as a small child, and the life review blew me away. For twenty-three years I thought that was his way of getting revenge. All those years, I saw the light every day, and there were times when I wished it would leave me alone. It was still just as beautiful, but I still have to go to work every day, I still have to live in this reality, and the light was always pulling me away from this reality toward one I only got a glimpse at during my NDE,'' he said.

''We were being interviewed for a documentary on West German television when all of a sudden it dawned on me. I was telling my story in front of the camera and realized that my grandfather had come to tell me that he loved me. That's why he sent me back.''

# 22

---

# John Loranger

During the fall of 1986, Laurie Peters, a friend of Barbara's, asked her to visit a patient in the intensive-care unit at John Dempsey Hospital. The patient had just undergone cancer surgery.

John Loranger was a man in his mid-thirties who had developed a tumor in his brain stem. Although it couldn't be totally removed, the surgeons had gone in and taken as much of it as they could to alleviate the pressure it was exerting on his spinal cord. Barbara felt sad for Laurie. "We had met just a year ago, when her best friend and business partner, Jean, had died.

"I had been called in to visit Jean just days before her death. It was there that I first met Laurie, and we became instant friends. Now, as she told me about her friend John, she had that same crushed look on her face that she had when Jean was dying."

228

After working in her office all day Friday at Dempsey, Barbara went upstairs to the second floor directly above psychiatry and found John's room in the intensive-care unit.

"It was hard for me to connect all the dynamic facts Laurie had told me about John Loranger," Barbara said. John was a successful building contractor and just thirty-five years old. He had also been a town planner, and his private business ventures grossed millions annually. "There was a different man lying in the bed in front of me. He weighed very little and was paralyzed from the neck down. His face reminded me of a concentration-camp victim—gaunt, tremendous pain, but behind all that I could still see remnants of strength," Barbara said.

Communicating with John was almost impossible. His ability to talk had deteriorated to garbled mumbling, and Barbara had to guess at answers to the questions she had posed. "What I gathered from our attempt to communicate was that his pain medication wasn't working," she said. "He seemed focused on constant pain and couldn't sleep at night. This once-powerful man in his prime was now totally paralyzed. The only obvious purpose his now-withered body served was to contain his pain. He had an incision in his throat so he could be connected to a ventilator that was breathing for him. There was a maze of tubes hooked up to pumps and bags, and monitors with electronic readouts and beeps," Barbara said. "Through his thick glasses I could see his pupils registering his pain through heavy drugs. His hair had the greased-over look of the intensive-care patient who has been there for a long time."

*Just a few minutes into standing at his bedside, and my body went cold. I felt totally helpless. No one seemed able to give this poor soul any comfort. He was trapped in a tortured body. The surgery was an attempt to relieve his suffering. It had failed to return this man to any kind of normal functioning. I drew the curtain between his bed and the glass facing the nurse's station. I put one hand on his forehead and one just below his navel. As I did a gentle tummy rock, it struck me that he couldn't feel it. I started stroking his forehead and hair hoping to give him some comfort. It seemed to agitate him more.*

*Memories of the Circle Bed I had been trapped in floated through my mind.*

*I suddenly felt very selfish. I had the need to comfort him, and it appeared as though I was making him worse.*

*"John, what would help you the most?" I asked, speaking directly in his face, three inches from his nose. I put the electronic voice box in his mouth and the vibrating sound that came out sounded like, "Sleep, help me sleep." I turned and looked behind me, in the direction that John faced. There on the wall was a large chalkboard with John's schedule on it, hour by hour. Next to it was a large electric clock. His sleep medications were scheduled for ten-thirty each night.*

*I looked back directly into his eyes. "John, at ten-thirty tonight we are going to pray for you. I'm in a prayer group tonight and we are going to pray for you to relax and have the pain medications work. You're going to sleep well tonight. Remember, at ten-thirty tonight, open up and feel our prayers!"*

*And I left, walking quickly out of the room. I was thankful that I wasn't working in those surroundings anymore. I felt weak, powerless, and unable to help John. My own words rang in my ears as I rode the elevator down to the main floor. Did John pray or even believe in the power of such things?*

\* \* \*

A month after Barbara had come to Connecticut, she had named Mary Ellen's home the Clubhouse. It was a gathering place for everyone they knew, and the gatherings usually occurred on Friday nights. They told stories, carried in pizza, played music, and used the time to catch up on each other's lives. Toward the end of each gathering, they would join hands and have what they called a "prayer circle." This Friday night, Barbara asked everyone to help her pray for John. After her brief encounter with him, she had seen enough to minutely feel his anguish. She poured out the scene to the others over pizza. It wasn't pleasant dinner conversation but Mary Ellen's brother, David, listened intently. Dave Doherty was a social worker for the Connecticut Department of Mental Retardation, so he had to witness this kind of hopelessness occasionally too.

*I must have gone on and on about John, and my own memories of the Circle Bed, something that still remains deeply embedded in my mind. I was hoping John could escape to other realities as I had done. Surely he would never escape in this reality. David patiently waited for me to wind down. Then he said, "It's almost ten-thirty, Barbara. Let's get into our circle and meditate. We'll know when it's time to pray for John."*

*There were only four of us that particular evening. David had brought his friend Healy, a tall man who stood at least six-foot-five. Mary Ellen and I joined hands with the two men in a circle on the floor. A fire burned brightly in the fireplace behind us, and there were lit candles on the table.*

*Soon I asked that John be able to sleep, that he become free of pain. I took a deep breath and asked that he be relieved of his useless body, something that I had never done before. In the past, I had always trusted in the wisdom of the Universal timing.*

"Can you see John, Barbara?" David asked. She could.

"I have a clear vision of him lying on his side," she said.

"Which side is he on?" David asked. It wasn't a particularly strange question, coming from a man who had been involved in the charismatic movement in the Catholic Church.

"The right side," she said weakly.

"He's not ready to die yet," David said. "Trust God, John needs to be here awhile longer. Maybe not for himself, but for others."

*Energy was racing through our circle, and it was most obvious in our hands. Gus suddenly bolted backward, disengaging his large frame from the circle.*

"I don't understand what's going on," he said. Intellectually, Gus understood the theories of quantum physics, in which science attempts to explain the mystical. He had always been able to talk about energy in terms of physics, but now he was experiencing it, and that made him uncomfortable.

*I was getting uncomfortable too. Nowhere in my past was there preparation for me to accept or understand what Mary Ellen and David calmly referred to as the Holy Spirit. I always felt this presence during hands-on healings, and sometimes during massage. But this was something stronger than anything I had ever experienced, and it made me uncomfortable. I had read the theory of quantum physics and so-called New Age literature in search of an explanation for the energy I knew coursed through my body. The Kundalini theory had become comfortable for me. Now I was hearing it explained from a Catholic perspective. David and Mary Ellen were comfortable in the presence of the immense energy they called the Holy Spirit. Gus and I, however, were overwhelmed by it and needed to stop.*

The four of them needed to lighten up. David and Gus played their guitars. They sang "The Wedding Song," words Barbara had never listened to before. "I'll always remember those lyrics that night, though, especially the phrase 'Whenever two or more of us are gathered in His name, there is love,' she said.

The next morning, still together, the four of them did fall chores, raking leaves and stacking firewood. It was a sunny fall day and the trees in New England were ablaze with the oranges, yellows, reds, and purples of autumn. In the afternoon they piled into a car and headed north to Massachusetts to show Barbara the Berkshire Mountains for the first time. They stopped in a little village, on the green, and sat in the town gazebo. Gus and David had brought their guitars and they sang folk songs. Then they went to Stockbridge and drank Bloody Marys on the front porch of the Red Lion Inn as the sun set. Despite all this, Barbara never quite forgot about John Loranger.

Sunday afternoon, she was headed back to U Conn and John, only ten minutes away from Mary Ellen and her house. She showed one of the nurses at the desk her identification and walked into his room. He was asleep, so she sat down and waited. "I prayed for a while and then left him," she said.

She went back on Tuesday and touched him lightly on the head, asking him how he was doing. He mumbled about pain, about not being able to sleep. Barbara asked him about his night medications, if the prayers were helping, and realized that he was not capable of understanding at all. "I remembered the feelings myself when I was on morphine, the tumbling around in what we call 'reality.'"

*As I was walking out of John's room I met a woman just entering. We exchanged smiles and then said hello. She asked me, "How is he doing?"*

*I answered, "Sleeping."*

*She looked relieved. Then I asked, "Do you know John well?"*

*"Yes," she sighed. "This is so awful for him, and has been such an ordeal for me to watch."*

*"Do you have anybody to talk to?" I asked.*

*"No, not really. I talk with his girlfriend, Joni, but that's me trying to help her. I don't get to really deal with my own feelings."*

*"Want to go sit in the lounge?"*

*As we walked toward the lounge, I introduced myself and asked Diane if she would like some coffee. I got us two cups and we sat looking at each other. Diane told me that she was a social worker, and now worked as director of the social-service agency in Vernon. John had been the president of the board of directors.*

*I asked her to tell me more about John.*

*"John was my supervisor as president of the board. It had really surprised me that someone that young had accomplished so much. He was only thirty-years old when we met in 1981, and yet he had worked as the Vernon town planner for several years and then built up his own multimillion-dollar development corp."*

*Diane went on to describe John as a man who on the one hand had lived a very fast-paced business and social life, jet-setting all over the country. At the same time, he was a caring family man who deeply loved his two young children. He was also concerned about his community, giving countless hours to her agency over the five years he was on the board. There were tears in her eyes occasionally, running down her cheeks, and her face was flushed as she talked about him working so hard to help keep the agency from closing.*

*"The last six months John and I worked together in 1982, things were very difficult for him. His father, who was terminally ill, lived with them for several months. His business was floundering temporarily because of the real-estate climate; and then his marriage ended. In the midst of all of this, John always made it to our weekly meeting even if he had just flown in on an early-morning flight, unshaven and exhausted. He said the agency was important enough that he got there no matter what. Or,"* she said laughingly, *"he would say, 'No big deal.'"*

*"I was afraid for him at that time. I had a sense that something like this would happen. I kept telling him to slow down, but he wouldn't."*

I said, *"He sounds like a very special person."*

*Diane couldn't speak for a few moments. She threw her head back, looked away, and then looked back. Her next few words were half-choked. "He was so bright, caring, and sensitive to the needs of others. He sure helped me, but he couldn't help himself, and now look at him. It's so unfair . . . ."*

*"It sounds like this was a lot more than a working relationship, Diane."*

*She sighed and said, "It was, but I didn't realize how much more until a few months ago. I had only seen him a few times socially for a year and a half after we stopped working together. After his first surgery he called me and asked for my help regarding his convalescence, and he needed to talk to me about his girlfriend. He really cares for her. He's afraid of how she will deal with his death, and asked for my help. I've spent a lot of time with them, but I don't know how much I've helped."*

*I dug into my purse to find tissues for Diane, and thought to myself: It's good to know more about him. I wish I could ease her pain, but at least she can talk to me about it.*

*Diane needed a few seconds to compose herself again, and then continued, saying, "I need to reassure him about Joni, but I can't quite grasp how to reach her. She just can't accept that he's terminally ill."*

*"Diane, listen, please. She's right where she needs to be. We can't get her out until she wants to, and right now he's dying, so she needs to be where she is. But how about you? You are worrying about everyone else and not taking care of yourself."*

*Through her tears, she started to laugh, and said, "Yeah, probably. It sure does feel good to talk."*

*"Well, I'm here a couple times a week. How about taking my number and giving me a call when you want to talk?"*

*"Or I'll see you again here."*

*We thanked each other for the help and left.*

There was a semester break at the Connecticut Center for Massage Therapy, so Laurie Peters, Mary Ellen, and Barbara went together to visit friends in California. On the first day back, Barbara faced a pile of mail in her office. It was much bigger than she had expected. Since *McCall's* magazine had done a big story on near-death experiences, Barbara had received over five hundred experiences in the mail. Barbara answered each letter and enclosed information on IANDS. There were also students needing help in writing high-school and college papers about NDEs.

As Barbara sat staring at the new pile of mail, the phone rang. It was Laurie asking her if she had seen John.

"No," she said, "But I am going upstairs in a few minutes." She and Laurie made plans to meet for dinner at the restaurant across the street from the U Conn Health Center at five-thirty.

Barbara hung up and went upstairs, trying to put on a

cheerful face before she got to John's room. As she looked at him for the first time in two weeks, she remembered it didn't matter if she was cheerful or not. John was beyond anything Barbara thought was important.

Sitting quietly next to the bed was John's brother. He had come thousands of miles to see him. Barbara and he talked long enough for her to know he was badly shaken and now numb over his brother's condition. "I told him how important it was for John to know he was there," she said. "I told him the best way to communicate this was to touch him. It was the only real way to communicate with him now.

"I put one hand on John's tummy and the other on his forehead and just stayed like that for five or ten minutes. I told him I did that with all my dying patients and I knew that John needed human touch now more than anything," she said.

"Are you here with anyone else?" she asked him.

"No, my wife is back home. I don't know if I should go back and wait or stay here."

"I wish I had some advice for you, but there's no way to know," Barbara said after a long pause.

"Since you're alone here, if you want to talk, give me a call," she said, writing down her number. "I'm here three days a week. Please feel free."

He never called and she didn't see him again until the day she saw John Loranger for the last time.

Barbara then went across the street to meet Laurie. When she sat down, Laurie looked at her intently, searching for something. Laurie talked about John for a long time.

"I wish I had answers for all your questions, but there aren't any," Barbara said. "We have to follow our hearts. The best we can hope for John is to help him get in touch with his own feelings right now. But John's so spaced-out on drugs that that's close to impossible," she said. "You've got to touch him when you're in there. He can't feel much, but let him see that your hands are on him. Look him right in the eye. Tell him that you love him, and when you feel comfortable with all this, tell him that you love him enough to let him go when he's ready. And remember, it doesn't matter if he's awake or asleep. We don't know what's happening inside his heart, or what he's experiencing. That hurts us," Barbara said. "But by touching and expressing our emotion, at least he's hearing or feeling our end and there's some communication going on."

Laurie sponged up every word Barbara said and left to visit John. When she got there, she found one of his doctors in his room. He asked her many questions about John, because John had asked to be unplugged from his life-support systems during a lucid moment.

His request had been clearly heard by his friends, and now the hospital committee had to meet and decide his fate. It was a historic situation at the U Conn hospital because it marked the first time a patient had asked to be taken off life-support systems. A year earlier, the State Supreme Court had ruled in favor of taking critically ill patients off life supports, but it was the first time it had to be considered at U Conn.

The committee decided to honor John's request. A week later, they planned to unplug him from any extraordinary systems that would sustain his life. They would take him off the ventilator, the breathing device that had been breathing for him for three months.

The night before doctors planned to unhook him, Barbara saw Laurie in the hospital on her way to a Friends of IANDS meeting. She had stopped in to see John once that day, but stayed only a short time. Laurie told her they were unplugging John the next day. When the meeting was over, about ten o'clock that night, Barbara went back to John's room. She knew there was nothing she could do, but she went anyway.

*I was stopped by one of the evening-shift nurses. She knew about Bruce's and my work and started firing questions at me. I could feel what a soft, caring woman she was. She told me how much she was hurting. She had asked for permission to come into work the next morning, wanting to be with John in his last moments. She wanted my opinion about their decision to unplug John from the life-support systems. She cared about this patient and knew John's friends and knew that John's friends and relatives had threatened to take the hospital to court if they did not comply with his wishes.*

Early the next morning, Barbara again visited John's room. John had been there for three months, and this was to be his last day. Between floors on the stairway, Barbara encountered a nurse who excitedly told her the news of John's planned death.

"A patient is going to be unplugged in intensive care at ten this morning," she said. "Isn't that weird?"

Barbara nodded. "Well, at least I know what time it's happening," she said to herself.

When she walked into John's room, she was startled to see so many people there. The nurse she had talked to the night before was in and out of the room. She looked exhausted. John's brother and sister-in-law were there. Laurie was there with Werner, a close friend of John's, and John's girlfriend, Joni. Joni was accompanied by her parents. Diane Mann was standing by the bed, quiet and pale. A priest came in for a few minutes and gave him the Last Rites. The hospital chaplain, a woman Barbara had seen often around the hospital, came in.

*Our eyes met and we smiled. John's day nurse was busy tending to him during all of this. He seemed much more alert, looking intently at each one of us, obviously registering who we were. Things started to take shape. The chaplain asked who wanted to take Communion with John. The group divided, some people stepping back, others moving in toward the bed. The chaplain wore a wooden cross, dark pants and sweater, and had an ease about her. She said a prayer and broke a wafer—first a piece for John, which she placed in his mouth, and then she gave each one of us around his bed a piece. As I put the bit of wafer in my mouth, I put my hand on John's foot and prayed silently that he would go toward the light.*

*I moved back and leaned into the corner of the room, trying to be as flat against it as I could. The only time I said anything was twice to translate for John. Just before the doctors came in, John said something loudly, but it wasn't easy to understand."*

"What did he say?" everyone asked.

"He said, 'They're coming for me at five-thirty.'"

"No, no, John," the day nurse said, "the doctors are coming in soon. They're supposed to come at ten o'clock."

At ten-fifteen the doctors hadn't arrived yet, and John said it again. "They're coming for me at five-thirty."

"John, you know this is hospital time," the nurse said. "We're always late. The doctors will be here in a minute." She looked so pained.

I repeated, "He said, 'They're coming for me at five-thirty,'" and I pointed up with my thumb. Finally the doctors came. Werner played a tape of George Winston's "December," and the room was filled with the music John had wanted played. The doctors asked most of us to leave the room. John's girlfriend, Joni, began to cry again, trying to say good-bye; then she walked out, partially slumped over, supported by her parents.

Werner was holding Barbara's right hand. She held John's foot with her left hand.

"It's been good, buddy," Werner told his friend. "I'll see you in the next life!"

John smiled. "Save the Porsche, I'm coming back!" he said, and everyone laughed. The nurse gave him an injection and his eyelids got heavy and he closed his eyes.

We watched them unplug the ventilator. The three doctors stood together by the window. Some people stayed by the bed. I sank back into the corner and watched his vital signs get weaker. Twenty minutes later, however, his vital signs grew strong again. John had slipped into a deep coma but he was breathing on his own. He had started to die, and we all felt joy that he was finally being freed of his pain. Now, a half-hour later, he had started breathing on his own, and it confused us. How long could he breathe on his own in a deep coma?

People milled around, sticking their heads into the room periodically all afternoon. Barbara went back to her office on the floor below. The whole staff at the hospital had heard what was going on in that room, and the units buzzed with gossip about it. People went to the chapel to pray for John. Others came into his room and joined the ongoing vigil.

*Around three in the afternoon, I bumped into a hospital administrator coming out of John's room. She told me a lot of the staff in the ICU knew about Dr. Greyson's and my work. She asked if I'd be willing to hold "an in-service meeting" at seven o'clock that evening, because the ICU staff was upset over what was happening. She felt a meeting should be immediately held to diffuse some of the intense emotion in the ICU.*

*I asked her why seven o'clock, and she said so both the day and the evening staff could come.*

*I agreed and put a notice of the meeting next to the phone at the ICU nursing station. I handed out some IANDS brochures to the staff and then went home to rest.*

*I was back at six o'clock, planning to stop in to see John before the meeting. John's brother and sister-in-law were on the telephone at the nurse's station. John's brother looked at me and said with tears in his eyes, "He just died, at exactly five-thirty."*

*I went to John's room and looked at him for one last time. I smiled and said, "They're coming for you at five-thirty." And I said a prayer, thanking God for John's release.*

*Then I went to the conference room where the in-service meeting was supposed to be held. When I got there, the room was empty. I waited until seven-fifteen. No one came. No one on the staff wanted to talk about it.*

*As I walked to the elevators to go home, I realized how thankful I was to be going home to be with Mary Ellen. Diane Mann and Laurie Peters were standing at the elevators together and crying.*

*Diane said, "He knew this morning they were coming for him at five-thirty. He was so alert, so peaceful—better than I had seen him in months. He was having a near-death experience this morning, wasn't he?"*

"Yes," I said, choked up too. "At ten o'clock this morning it was a near-death experience, and at five-thirty this afternoon he continued his journey."

# III

## FULL
## CIRCLE

# Epilogue

In November 1987 my son Steven, then twenty-two, moved north to attend the University of Connecticut in Storrs. He pulled in during the night and I helped him unpack his car, filled with all his worldly possessions, his clothes, and, yes, his stereo. Another full circle.

Steven graduated from the university in May with honors and moved in with me. He's going to be teaching music at Central Connecticut State University and at nearby Manchester High School in the fall. I graduated from a one-year full-time course at Connecticut Center for Massage Therapy as a massage therapist last December. I've incorporated my respiratory-therapy background into a breathing technique similar to Dr. Grof's holotropic breathing. Putting together the breath work and massage, I have a small practice specializing in bio-energy balancing.

My son Gary, nineteen, came here last October for what was to be a few months to help me move. He still hasn't left. He just recently received his GED and is planning to attend the university too.

Those horribly painful memories of leaving Florida alone have melted as we function as a family again.

Beth graduated from the University of Florida. She's twenty-six now and is enthusiastically working her way up in advertising in South Florida. She comes up here for all the holidays and, most recently, for Steven's graduation. There are just no words for these precious moments when we are back together again.

I live with my two boys in a wonderful small flat above Sharon Grant and her thirteen-year-old son, Brian. I never had to look for a place to live. When I knew it was time for my own place, this flat became available and Sharon and I just laughed and said, "Synchronicity!"

Sharon and I have given talks together on the near-death experience, and more recently, workshops introducing touch as the basic element of healing. We call our one day intensive Healing Yourself, Healing the Planet.

Bruce Greyson and I recently co-authored a paper entitled "Counseling the Near-Death Experience." It is going to be published in Christina and Stan Grof's next book: *Spiritual Emergency: When Personal Transformation Becomes a Crisis* (J. P. Tarcher, 1990).

The first annual IANDS conference will be held in Philadelphia in two weeks. I'm giving a workshop there called "The NDE: Working with the Aftereffects Through Energy Balancing." In August 1990 we are having an international IANDS conference in Washington, D.C., with delegates from the United Kingdom and France, and possibly West Germany, Holland, Australia, Japan, and Canada. There are now twenty-four IANDS local chapters all over the United States, and more are forming.

In *Heading Toward Omega: In Search of the Meaning of the Near-Death Experience*, Ken Ring broke new ground in exploring the deepest, most intense near-death experiences, and the implications of their transformative effects. In his theory, that the NDE and other transformative experiences like it are a catalyst, he explains the possible next step in human evolution.

Given the frightening possibilities of nuclear destruction faced by the world today, Dr. Ring holds out the hope that the increasing prevalence of NDEs and their aftereffects holds great promise for a more peaceful future. Drawing on Rupert Sheldrake's morphic resonance theory, which holds that when a phenomenon is experienced a certain number of times by a given species, it becomes more common for other members of the species, even if they have not been previously exposed to it, Dr. Ring, both in his book and now at conferences on consciousness all over the world, maintains that: "The increasing number of NDEs means humans may be approaching the 'critical mass' necessary for significant evolutionary change. If more and more people develop a direct inner awareness of the 'core' NDE—the sense of Cosmic Unity that empathetically transmits total unconditional love—the threat of planetary disaster can be overcome and a more compassionate world society of humans can celebrate life on the planet."

Three documentaries have now been shown on European television about the near-death experience, with Dr. Ring's theory as the theme. Each has featured interviews with him as well as with Bruce Greyson, Rupert Sheldrake, Sharon Grant, Steve Price, Tom Sawyer, and me, plus many others. "Unsolved Mysteries," "The Reporters," "The Sunday

Today Show,'' "Larry King Live,'' and many more television shows in the United States have dedicated segments and entire programs to NDE research and education, featuring all of the above researchers and experiencers. *McCall's* magazine, the *New York Times*, Associated Press, *Special Reports* magazine, and the *National Enquirer*, to name a few, have run feature stories on the latest research and education into the near-death experience. Several of these articles have been syndicated in newspapers and magazines all over the world.

Unfortunately, no funding has been made available at this time for medical research in a laboratory setting. To quote Bruce Greyson, recently writing about future research: "As director of research for IANDS, I have been engaged in the scientific investigation of the psychological and phenomenological effects of near-death experiences like Ms. Harris'. Together with Dr. Ring and Ms. Harris, I am embarking on a program of research into the physiological changes brought about by NDEs such as hers . . .''

When the funding is made available, we hope to bring subjects into the lab to test objectively with EEGs, CAT scans, and evoked potentials. This testing will center around those who claim to have healing abilities or who experience strange energy sensations after an NDE or similar experience.

To finish this epilogue, I'll take you back to a lunch shared by Ken Ring, Bruce Greyson, and me just a few weeks ago. We were talking about what I was going to say in this epilogue, and Ken said to me: "We may not have the physiological research yet, but we do know that these experiences do happen and that they're absolutely real to the people who have them. And we also have impressive statistics that they have a great impact on these people's lives. And, my dear, now that we are hearing from these people all over the world, we realize that the near-death experience is no longer *only* research. It's a social movement that is spreading all over this planet!''

Newington, Connecticut
Memorial Day, 1989

# Scientific Commentary

## by Bruce Greyson, M.D.

In attempting to provide a scientific commentary to this story, the first question that arises is whether science can in fact understand this kind of experience. The NDE itself, obviously, is not something that onlookers can watch or measure. And many of what seem to be the important questions about NDEs—"What do they mean?" or "What is the nature of the reality in the NDE?"—are not observable and therefore not appropriate questions for science. The scientific method answers "how-much" questions—how big, how many, how fast, how powerful—but not "why" questions. We can't expect science to address the philosophical questions about NDEs, but only the empirical questions about them.

Are there empirical questions worth asking about NDEs? I think there are, and I believe that in answering some of these empirical questions about NDEs, we can refine what we think we know about the experience and clarify how we regard these events, so that it may become much easier to address the philosophical questions by other means.

The first point to make in exploring a scientific or empirical approach to NDEs is, if we can't observe the NDE itself, what can we observe? We can certainly observe the reports of what near-death experiencers, or NDErs, remember of their experiences. Of course, what they remember may not be the same as what they actually experienced, and what they choose to tell a researcher may not be the same as what they remember. In addition to what they say, we can also observe how NDErs act. So the question "Can science explain the NDE?" now becomes "Can science explain what people say and do after an NDE?"

There are a number of general categories of empirical questions about NDEs; for example: (1) What do NDEs consist of? (2) What influences who will have an NDE? (3) What are the aftereffects of NDEs? (4) What practical applications do NDEs have? (5) How are NDEs similar to or different from other experiences? and (6) How reliable are NDE reports?

A number of scientific studies have been conducted in an attempt to answer these questions. The first category of empirical question I mentioned was "What do NDEs consist of?" When you operationalize this question, it becomes "What do NDErs report their NDEs to consist of?" Within that general category, there are a number of issues that science can address. The first is: Can NDEs be broken down into a few meaningful components or parts?

When I first began this work fifteen years ago, I read what had been written up to that point by the early pioneers of near-death research, such as psychiatrists Raymond Moody and Russell Noyes and parapsychologist Karlis Osis.

I collected from that early literature over a hundred different features—feelings, sensations, encounters, and events—that had been reported as part of an NDE. Through a process of collecting reports from hundreds of NDErs like Barbara Harris, and refining those reports through statistical techniques, which are really just another type of observational instrument, I was able to describe the NDE as containing four separate parts.

I labeled these four component parts: (1) a Cognitive Component, including time distortion, thought acceleration, life review, and sudden understanding; (2) an Affective Component, including feelings of peace, joy, and cosmic unity, and an experience of a brilliant light; (3) a Paranormal Component, including enhanced vision or hearing, apparent extrasensory perception, precognitive vision, and an out-of-body experience; and (4) a Transcendental Component, including encounters with an apparently unearthly realm, a mystical being, and visible spirits and a barrier or "point of no return" that, had the NDEr crossed it, would have precluded his or her return to life.

Obviously, not all NDEs include all of these features, but all NDEs can be described as having so many Cognitive elements, so many Affective elements, so many Paranormal elements, and so many Transcendental elements. Furthermore, each individual NDE can be classified as to whether it is *predominantly* Cognitive, Affective, or Transcendental experience. (As it turns out, almost no NDEs are predominantly Paranormal.) The importance of this is that when we compare NDE reports with physiological and psychological variables, we can look at these distinct parts separately.

For example, I have developed a thirty-two-point scale on which to "rate" the depth of NDEs, with eight possible points for each of the four components. On this NDE scale, Barbara's NDE has a "depth" of twenty-one out of thirty-two. Her NDE could be "rated" as having seven out of eight Cognitive points, since it included time distortion, thought acceleration, a life review, and sudden understanding about herself, but not about the workings of the universe, which some NDErs report. It would rate six out of eight Affective points, for feelings of peace, mild feelings of happiness, cosmic unity, and a glowing light—but not the brilliant light often described by NDErs.

It would rate six out of eight Paranormal points, for enhanced vision and hearing, apparent extrasensory perception of facts later confirmed by others, and an out-of-body experience, but no precognitive visions. And it would rate only two out of eight Transcendental points, for a sense of being in an unearthly realm of existence, but no encounter with a mystical being or voice, no visible deceased spirits, and no barrier or "point of no return."

Another question about what NDEs consist of is: Do the different parts of an NDE unfold simultaneously or in some temporal sequence? Psychologist Kenneth Ring formulated a model of the NDE unfolding in five sequential stages: peace, separation from the body, the tunnel, seeing the light, and entering the light. Looking at the NDE in temporal stages is quite different from looking at separate parts of the NDE. Which way of looking at the experience is right?

The modern inductive scientific method does not allow us to regard any of our conclusions as absolute truth. From our observations—what NDErs tell us—we build generalizations that are imperfect models of the way things are. There is no meaning to the question of which model is the right one, since they aren't intended to be truths. The only meaningful question is how helpful these models are in predicting new information and new answers. Temporal stage models can predict some new information, and component models can predict other information.

As an analogy, consider our scientific models for understanding the behavior of light. One model that pictures light as a particle, or ''photon,'' predicts some events, like the casting of shadows. Another model that pictures light as a wave predicts other events, like the diffraction of white sunlight into multicolored rainbows. The photon model doesn't predict rainbows, and the light-wave model doesn't predict shadows, so science regards both models as incomplete.

Instead, the scientist searches for more comprehensive models: for example, a model that pictures light as being *sometimes* a wave and *sometimes* a particle, or a model that pictures light as a ''wavicle,'' with some properties of waves and some properties of particles. But until we develop a more useful single model, we're left with two models of light, each of which is useful for predicting different phenomena about light.

The same may be true for NDEs. Perhaps a temporal stages model will be more helpful in predicting some features of NDEs, and a parallel components model more helpful in predicting others. But inductive science views *all* models as just models, rough approximations of reality that are never right or wrong, but only approximations that are closer to or farther from the truth.

We can also ask empirical questions about different parts of the NDE, about different kinds of NDEs, and about NDEs in different people. For example: What paranormal or mystical elements occur in NDEs? How do unpleasant, negative, or hellish NDEs differ from others? How do NDEs vary among different cultures? Cross-cultural studies have tended to support the similarity of the basic near-death experience across a wide range of societies, but such studies are few in number and generally have included too few cases to provide definitive comparisons.

Within our own culture, we can ask how NDEs differ among different segments of the population. Barbara devoted one chapter of this book to pediatrician Melvin Morse's research, which found children to have essentially the same kind of experience that adults report. Larger studies of NDEs, such as those of Kenneth Ring and cardiologist Michael Sabom, categorizing subjects by age, sex, race, religious and educational background, have never shown any effect of these variables on either the frequency with which people report NDEs or on the type of experiences they report.

The second category of empirical question I alluded to above was "What influences who will have an NDE?" To answer these questions, we need not only a group of near-death experiencers but also a "control group" of people who have not had NDEs. For my research, I anticipated a control group of people who came close to death but did not report NDEs. In the process of recruiting such a control group, I unexpectedly came across two further groups of subjects.

The first unanticipated group were those who claimed to have had NDEs, but whose descriptions of what they experienced scored close to zero on an instrument like my NDE scale. Did those people have NDEs, or didn't they? *Something* happened to these people that made them label their experiences NDEs, but in the interest of research I kept them in a separate group.

The second unanticipated group were those who denied having had an NDE, but whose descriptions of what did happen when they came close to death scored quite high on the NDE scale. Did *these* people have NDEs, or didn't they? Despite their experiencing many of the common features of NDEs, something prevented them from labeling their experiences as NDEs. Again, in the interest of research, I have kept these people in a separate group.

How NDErs compare with the control subjects on a variety of variables can then tell us what factors influence who will have an NDE, and, by looking at the separate parts of the NDE, it can tell us what factors will determine who will have what kind of an NDE. Furthermore, including in the analysis my two unanticipated groups of ambiguous NDErs can tell us what factors will determine who will label an experience as having been an NDE and who will be reluctant to do so.

Several factors that might potentially influence the NDE can be observed. We can ask, for example: What socio-cultural variables influence the NDE? How do religious beliefs and practices influence the NDE? As I mentioned above, none of the larger studies of near-death experiences have shown any effect of these variables. We can also ask how previous paranormal or mystical experiences might influence the NDE. My own research has found that such experiences are no more or less common in NDErs *before* the NDE than they are in the general population.

We can also ask: How do prior expectations of death and dying influence the NDE? Again, research that I carried out with psychiatrist Ian Stevenson showed no effect of prior expectations of death or an afterlife, and no effect of prior knowledge about NDEs. And how do circumstances of the close brush with death influence the NDE? No particular way of approaching death has yet been shown to lead to any particular type of NDE. However, it does seem to matter whether a close brush with death was sudden and unexpected, such as in many accidents and heart attacks, or whether it was possibly anticipated, such as in suicide attempts or complications of surgery.

My research has shown that sudden, unexpected near-death events lead to roughly equal numbers of Cognitive, Affective, and Transcendental experiences. However, Cognitive NDEs—where time distortion, thought acceleration, life review, and sudden understanding are most prominent— tend not to occur in people who had expected to die and had had time to prepare for it. While I hadn't anticipated that finding, it makes sense: you're more likely to survive a sudden unexpected accident if you stop time, think faster than usual, and acquire sudden insights. On the other hand, people who expect they may die soon often review their lives in preparation for death, so that a life review during the near-death event becomes unnecessary.

We can also ask how physical details of the close brush with death influence the NDE. What effect does brain functioning have, as measured by EEGs? Though a number of writers have reported anecdotes about NDErs who recovered from "flat EEGs," no physician or scientist has yet published a firsthand report with EEG findings. What is the effect of level of consciousness? Michael Sabom studied NDEs only in people who were unconscious, whereas Russell Noyes studied NDEs only in people who had *not* lost consciousness. My own research has shown no influence of level of consciousness on the NDE.

We can ask more specific questions, such as: How does anoxia, as measured by blood levels of oxygen, influence the NDE? Though skeptics often attribute NDEs to anoxia, Michael Sabom, who alone has reported actual levels of blood gases in NDErs, found no effect of anoxia. How do endorphins, morphinelike compounds produced in the body under stress, influence the NDE? Again, endorphins are widely implicated in theories of NDEs, but they are extremely difficult to measure directly. However, in some emergency settings comatose patients are given narcotic antagonists, which would block the effect of endorphins. By studying the incidence and type of NDEs in people who have been given these drugs while close to death, we might infer the role of endorphins in NDEs.

The questions we can ask about the effects of drugs on the NDE are limited only by the number of different drugs available, but we can ask generally: Do drugs seem to influence the occurrence or type of NDE? Once again, while a number of drugs can produce states that have features in common with NDEs, studies of near-death experiencers by Michael Sabom, by Karlis Osis and Erlendur Haraldsson, and by myself have concluded that NDEs occur *less* often when people near death are given drugs.

Perhaps the ultimate question we can ask about the near-death event itself is: Is it even necessary to come close to death to have an NDE? Melvin Morse and his colleagues did find that children who were near death reported NDEs quite frequently, while equally sick children who were not near death did not report any NDEs. However, studies of adult NDErs, including my own, those of psychiatrists Glen Gabbard and Stuart Twemlow, and those of Ian Stevenson and his colleagues have suggested that NDEs may be as common among people who *think* they are near death as they are among people who actually *are* near death. In fact, Stevenson's group has suggested, perhaps tongue-in-cheek, that we call these events "*fear*-death experiences." It seems clear that being near death is not the only trigger for an NDE-like experience; it may just be the most reliable trigger.

We can also ask: How does the individual's personality influence the NDE? Though the studies of Glen Gabbard and Stuart Twemlow and of psychologist H. J. Irwin suggest that people who have out-of-body experiences tend to be psychologically healthy, very little work has been done on personality traits of near-death experiencers per se. Psychologists Thomas Locke and Franklin Shontz found no differences in intelligence or personality between a small group of NDErs and a control group who had come close to death. Preliminary research that I conducted with psychologist James Council showed that NDErs score higher than control groups on measures of "absorption" and "fantasy-proneness," two related traits that measure the ability to focus attention narrowly, and on imagined or internal stimuli.

The third category of empirical question that I mentioned earlier is: What are the aftereffects of NDEs? How do NDEs influence personality traits? How do NDEs influence attitudes and beliefs? How do NDEs influence apparent psychic abilities? What parts of the NDE exert these aftereffects? How long do these aftereffects last? This has proved to be the most fertile area of near-death research, for two very different reasons.

The first reason is practical: since the occurrence of NDEs can't be predicted, investigators can't often be there when they occur, but can only study them retrospectively, when the only available data may be the NDErs' recollections. Aftereffects, on the other hand, since they predictably follow the NDE, can be studied prospectively as they evolve, and can often be observed by others.

The long-term effects of NDEs to increase spirituality, concern for others, and appreciation of life, while decreasing fear of death, materialism, and competitiveness, are well-documented in Kenneth Ring's *Heading Toward Omega*, sociologist Charles Flynn's *After the Beyond*, psychologist Margot Grey's *Return from Death*, Michael Sabom's *Recollections of Death*, P.M.H. Atwater's *Coming Back to Life*, and numerous articles by these authors and many others, including Russell Noyes, Martin Bauer, and myself. Kenneth Ring's work in particular is notable for his systematic interviewing of "significant others" who can independently confirm the NDErs' claims of altered attitudes, traits, and life-styles.

The second reason that studying the aftereffects has been the most fertile facet of near-death research is that it is also the most meaningful facet. The NDE itself, striking though it may be, does not sound to the investigator all that different from hallucinations or dissociative states. Its aftereffects, on the other hand, are uniquely profound, pervasive, and permanent, totally unlike the aftereffects of any phenomenologically comparable experience. NDEs are seed experiences, and it is only by studying the fruits that eventually grow from those seeds that we can understand their full meaning.

And we can go further, asking questions about the aftereffects on people other than the NDErs themselves: How do NDEs influence marriages or other relationships? While this is a largely unstudied area, P.M.H. Atwater has documented profound "ripple effects" on those close to the NDEr. And how do NDEs influence people who hear or read about them?

While it had been speculated in the infancy of near-death research that hearing about NDEs might make suicide more attractive to some people, psychologist John McDonagh actually found the exact opposite effect: suicidal patients reading about NDEs as a result found life more meaningful and suicide *less* appealing. And sociologist Charles Flynn found that teaching college students about NDEs tended to instill some of the same changes as having an NDE.

Finally, we can ask: How do NDEs influence society? On this point we have no data, but Kenneth Ring and philosopher Michael Grosso have argued that the personal transformations brought about by NDEs are precisely what are needed now on a planetary level to avoid global catastrophe.

The wider influence of NDEs on others leads directly into the fourth category of empirical question that I mentioned: What practical applications do NDEs have? What do NDEs and their aftereffects tells us about how we can better help dying patients—including comatose ones; about how we can better help grieving families; about how we can better help suicidal people; and how can the beneficial effects of NDEs be safely induced or replicated?

The fifth category of empirical question was: How are NDEs similar to or different from other experiences? For example, how do NDEs compare with out-of-body experiences occurring in other settings? Glen Gabbard and Stuart Twemlow, in making just this comparison, found the NDE to contain no single unique element, but rather a unique pattern of features, most prominent being its profound aftereffects. And do NDEs compare with mystical experiences that occur in other situations, or with other experiences of "alternate realities"?

In the research Barbara and I did on suicide-induced NDEs, psychiatric patients used many of the same words to describe their NDEs as they did to describe their psychotic or drug-induced hallucinations; yet they insisted that those experiences were in fact nothing at all like the NDE. Our data suggest that the mentally ill have neither more nor fewer

NDEs than the mentally healthy; and for both groups, the NDE is a unique experience, unlike anything else they have known.

In comparing NDEs to comparable events, we can also ask how NDErs' impressions of death and an afterlife compare with purported evidence of an afterlife from other sources, such as alleged mediumistic communications and reincarnation memories.

And finally, the sixth category of empirical question that I mentioned earlier was: How reliable are NDE reports? How similar are recountings of the same NDE? How does hypnosis or sodium amytal influence recall of NDEs? How does prior knowledge of NDEs influence the NDE report? How does the interviewer influence the NDE report? How does the NDEr's motivation influence the NDE report? Many factors may make an NDEr more willing or less willing to talk about an NDE or to disclose certain aspects of it.

While my studies show that NDE accounts are remarkably reliable over time, and not influenced by previous knowledge about NDEs, there is no doubt that an interviewer's encouragement or hostility can markedly influence what an NDEr will reveal. As there is some evidence that NDErs benefit from sharing their experiences with others, the question of how to encourage that sharing becomes a very practical one with therapeutic as well as research implications.

One of the most remarkable chapters in this search has been our study of NDEs and suicidal attitudes that Barbara described in Chapter 18. In the early days of near-death studies, some critics of the field as well as some near-death researchers feared that publicizing NDEs would encourage people toward suicide. We worried that near-death experiences would "romanticize" death, that the accounts of overwhelming peace, unconditional love, and reunion with loved ones who had died earlier would make death seem irresistible.

When you tally up all the adjustment problems NDErs may face, their concerns about being misunderstood or rejected by others, their difficulty finding a meaningful role in our competitive society, add in the pain and disability they may have from the illnesses or accidents that brought them close to death, and then take away their fear of death, which often stops people from considering suicide seriously, we might expect NDErs to have a high suicide rate.

In fact, though, our own studies as well as those of Kenneth Ring and of psychiatrist David Rosen all suggest that suicide attempters who have NDEs do not repeat their attempts after the experience. This paradoxical finding led me on a search for the reasons why NDErs, despite looking forward to their own eventual deaths, do not try to kill themselves. The scientific literature offered interesting speculations but very little data to support them. I therefore began asking suicide attempters why they felt less suicidal after their attempts (if, in fact, they did); and I compared the answers of those who had had a near-death experience as a result of their suicide attempts with those who hadn't had an NDE.

The reasons people mentioned for no longer being suicidal could be lumped statistically into three categories. The first group were "transpersonal" effects of the suicide attempt and the experience that followed, effects that made the attempter feel a part of something greater than him- or herself. This included feeling, after the attempt, a sense of "cosmic unity," of being part of nature or part of the universe; feeling that the personal losses and failures that led to the attempt were no longer important from that cosmic or transpersonal perspective; that life seemed more meanful or valuable than it had before; that the individual felt more alive than previously; and that the individual felt closer to other people than he or she had before the attempt.

The second category was also otherworldly or mystical in nature, but without the transpersonal perspectives. This included feeling better about yourself, knowing that death is not the end, or having been "sent back" for a reason, believing that suicide would not lead to an escape from the problems that led to the attempt; believing that suicide is morally wrong or might lead to punishment after death; and fearing a repeat of a frightening or painful experience.

The third group were aftereffects relating to this world. They included feeling that, since the attempt, the individual had reevaluated his or her life and could now see it from a different (but still worldly) perspective; that the problems that led to the attempt had gotten better or that help with those problems had become more available; and that now that the attempter's "bad" part had been punished or even killed off, the "good" part was free to go on living.

As reasons for becoming less suicidal after an attempt, "worldly" reasons from this third category were mentioned equally often by those who had had a near-death experience as a result of the suicide attempt and by those who hadn't. Likewise, "otherwordly" reasons that were not derived from a transpersonal perspective—those in the second category—were mentioned with equal frequency by those who had and hadn't had an NDE after their suicide attempt.

However, the "transpersonal" reasons that made up the first category were mentioned more than twice as often by those who had had an NDE following their suicide attempt as they were by the non-NDErs. In other words, the only suicide-inhibiting effects that having an NDE seemed to add to simply making a suicide attempt were those that implied a transpersonal perspective on life and its value.

We know, then, that while many suicide attempters will repeat their self-destructive acts, they are *not* likely to do so if their attempts led them into a near-death experience. And we know that those who do have suicide-induced NDEs differ from other suicide attempters in adopting a transpersonal view, but not in terms of other potentially suicide-inhibiting effects. The obvious conclusion is that feeling yourself to be a part of something greater than yourself, experiencing "cosmic unity" or a sense of oneness, is what stops NDErs from being suicidal.

How does this apply to non-NDErs? If in fact we can generalize from near-death experiencers to other people, this finding casts suspicion on the effectiveness of our traditional suicide-prevention tactics. Crisis intervention and suicide prevention, as we usually practice them, tend to focus on "reality"-oriented problem solving, on the practical, worldly coping skills that don't differentiate the high-risk suicide attempters from the low-risk NDErs.

This research suggests that fostering a transpersonal perspective on problems, focusing on the meaning and purpose of life, are what reduce suicidal thinking, rather than coping skills. The problems that lead people to attempt suicide will always be there. Teaching people how to cope with those problems doesn't seem to reduce suicide risk as much as showing them the "larger picture," in which those problems become insignificant or perhaps even blessings in disguise.

# Future Research

What does the future of near-death research hold? Obviously, many of the questions I outlined earlier in this commentary remain unanswered. But I think we know enough now about the phenomenology of NDEs, and have seen enough hints as to their meaning and potential, for us to focus our efforts on the role of the experience in personal transformation. This may lead us away from the "near-death" feature of the NDE and toward those features it shares with other transformative experiences. And it may lead us away from collecting further stories and verbal reports and toward laboratory investigation of the more profound aftereffects.

Several investigators in the field of consciousness and near-death studies have suggested that the significance of the NDE may be its role as a catalyst for human evolution, and that NDErs may collectively be a prototype of a new kind of human being that is emerging in our time. Those speculations are based on the reported aftereffects of NDEs, mental, physical, and spiritual, suggesting that NDErs may undergo an accelerated development of different-order intuitive mental functioning.

The configuration of cognitive, psychic, and spiritual aftereffects following NDEs is similar to that traditionally reported in people awakening to a a higher-order state of consciousness. Several consciousness researchers have argued that the increasing number of people experiencing those higher states of consciousness heralds the emergence of a new type of human being, a new personality that Kenneth Ring called the Omega Prototype.

If evolution of consciousness implies the continuing biological evolution of humanity, then personality transformations should be matched by signs of biological transformation. The next step in near-death research may be to measure objective and reliable physiological changes in NDErs.

At this point I need to elaborate on the Kundalini hypothesis that Barbara mentions several times in her narrative. The Sanskrit word "Kundalini" means "coiled-up," and refers to the potential energy within each of us, symbolized in Hindu tradition as a snake coiled up at the base of the spine, waiting to strike. When that energy is awakened, it can produce a variety of mental, emotional, physical, and psychic effects that are collectively called a "Kundalini experience," which is traditionally regarded as the path to enlightenment of the individual and to evolution of the species toward higher consciousness.

In Eastern traditions, your Kundalini would ideally be awakened at the appropriate time by a guru who can guide you properly in the development of that energy. If awakened without proper guidance, as Kenneth Ring believes happens in a near-death experience, Kundalini can be raw, destructive power loosed on the individual's body and psyche.

Though the vocabulary of the Kundalini hypothesis is foreign to Westerners, the concept bears some resemblance to the more familiar Holy Spirit. The process of Kundalini awakening is essentially a spiritual one, outside the domain of science. However, its traditional roles as the vehicle of evolution, if guided, or of psychosomatic havoc, if spontaneous, imply scientifically verifiable physical and psychological effects.

A little over a decade ago, biomedical engineer Itzhak Bentov formulated a scientifically verifiable version of the Kundalini concept, which he called the physio-Kundalini hypothesis. Psychiatrist and opthalmologist Lee Sannella developed the physio-Kundalini model further, collecting cases, experimenting with ways to help channel it, and outlining research strategies. While both scientists acknowledged that the physio-Kundalini concept is less complete than the classical Kundalini model, they argued that its limitations are what made it accessible to scientific study.

Following up on Kenneth Ring's suggestion that NDEs can awaken the Kundalini, I analyzed responses of NDErs and control subjects on a nineteen-item questionnaire that I based on the Bentov-Sannella physio-Kundalini model. This questionnaire includes motor "symptoms," such as spontaneous body movements, strange posturing, breath changes, and the body getting locked into certain positions; sensory symptoms, such as spontaneous tingling or vibrations, orgasmic sensations, progression of physical sensations up the legs and back and over the head, extreme heat or cold, pain that comes and goes abruptly, internal lights or colors that light up the body, internal voices, and internal whistling, hissing, or roaring noises; psychological symptoms, such as sudden bliss or ecstasy for no reason, sudden anxiety or depression for no reason, and speeding or slowing of thoughts; and expanding beyond the body and watching the body from a distance.

As you might have guessed from Barbara's vivid descriptions of her Kundalini manifestations, she experienced all nineteen items on the physio-Kundalini questionnaire. As a group, near-death experiencers reported experiencing almost twice as many physio-Kundalini items as did people who had had close brushes with death but no NDEs, and people who had never come close to death. As a check on whether the physio-Kundalini questionnaire might be measuring nonspecific strange experiences, I threw into the analysis the responses of a group of hospitalized psychiatric patients; they reported the same number of physio-Kundalini items as did the non-NDEr control group.

I mentioned earlier two unexpected and ambiguous "control" groups in my studies: people who claimed to have had

NDEs but described experiences with virtually no typical NDE features; and people who denied having had NDEs but then went on to describe prototypical near-death experiences. In their responses to the physio-Kundalini questionnaire, the group that made unsupported claims of NDEs were comparable to the non-NDEr control group, while the group that undeservedly denied having NDEs were comparable to the group of NDErs. In regard to awakening Kundalini, then, *having* an NDE mattered, but *thinking* you had one didn't.

Here, then, we have near-death experiencers reporting precisely the kind of physiological changes that are associated in Eastern traditions with the bio-energy that drives evolution. From verbal reports of such evidence as patterns of physiological functioning and disease history, as well as physio-Kundalini manifestations, we can identify which items best differentiate NDErs from control groups.

Based on those findings, people who seem to fit Kenneth Ring's Omega Prototype can be tested in the laboratory to measure objectively those physical and physiological characteristics highlighted by the verbal reports. Those characteristics that are confirmed by laboratory testing can then be used to compare biochemical and electrophysiological factors in NDErs, in people who have had other profound spiritual experiences, and in people who have followed systematic spiritual disciplines, as well as control subjects.

It is possible that future work in this area could lead to vital new insights into the evolution of humanity toward a different order of consciousness, echoing a major theme in Barbara's story: that the importance of the near-death experience is not its association with death, but its implications for life.

# Appendix:

## Clinical Approaches to the NDEr; Bibliography

## by Bruce Greyson, M.D.

The experience of leaving the body and encountering some other realm or dimension can permanently and dramatically alter attitudes, beliefs, and values. Near-death experiences are often the seeds that eventually flower into profound spiritual growth. Thanks to medical technology, the NDE may become our most common doorway to spiritual development.

But it is perhaps unique among doorways in that it opens to people regardless of whether or not they are seeking enlightenment. And precisely because it often occurs to people who are not looking or prepared for spiritual growth, it is particularly likely to lead into a spiritual crisis.

The growing literature on the aftereffects of the NDE has focused on the beneficial personal and spiritual transformations that often follow. But we know considerably less about the emotional and social problems NDErs often face.

Although NDErs might naturally feel distress if the NDE conflicts with their previously held beliefs and attitudes, the emphasis in the popular press on the positive benefits of NDEs inhibits NDErs who are having problems from seeking help.

Sometimes people who are totally unprepared to face a spiritual awakening, as in an NDE, may doubt their sanity; yet they are often afraid of rejection or ridicule if they discuss their fear with friends or professionals. Too often, NDErs do receive negative reactions from professionals when they describe their experiences—which naturally alienates them even further from seeking help in understanding the experience.

Many NDErs gradually adjust on their own, without any help, to their experience and its effects. However, that adjustment often requires them to adopt new values, attitudes, and interests. Family and friends may then find it difficult to understand the NDErs' new beliefs and behavior, and may avoid the NDEr, who they feel has come under the influence of some evil force.

On the other hand, family and friends who have seen all the popular publicity about positive effects of NDEs may place the NDEr on a pedestal and expect unrealistic changes. Sometimes friends expect superhuman patience and forgiveness from the NDEr, or miraculous healing and prophetic powers. They may then become bitter and reject the NDEr who does not live up to the new role as a living saint.

It is not unusual to see NDErs angry and depressed at having been returned, perhaps against their will, to this physical dimension. NDErs may find it difficult to accept that return, and experience "reentry problems" like those of an astronaut returning to earth. They often have problems fitting the NDE into their traditional religious beliefs, or into their traditional values and life-styles.

Because the experience seems so central to their "core," and seems to set them apart from other people around them, NDErs may identify too strongly with the experience and think of themselves first and foremost as "NDErs." Since many of their new attitudes and beliefs are so different from those around them, NDErs can overcome the worry that they are somehow "abnormal" only by redefining for themselves what is "normal."

The NDE can also bring about social problems. NDErs may feel a sense of distance or separation from people who have not had similar experiences; and they may fear being ridiculed or rejected by others—sometimes, of course, with good reason. It can be difficult for the NDEr to reconcile the new attitudes and beliefs with the expectations of family and friends; as a result, it can be hard to maintain the old roles and life-style that no longer have the same meaning after the NDE. NDErs may find it impossible to communicate to others the meaning and impact of the NDE on their lives. Frequently, having experienced the unconditional love of the NDE, the NDEr cannot accept the conditions and limitations of human relationships.

Above and beyond these problems that all NDErs may face to one degree or another, people who do have unpleasant or frightening NDEs may have additional concerns about why they had that kind of experience, and may be troubled by terrifying flashbacks of the experience itself.

The way a counselor or therapist—or a friend—responds to an NDEr can have a tremendous influence over whether the NDE is accepted and becomes a stimulus for further growth or whether it is hidden away—but not forgotten—as a bizarre experience that must not be shared, for fear of being labeled mentally ill.

These were the issues addressed by the 1984 IANDS

conference with which Barbara starts Part II of *Full Circle*. As she describes in that section of the book, a number of strategies and techniques for dealing with these problems came out of that pioneering group's own struggles. What follows here is a summary of those strategies and techniques.

While many of the notions described here apply uniquely to helping the near-death experiencer, others reflect common sense or approaches that would be helpful in any spiritual crisis. Keep in mind that these are not therapeutic techniques that have been validated by controlled studies, but rather are helpful approaches that emerged by consensus from some three dozen professional helpers, one-third of whom were NDErs themselves.

During or immediately after the near-death event, professional staff resuscitating a patient should be careful of insensitive comments and actions. Patients who seem to be unconscious may be aware of what's going on around them, and may later remember offensive actions or statements. When you have to say or do things during a resuscitation that may be misinterpreted, explain to patients what you're doing, even though they appear unconscious; if you don't, you may have to help them untangle frightening memories after they awaken.

During and immediately after being unconscious, physical touch is very helpful in orienting a patient. Talking to patients while touching them, outlining their bodies with your hands while you describe what you're doing, may help unconscious ones refocus their attention on their bodies after an NDE.

When talking with people immediately after a close brush with death, be alert for clues that they have had an NDE. People often drop subtle hints to test your openness to listen, before they risk sharing the experience with you. Don't push for the details of an NDE, but wait for clues that the person wants to talk further. NDErs may not want to share the details until they trust you. Let them describe their experiences at their own pace, while watching for those subtle hints—tests of how open you are—that they want to tell you more.

Before approaching an NDEr, you should explore your own attitudes toward the NDE. Be aware of your own prejudices, both positive and negative, about what NDEs mean and about the people who have such experiences. You should not press your own beliefs or interpretation of the experience on the NDEr, but let your conversation be guided by the individual's own account and understanding of the experience.

Listen for clues as to how he or she makes sense of the experience, and help the experiencer clarify that interpretation, using his or her own words. You each have to develop your own personal ways of encouraging talk about the NDE. Using your own personal style of speaking, both verbally and nonverbally, is the best way to get across your willingness to listen openly.

Whatever you think of the ultimate meaning or cause of the NDE, you must respect it as an extremely powerful agent of transformation. If you ignore the NDE's profound potential to bring about both positive and negative changes in personality, beliefs, and bodily activity, you ignore what is often the individual NDEr's most pressing concern. You must respect not only the experience but also the experiencer. All types of people have NDEs, and the NDEr's rich personal and spiritual background should not be ignored by focusing solely on that person's role as an "NDEr."

Labeling the NDE, or giving the NDEr a clinical diagnosis based on having had an NDE, is more likely to get in the way of understanding and to push the NDEr away than it is to help. When an individual NDEr does seem to have a mental or emotional disease, both you and the NDEr must be clear that the disease is not related to the NDE itself. Trying to label the experience as a symptom of illness is not accurate or helpful.

Honesty is critical in establishing an NDEr's trust. If it seems appropriate, you can share your own reactions to the NDE, without discrediting the NDEr's own perceptions and interpretation. You must reassure the NDEr that you can treat what you are told confidentially; the NDEr must be able to trust that you will not tell others about the NDE without permission. People are often cautious about sharing something as unusual and intimate as an NDE until they are sure you will respect it, and they will have reasonable concerns about the respect or attitudes of other people with whom you might share information about the NDE.

The most helpful thing you can do after an NDE is to listen carefully to whatever the person wants to say. People who seem to be upset by an experience usually feel pressure and urgency to understand it. They often become *more* frustrated if you tell them *not* to talk about it, or if you sedate them into silence. Allowing NDErs to talk lets them share and get rid of frightening feelings. Unlike hallucinating patients, who may become more upset by talking about their fears and confusion, NDErs are usually relieved if you allow them to struggle until they find the right words to describe their experiences.

You should encourage the NDEr to express whatever emotions were brought on by the experience. Most NDEs include very intense emotions, and the NDEr might still have those unusually intense feelings afterward. Mirror the person's feelings, but don't analyze them. Feeding back to

NDErs their own descriptions and emotions will help them clarify what at first may seem like unexplainable feelings, while analyzing and interpreting those emotions prematurely may only increase the NDEr's fears of being misunderstood.

In hospitals or other places where people often come close to death, it might be helpful to rotate "listeners" to prevent "burnout." NDErs are often excited about their experiences, and often need fresh listeners who can take the time, and have the patience, to hear them out.

One of the most helpful things you can provide for an NDEr is accurate information. Facts about NDEs and their aftereffects, shared in a straightforward, nonjudgmental way, will greatly reduce the experiencer's immediate concerns about the implications and consequences of the NDE. Near-death experiencers are usually relieved to learn how common NDEs are. On the other hand, no matter how universal the experience is, it is unique for each individual, and you must guard against using the NDE's commonness to trivialize any individual's experience or its unique impact on his or her life.

When NDErs seem upset immediately following the experience, help them identify exactly what it is about the NDE that is causing the problem. Explore the possible problems listed in the opening paragraphs of this commentary, using the individual NDEr's understanding of his or her own personality and situation. Once the specific problem is identified, tailor the situation to the specific person and problem. No two NDErs have the same experience, the same personality, or the same life situation to return to.

Finally, NDErs may need help immediately after the experience in dealing with what brought them close to death. Focusing on the NDE itself and its meaning, they may find it hard to arrange practical medical and social details. For concerns centered on the experience itself, put them in touch with other NDErs or with local professionals who have worked with other NDErs. Many cities have Friends of IANDS support groups, in which NDErs and their families and friends regularly discuss issues around the experience; you can get the address of the nearest support group from the International Association for Near-Death Studies (IANDS), P.O. Box 7767, Philadelphia, PA 19101.

Beyond these guidelines for working with people immediately after a near-death experience, if you expect to work with an NDEr past the initial contacts, you must be prepared for the NDE to raise issues about life and its purpose that may not come up in other clinical relationships. The profound aftereffects of an NDE may affect your own psychospiritual growth as much as the NDEr's. Decide whether you want to accept that risk before starting to work with an NDEr on an ongoing basis.

Once you have made that decision, you need to clarify what you expect from the work, and what the NDEr expects. Make sure you understand what help the NDEr wants from you, and that the NDEr understands what you want from him or her, and what you hope will come out of the relationship.

Be especially careful of jumping to conclusions about people you knew before their NDE, particularly clients you may have helped prior to their NDE. Don't assume that work you began before the NDE will continue on the same course after the experience. Even though the person's underlying problems and personality may be the same, the NDE may dramatically change his or her goals and priorities in life and in your work together.

You may need to limit what areas you will address in your work together. Taking into account the NDEr's personality and situation before the experience, clarify what problems are new as a result of the NDE. You may find it impossible to help someone with both NDE-related problems and unrelated emotional or psychological problems; the techniques and the goals of one kind of counseling may conflict with those of the other.

For example, helping your client adapt to social norms may reduce his or her long-standing psychological problem, while helping that same client to adapt to values that no longer have meaning after the NDE might increase his or her problems dealing with the experience. If you choose to work with someone around NDE-related problems, you may need to refer that person's problems that are not related to the NDE to someone else.

You and the NDEr must continually work toward mutual trust. Because the NDE is so different from daily reality, it may take longer than usual for an NDEr to trust even the most sensitive helper with some parts of the experience and its aftereffects. The otherworldly reality of the NDE also makes it hard for even the most open-minded helper to trust some of the NDEr's recollections and interpretations of the experience.

Don't be too concerned about traditional clinical roles; rigid adherence to form and appearances may undermine your relationship with the NDEr. Since many of our labels and definitions lose their meaning after an NDE, you must rely more on your direct experience with the NDEr and less on your formal training and knowledge of clinical techniques. Labeling the NDEr's problems and separating yourself from the NDEr for the sake of objectivity are more likely to interfere with your understanding of his or her problems than they are to help.

In particular, be flexible with how long and how often

you see an NDEr you are helping. Since the NDE is so different from other experiences and is very difficult to describe in words, exploring it may take unusually long sessions, and may unleash overwhelming emotions and thoughts that require frequent sessions.

Be prepared to stick with NDErs. They often feel frustrated in trying to describe the NDE and its aftereffects, and may give up trying if they see you as giving up. Particularly, those who feel they were ''sent back'' to this life against their will may feel rejected and undeserving of the NDE, and may be on the lookout for rejection from you.

It is not helpful to think of the NDEr as a passive victim of the experience. Helping the NDEr see his or her active role in creating or unfolding the NDE will help in understanding and dealing with problems arising from the experience.

Remember that parts of the ego that may have died in the NDE need to be grieved for. Even though NDErs may be happy to be rid of parts they transcended or were freed from, they still need to deal with that loss.

The major features of an individual's NDE may give you clues as to the sources of problems continuing after the experience. For example, if the NDE was composed largely of a life review, or of precognitive visions, or of certain strong feelings, exploring those particular features with the NDEr may shed light on continuing problems. Particularly explore details of the NDE that seem bizarre or unexplainable, as well as the NDEr's mental and emotional associations to those details. You can interpret NDE imagery on many levels, just as you can do with dream imagery.

Any techniques that you use for inducing altered states of consciousness may help the NDEr recall further details of the experience, and may help the NDEr learn to shift at will between different states of consciousness. Any techniques you use for integrating the left and right hemispheres in particular may help NDErs find practical ways to apply what they learned in the experience. Imagery, projective techniques, breath and body work, and nonverbal expressions such as art, music, and dance may help uncover and express feelings that are hard to put into words.

Explore the NDEr's sense of a specific purpose or mission after surviving death. The "unfinished business" of that mission may be a source of continuing problems. Those NDErs who chose to "return" to this life may feel ongoing regret or mixed feelings about that decision. On the other hand, NDErs who chose *not* to return to this life may feel ongoing guilt or anger at having been "sent back." Some NDErs feel "manipulated" by a higher power in being "sent back," and that feeling may cause continuing problems.

Explore fully the NDEr's fears about unwanted aftereffects. Whether or not fears about the consequences of an NDE are realistic, they can cause continuing problems. It is important to distinguish the NDE from its aftereffects. The NDEr must feel free to reject or resist unwanted aftereffects without having to devalue the NDE itself. While the NDE is going to be a permanent part of the individual's life from now on, various aftereffects may come and go in a natural course, or may be developed or eliminated through counseling.

The changes in values and attitudes following an NDE often lead to subtle changes in family interactions that can cause continuing problems. Meeting with the NDEr and the entire family together, ideally in their home, may be the only way to understand how the family has changed, and to get the reactions of family members to the NDEr. If the family dynamics have been greatly changed, family therapy may help.

Avoid glorifying or idealizing the NDE and its after-effects. The newness and uniqueness of the experience may lead both you and the NDEr to see it—and sometimes the NDEr as well—in unrealistically romantic ways. Similarly, it is tempting to see the remarkable aftereffects—physical, emotional, and mental—as more important than they are, simply because they are so dramatically different from the way the NDEr was before the experience.

The NDEr must learn to see the striking aftereffects in the greater context of the entire NDE. Paranormal effects in particular may capture your interest and the NDEr's simply because of their novelty, and blind you to other important parts of the experience or other aftereffects that are more important in fostering psychospiritual growth.

In the same way, the NDEr must learn to see the NDE in the greater context of his or her entire life. Obviously, you can't ignore the experience and its aftereffects, but neither should you allow the NDEr to focus on them to the neglect of other parts of his or her life. The overwhelming need to understand the meaning or message of an NDE can lead the experiencer to overvalue its content or its after-effects.

If the NDEr overidentifies with the experience, he or she may not be able to deal with any issues not directly related to the NDE. Talking with other NDErs is very helpful in normalizing the experience, but identifying *only* with other NDErs can lead to feeling alienated from people who have not had the experience, to feeling that the physical realm is not meaningful or important, and to ignoring basic problems of living in the physical world.

You may need to help those who become "addicted" to the NDE or its aftereffects to withdraw from it gradually. It may help to point out that problems often can't be solved on the level that created them. NDErs often say that physical-plane problems they had for years were resolved only by what they learned in the NDE. By the same token, problems created by the NDE may be resolved only by working on the physical plane.

Some NDErs have to relearn how to handle daily responsibilities that no longer seem relevant after the NDE, but are still necessary. The timeless quality of the NDE makes it hard for some NDErs to remain grounded in the present once they return. After a profound life review, NDErs may remain focused on the past, while after profound precognitive visions they may fixate on the future. You may need a very firm here-and-now focus to help the NDEr function in the present.

On the other hand, you can't expect NDErs to take up life as usual after an NDE; their outside circumstances may have to be changed to meet their internal changes. If the NDEr's new attitudes, beliefs, and values don't fit with old roles and life-style, then he or she needs to find a new role and life-style that will meet the new goals and priorities. You may need to help the NDEr through major changes in careers and relationships.

Finally, your ultimate usefulness to the NDEr may be in helping to channel what he or she learned in the NDE into practical use. The same new attitudes, beliefs, and goals that create problems in the NDEr's surroundings can also be important in changing those surroundings for the better. The best way for many NDErs to feel comfortable with the experience and its aftereffects is to use what they have learned to help others. Your work is finished when the NDEr finds a way to bring into daily life the love that he or she received in the NDE.

*   *   *

For those who wish to pursue the near-death literature further, an excellent resource is the International Association for Near-Death Studies (IANDS), P.O. Box 7767, Philadelphia, PA 19101, which publishes a quarterly newsletter, *Revitalized Signs*, and the only scholarly journal devoted to this topic, the quarterly *Journal of Near-Death Studies* (formerly called *Anabiosis*). In addition, the following books, arranged chronologically, have become or, I believe, will become, classic references in the field:

*Life After Life*, by Raymond A. Moody, Jr., 1975 (New York: Bantam Books).

*Reflection on Life After Life*, by Raymond A. Moody, Jr., 1977 (New York: Bantam Books).

*Life at Death*, by Kenneth Ring, 1980 (New York: Coward, McCann & Geoghegan).

*Adventures in Immortality*, by George Gallup, Jr., 1980 (New York: McGraw-Hill).

*A Collection of Near-Death Research Readings*, edited by Craig Lundahl, 1982 (Chicago: Nelson-Hall).

*Recollections of Death*, by Michael Sabom, 1982 (New York: Harper & Row).

*Heading Toward Omega*, by Kenneth Ring, 1984 (New York: William Morrow).

*The Near-Death Experience*, edited by Bruce Greyson and Charles Flynn, 1984 (Springfield, IL: Charles C. Thomas).

*The Final Choice*, by Michael Grosso, 1985 (Walpole, NH: Stillpoint Press).

*Return from Death*, by Margot Grey, 1985 (London: Arkana).

*After the Beyond*, by Charles Flynn, 1986 (Englewood Cliffs, NJ: Prentice-Hall).

*Otherworld Journeys*, by Carol Zaleski, 1987 (New York: Oxford University Press).

*The Light Beyond*, by Raymond A. Moody, Jr., 1988 (New York: Bantam Books).

*Coming Back to Life*, by P. M. H. Atwater, 1988 (New York: Ballantine Books).

*The Return from Silence*, by D. Scott Rogo, 1989 (Wellingborough, England: Aquarian Press).

*Spiritual Emergency*, edited by Stan Grof, M.D. and Christina Grof, 1989 (Los Angeles, CA: J. P. Tarcher).